CORPORATE CRIME AND PUNISHMENT

Corporate Crime and Punishment

THE CRISIS OF UNDERENFORCEMENT

John C. Coffee Jr.

Adolf A. Berle Professor of Law and
Director of the Center on Corporate Governance
at Columbia University Law School

BERRETT-KOEHLER PUBLISHERS, INC.

Berrett-Koehler Publishers, Inc.
1333 Broadway, Suite 1000
Oakland, CA 94612-1921
Tel: (510) 817-2277
Fax: (510) 817-2278
www.bkconnection.com

ORDERING INFORMATION

Quantity sales. Special discounts are available on quantity purchases by corporations, associations, and others. For details, contact the "Special Sales Department" at the Berrett-Koehler address above.

Individual sales. Berrett-Koehler publications are available through most bookstores. They can also be ordered directly from Berrett-Koehler: Tel: (800) 929-2929; Fax: (802) 864-7626; www.bkconnection.com.

Orders for college textbook / course adoption use. Please contact Berrett-Koehler: Tel: (800) 929-2929; Fax: (802) 864-7626.

Distributed to the U.S. trade and internationally by Penguin Random House Publisher Services.

Berrett-Koehler and the BK logo are registered trademarks of Berrett-Koehler Publishers, Inc.

Printed in Canada

Berrett-Koehler books are printed on long-lasting acid-free paper. When it is available, we choose paper that has been manufactured by environmentally responsible processes. These may include using trees grown in sustainable forests, incorporating recycled paper, minimizing chlorine in bleaching, or recycling the energy produced at the paper mill.

Library of Congress Cataloging-in-Publication Data

Names: Coffee, John C., Jr., 1944– author.
Title: Corporate crime and punishment : the crisis of underenforcement / John C. Coffee, Jr.
Description: First edition. | Oakland, CA : Berrett-Koehler Publishers, [2020] |
    Includes bibliographical references and index.
Identifiers: LCCN 2020002383 | ISBN 9781523088850 (hardcover ; alk. paper) |
    ISBN 9781523088867 (pdf) | ISBN 9781523088874 (epub)
Subjects: LCSH: Criminal liability of juristic persons—United States. |
    Corporate governance—Law and legislation—United States—Criminal provisions.
Classification: LCC KF9236.5 .C64 2020 | DDC 345.73/0268—dc23
LC record available at https://lccn.loc.gov/2020002383

First Edition
26 25 24 23 22 21 20   10 9 8 7 6 5 4 3 2 1

Book producer: Westchester Publishing Services
Text designer: Laurel Muller
Cover designer: Peggy Archambault

This book is dedicated

to the love of my life (and wife of fifty years):

Dr. Jane Purcell Coffee, professor of mathematics

at the City University of New York.

Contents

Preface

This is *not* an "academic" book. If it were (and I have written several such books), it would have three times the footnotes and much more jargon. Instead the footnotes have been trimmed (reluctantly) and the jargon avoided (hopefully) to reach a broader audience. At least by design, this book is intended to be accessible to anyone interested in (1) white collar crime, (2) criminal justice administration in the real world, (3) why high-ranking executives seldom seem to be prosecuted, and (4) why certain aspects of contemporary corporate governance tend to be criminogenic. Thus, this book's focus is on both corporate and criminal law, and this book is the product of the author's work in the field of white collar crime for over forty years and in the field of corporate law and governance for even longer.

This combination produces a special perspective. For example, others have explained the persistent phenomenon that high-ranking executives are seldom prosecuted using primarily political explanations—for example, the enforcers were "captured" or the prosecutors were too risk averse. Without rejecting these explanations (which could sometimes be true), the more fundamental problem is that prosecutors function within understaffed, overworked bureaucracies that cannot normally undertake intensive investigations. Those who rise to managerial positions in such a bureaucracy are those who have learned how to stay within budget and achieve early settlements that allow their agency to claim a victory. This need to claim a victory (and quickly) is part of the unending struggle for credit in which agencies engage in order to justify a greater budget, and this need explains much about the behavior of enforcement agencies, including the recent popularity of deferred prosecution and nonprosecution agreements, the tendency for internal corporate investigations to be run by defense counsel (and not the prosecutor), and the desire of enforcement agencies to avoid protracted litigation. Bureaucracies, including U.S. Attorneys and the Securities and Exchange Commission (SEC), need to celebrate claimed victories, while staying within budget, if they are to convince legislatures to allocate them greater funds. This is a difficult balancing act and sometimes an impossible one when a major new crisis arises.

Although this diagnosis that prosecutors are too logistically constrained to undertake intensive investigations applies easily to such cases as Lehman Brothers and the other major firms that failed in 2008, the same pattern is also evident in more recent cases, such as the Boeing 737 MAX crisis, the behavior of major opioid manufacturers in selling on a wholesale basis to drug mills, the Volkswagen emissions scandal, and the failures of Pacific Gas and Electric Company (PG&E), where the organization knew at all levels that its equipment was aged and its forests were overgrown and vulnerable to major forest fires. In none of these cases were prosecutors in a position to take on lengthy investigations that necessarily would have occupied a large staff for many months. Instead, they were under pressure to reach a quick settlement—and they did. In large part, this was because experienced defense counsel understood the prosecution's logistical limitations and exploited them. The result is what this book calls "underenforcement."

If this is the problem, what is the answer? This book explores alternative arrangements and strategies that could be used to redress the logistical imbalance that cripples white collar law enforcement. In this regard, this book is ultimately as much about corporate law as criminal law. What forces within the modern public corporation are criminogenic? What causes corporate executives to take high risk? A principal answer of this book is that high levels of incentive compensation induce managers to accept high risk—both operationally and legally. That is not an answer that an academic versed only in criminal law would give. In turn, it follows that a logical way to reduce excessive risk taking at a convicted corporation may be to restrict incentive compensation, and this is most feasibly done by imposing restrictive conditions of probation on the convicted corporation. This is a corporate solution to a criminal law problem, and this is the type of solution that this book will repeatedly offer.

Similarly, much of this book will be about procedure, but not traditional criminal procedure. For example, it will ask: How can we economize on the costs of investigation and prosecution? How can we induce or compel the corporate defendant to conduct an adequate investigation on which the prosecution can rely? Again, these are not the standard problems that traditional criminal procedure addresses. Current internal investigations, this book argues, tend to discover who was responsible only down at the base of the corporate pyramid, rarely going much higher. Although many recent commentators have justly criticized deferred prosecution and nonprosecution agreements, the better policy goal should not be to prohibit such agreements but rather to use them as the carrot that induces much greater cooperation by the corporation against its own executives. This "divide and conquer" strategy requires several steps that have not yet been taken and on which this book focuses.

Consistent with many other recent critics, this book argues that the corporation itself should not be the principal target of law enforcement. This is true for three entirely different reasons: First, corporations are hard to deter; they can (and do) absorb enormous penalties as a cost of doing business. In contrast, individuals tend to be more risk averse, and empirical evidence shows they are easier to deter. Indeed, senior executives may be happy to use the corporate entity as a buffer and shield. Second, the corporation has an enormous comparative advantage over prosecutors: it can investigate internal corporate misconduct much more quickly and efficiently than the government, which is restrained by a variety of constitutional protections. This advantage needs to be harnessed and put to the service of prosecutors much more effectively than it is today. But there are subtle problems here. Third, the moral failures underlying corporate crime are those of individuals, not artificial entities (such as the corporation), and currently these individuals usually escape exposure. Convicting the corporation should not be the end goal, but it can be a principal means by which the goal of identifying and convicting responsible individuals is achieved.

Much of this book addresses the question of how regulators and prosecutors can obtain adequate resources to contest corporate misbehavior, given the reality that public bureaucracies are always constrained by budgetary limitations. It advocates two controversial strategies.

First, civil regulators (such as the SEC, the Federal Trade Commission [FTC], and other consumer-oriented agencies) should employ private law firms as their counsel, on a contingent fee basis, to handle the largest cases that these agencies cannot afford to staff or conduct themselves. Empirically, private law firms are able to undertake two to five-year campaigns to prosecute corporate misconduct (and regularly to do so in class action litigation today). Compared to public agencies, such firms are superior risk bearers because they can face the risk of defeat and come back undeterred (and have done so many times). Also, because they eat only what they kill (meaning that their fees are contingent on the outcome and they understand that there is no fee if they lose), they impose low costs on taxpayers. The counterargument to this approach is that use of private counsel would require a sacrifice of prosecutorial discretion. If such a loss were truly necessary, that would be a strong reason for public agencies not to employ private counsel on a contingent fee basis. But this is a makeweight argument. As will be seen, many public agencies already employ such counsel and do very well. The insistence of civil service attorneys in federal agencies that private counsel not be employed is sadly self-interested.

Second, the one new law enforcement tactic that appears to work in white collar cases is paying bounties to whistle-blowers for information. Law enforcement agencies could make far greater use of the whistle-blower as a means of economizing on investigation costs than they do today. Although no one denies that whistle-blowers provide valuable information, few federal agencies make serious use of them, and those agencies that do use them seem equivocal and inclined to compensate these agents only parsimoniously.

Realistically, some of the reforms proposed in this book may never be adopted (although they are beginning to be discussed). The premise to this book is not that their adoption is imminent but that we need a new way of thinking about corporate crime and misconduct. Both prosecutors and defense counsel (including those who later enter academia) tend to view these problems through the narrow prisms of their professional roles and experience. Although that is understandable, the intent of this book is to develop new strategies and a broader inventory of tools. Even if these tools are not adopted, they can give us a fuller sense of what is possible.

Finally, a preface should acknowledge those who have helped the author to formulate his ideas. For over thirty years, I have taught a seminar on white collar crime with Senior U.S. District Judge Jed Rakoff. We agree more than we disagree, but we dispute much, and his cogent thinking and strong focus on the underlying moral values in criminal law have helped me crystalize my thinking. The work of several contemporary legal scholars has also influenced me, including, most notably, Professor Brandon Garrett, whose book, *Too Big to Jail: How Prosecutors Compromise with Corporations*, set a new standard for scholarship in this field. Others who helped me shape my ideas (or at least refine them) include my colleagues Reynolds Holding, the editor of the *CLS Blue Sky Blog*; Professor Henry P. Monaghan, the Harlan Fiske Stone Professor of Constitutional Law; Professor Harold Edgar, the Julius Silver Professor of Law, Science and Technology Emeritus; and Professor Joshua Mitts. Lastly, my research assistants, Roy Cohen and Amy Burr Hutchings, deserve special credit for diligent research, thoughtful criticism, and putting up with me.

CORPORATE CRIME AND PUNISHMENT

PART 1

The Factual Story

Introduction to Part 1

ONCE UPON A TIME, corporate criminal liability was very simple: the corporation was liable for any act, committed by an employee or agent, intended at least in part to benefit it. This rule—known to lawyers as *repondeat superior*—meant that if the employee or agent was guilty, so was the corporation.

That rule is still the formal law, but over the past twenty years, it has been overwhelmed by a new practice: the corporation can escape liability for its employees' acts and instead receive a *deferred prosecution agreement* under which it may pay a fine but is not convicted or formally sanctioned. The price for this disposition is that the corpoation may have to cooperate with the prosectuion to some degree and typically conduct an internal investigaiton, which could result in prosecutors instead indicting corporate employees.

Such dispositions have now become presumptive, but they are rarely accompanied by the prosecution of higher-level corporate officers or executives. Part 1 of this book describes how this practice developed and why it has become controversial. It principally focuses on events preceding and following the 2008 financial crisis, including the complete failure of the federal government to prosecute, either civilly or criminally, anyone at Lehman (or any other senior executive at any Wall Street investment bank). Then, it turns to subsequent scandals at Volkswagen, General Motors, and the pharmaceutical firms that produced or distributed opioids and finds that the same pattern prevails.

Part 1 examines each of these cases briefly and analyzes what has caused this pattern. Was it corruption, political cowardice, risk aversion, or logistical inability to take these cases on? Tentative answers are offered. Part 1 then moves on to the Trump administration and finds that corporate prosecutions are rapidly declining. In short, American law faces a problem of underenforcement, as corporations now receive leniency as a matter of course.

ONE

The Regulatory Shortfall

SINCE THE 2008 CRASH, one question has dominated the public debate over it: Why were no senior executives on Wall Street prosecuted? How did those guys escape prison? Politicians, scholars, television commentators, and participants in nearly every cocktail party at which the 2008 crash was discussed have asked this question—usually in tones suggesting outrage, suspicion, or, at the least, pure puzzlement.[1]

Indeed, this suspicion is understandable because earlier financial debacles did produce high-profile and sometimes massive prosecutions. When Enron and WorldCom collapsed in 2001–2002, their chief executives (among others) were indicted, convicted, and sentenced to lengthy prison terms.[2] Similarly, the collapse of savings banks in the 1980s elicited wholesale prosecutions with (by some estimates) over one thousand savings bank employees and executives being convicted of felonies in federal court (with most going to prison).[3] Yet the failure of Lehman not only produced no federal prosecutions of the executives at that firm, but the SEC similarly brought no civil actions against its senior executives. Although it is an overstatement to say that no one was prosecuted as a result of the crash (as a host of lower-echelon persons were), no senior executive on Wall Street or at a major financial firm was convicted (or even prosecuted).[4]

Given the public's strong desire for retribution and the personal interest of many federal prosecutors in conducting high-profile criminal prosecutions (upon which one can build a career), this absence seems anomalous. Many have offered plausible explanations to account for this joint failure of prosecutors and regulators. The most popular theory has been that the federal government was either "captured" by the financial industry or that prosecutors were too risk averse to take on major cases that might have been lost. Jesse Eisinger, an able and respected journalist, has been the most outspoken

3

proponent of this view, arguing in his 2017 book a thesis that is largely conveyed by that book's title: *The Chickenshit Club: Why the Justice Department Fails to Prosecute Executives.* As he sees it, the "revolving door" practices at the Justice Department and the cautious attitudes of its leaders (who were soon to rotate back to "establishment" law firms) explain this failure. Unquestionably, he makes a cogent and plausible case for his position. Even if one doubts his view that the Justice Department's leadership was cowardly or conflicted, one can still understand why the Federal Reserve and other banking agencies might have wanted more to calm troubled waters than to impose retribution. Having poured trillions into these banks pursuant to a variety of bailouts, the federal banking agencies likely saw little point in imposing massive fines on these same banks that ultimately would be paid from the funds they had advanced; the net result would only have been circular.

Of course, this does not explain why individuals were not also prosecuted. Financial regulators possibly feared that indicting senior bank officers might slow a return to normalcy and keep the banking system destabilized. Some foreign governments openly made this argument (in the case of their own banks), and some evidence suggests that federal officials also cautioned the Justice Department against a punitive pursuit of Wall Street.[5] But what does this mean? It can be read as a somewhat more polite and palatable reinterpretation of Eisinger's blunter thesis that prosecutors were simply "chicken." Still, this does not necessarily imply that federal prosecutors were "captured" but only that they proceeded more cautiously in the case of the nation's largest banks, recognizing that major banks presented a different and more problematic case for enforcement than did Enron and WorldCom.

At the other end of the spectrum from those who see the Justice Department as being overly constrained (whether by politics or innate caution) are those who deny that there was any enforcement failure at all. Within the banking industry and among economists, some believe that few prosecutions occurred because there were no true crimes committed.[6] They will argue: "It was a bubble, not a fraud." In their view 2008 was a "perfect storm"—a classic banking panic that arose outside the banking system because the "shadow banks" of Wall Street (including Lehman, Bear Stearns, and Merrill Lynch) were largely beyond the Federal Reserve's supervision. Some in this school will blame market forces; others, regulatory laxity. Clearly, these are at least colorable arguments, and one can buttress them with the observation that normally prosecutors would be eager to prosecute high-profile bank executives, either because they were "headline happy" or because they had careerist motives. Although this book believes that fraud was both present and pervasive, it recognizes that there are two sides to this argument, and neither the claim that prosecutors failed nor the counter-position that banking panics need not involve fraud can be dismissed or ignored. To date, there has yet to be a cool-headed, objective analysis that compares these rival explanations for why both prosecutors and regulatory enforcers were so equivocal (or worse) after 2008.

But the goal of this book is not to rehash a crisis that is already a decade in the past. Our starting point begins with the observation that this pattern of underenforcement that was so clear during the 2008 financial crisis has persisted, and recent crises (such as the opioid epidemic) have elicited only a few criminal prosecutions, notwithstanding deaths from prescription opioid overdoses in the range of 400,000 or more. Other disasters have produced even less of a response from public enforcers. Consider the record forest fires that swept California in 2018 and killed many. Was California's leading public utility responsible? Did it know and ignore the risks? Now in bankruptcy, Pacific Gas and Electric Company is beyond the reach of monetary sanctions, but should its executives have escaped liability? No one can answer this question without an objective investigation that probes deeply into a complex bureaucracy. In that light, the focus of this book is on the obstacles to effective investigation and enforcement, now and in the future, in the case of large-scale organizational misconduct. As we will see, the prosecutorial abdication that followed 2008 could easily happen again—and may have. In the arena of consumer safety, one may point to the cases of Boeing or General Motors where vehicles arguably known to have been unsafe were tolerated with consequent loss of life. In the case of the opioid crisis, the leading candidate would be Purdue Pharma Inc., which marketed a risky product broadly for a wide range of ailments, and overdoses potentially caused by it killed tens of thousands. In the case of environmental disasters, the examples of PG&E and British Petroleum (BP) stand out, as each recklessly caused epic destruction.

A recent popular movie—*Dark Waters*—alleges that DuPont for an extended period hid its chemical contamination of the water supply affecting at least 70,000 persons in an area of West Virginia. The movie, which grew out of a *New York Times Magazine* story,[7] asserts that DuPont long knew that the chemical was unsafe and was leaking into the water supply but concluded that the product involved was just too profitable. So it gave no warnings. Are these charges true? No judgment is here reached, because the more relevant point here is that only an extended investigation could uncover the true facts, and that is generally beyond the capacity of most prosecutorial offices. Even though a private civil settlement was reached, this is not a fully satisfactory resolution, as the settlement remains under seal and thus the goals of transparency and individual accountability are subordinated to that of victim compensation. Only public enforcement is likely to reveal the fuller truth.

Similarly, massive money laundering schemes have escaped federal prosecution (for example, HSBC), and we simply do not know how many foreign corrupt practices cases have not been pursued that should have been. The scope of these cases is simply too global for most prosecutors to pursue on their own. Overall, the more extensive and systematic the corporate corruption, the more it will likely produce a settlement, not a trial.

Politically, it is not enough in such cases that the corporate entity plead guilty to something. Accountability requires more, and the public particularly wants to know what individuals were culpable. Still, formidable obstacles constrain the ability of prosecutors and regulators to investigate, deter, and prosecute organizational crime (at least when the misconduct involves conduct that is subtler and less obvious than behavior that is aimed simply at personal profit[8]). The problem is less that prosecutors are "chicken" than that they confront a logistical nightmare when they face an engrained and systematic corporate practice (which often is industrywide). Even if prosecutors and regulators were motivated by uncompromising zeal, it will still often be beyond their ability to prosecute senior executives in complex cases. This is true whether the underlying misbehavior be securities fraud at a firm like Lehman or even more deadly crimes at a pharmaceutical firm that was supplying opioid mills or a public utility that was turning a blind eye to the risk of forest fires. For both legal and logistical reasons, these cases today are mismatches—a David-versus-Goliath battle, in which the slingshot is seldom mightier than the sword.

The worst-case scenario is that meaningful deterrence may be largely beyond the capacity of our existing institutional structure to achieve. Today, as will be shown, our existing institutional network of enforcement—both civil and criminal—succeeds mainly in imposing a steadily increasing level of fines on corporations, fines that are imposed by a large number of federal agencies, sometimes in a coordinated fashion, more often not. Unfortunately, monetary fines against large organizations are unlikely to generate adequate deterrence. This is evidenced both by the fact that these fines (even when they exceed $1 billion) amount to only a trivial percentage of the corporation's market capitalization (less than one-tenth of 1 percent on average) and by the fact that the public corporation's stock price usually goes up on the announcement of the sanction (as we will see in more detail in chapter 4). If adequate deterrence cannot be achieved through monetary penalties imposed on the corporation, it follows that a refocusing of penalties on individual officers and managers within the corporate hierarchy is necessary. But this is much harder to achieve than has been explained to date, and it requires that we enlist the corporation in the prosecution of its own officers and agents. Thus, this book's aim is less to assign blame for past scandals than to map a path to reform to deal with future crises.

This contention that logistical reasons, rather than motivational reasons (such as risk aversion or a conflict of interests), may better explain the enforcement failures after 2008 leads logically to a further contention: we need to focus more on what motivates or dissuades enforcement agencies. Enforcement agencies—civil and criminal—are bureaucracies. Two key facts must be understood at the outset about enforcement agencies as bureaucracies.

First, they are constrained by budgets given to them by legislatures that rarely award them all they want (or need). Thus, in the real world, the job of the efficient manager within an enforcement bureaucracy becomes that of handling any new crisis within the budget. The simplest means to this end is to seek a settlement with the defendants (and counsel for the defendants know and exploit this need).

Second, to obtain the budget that they desire, enforcement bureaucracies—both civil and criminal—need to satisfy both the legislature and the public. This means that if they cannot convince the press and other media that they are doing an effective job, they will likely encounter public skepticism, which can quickly translate into legislative resistance when they seek enhanced budgets.

The bottom line then is that enforcement agencies are locked into a never-ending struggle for credit. Obtaining credit and public approbation is a pre-condition to enhanced future funding. Particularly in the case of civil enforcement agencies (such as the SEC), this may require public enforcers to demonstrate that the number of cases their agency has brought and the ag-gregate recoveries they obtained have grown year after year. Beyond any doubt, such numbers are not good proxies for the total deterrence generated (which in theory should be the end goal that guides rational prosecutors). Nonetheless, what Congress wants Congress gets. Thus, regulators and pros-ecutors feel a need to show constantly improving statistics if they are to sat-isfy Congress.

Statistics can, of course, be manipulated, and the experienced bureaucrat is likely skilled at doing so. Efficient bureaucrats managing enforcement agen-cies know that they need victories (and will be injured by defeats), but they particularly need timely victories—ones that can be shown to Congress to in-fluence the budget cycle. Long, drawn-out investigations seldom advance this goal. In this light, the deferred prosecution agreement (which will be dis-cussed in detail later but is essentially a plea bargain that does not result in a felony conviction) has grown in popularity because it enables the agency to stay within budget and produce a timely victory (or at least an outcome that can be described as a victory) in order to generate the credit that justifies in-creased funding. In turn, those firms subject to such investigations (and their white collar counsel) can anticipate and manipulate this need by offer-ing symbolic victories that seem to show prosecutors succeeding gallantly, even though the settlements are weak and bloodless compromises.

There is, of course, a tension here. Hollow victories will eventually attract media criticism and hence congressional disfavor. But the efficient manager within the enforcement bureaucracy must balance these two goals. Often a timely resolution, achieved within the budget, is more useful than a delayed complete victory.

All this may sound obvious and too general to produce specific policy responses, but it has immediate implications for our context of organizational misconduct. Following the 2001 terror bombing of the World Trade Center on 9/11, the federal government shifted its priorities and understandably reallocated its prosecutorial resources away from white collar crime.[9] Terrorism now was given the highest priority, and white collar criminal prosecutions were deemphasized. That reallocation had just been fully implemented when the 2008 crisis erupted. This shift implied that U.S. Attorneys had more limited manpower and funding—and thus needed to pursue less costly settlements than in the past.

Next, add to this equation the fact that individual prosecutions of senior executives at Lehman, AIG, Countrywide, or Merrill Lynch (to name just a few of the financial institutions most criticized as playing a causal role in the 2008 crash) would have necessitated very manpower-intensive investigations. Particularly difficult would have been the attribution of culpable knowledge to these senior executives, who are typically remote from operating levels and generally insulated at the top of the corporate hierarchy from knowledge of operational details. For example, most CEOs at major investment banks can credibly deny knowledge of what was in those toxic securitizations that their banks marketed.

This is said not to justify the failure to prosecute senior executives but as the necessary prelude to opening a discussion of the controversial strategy that federal prosecutors did adopt. In the wake of 2008, federal prosecutors came to rely heavily on deferred prosecution agreements (or DPAs), which they used as a substitute for a criminal trial.[10] Essentially, DPAs amount to a written plea bargain under which the prosecutor agrees that if the defendant corporation pays a fine and completes a short period of probation (and possibly accepts a corporate monitor with modest powers), its conviction will be expunged—in effect, erased—at the end of this probationary period. Although an extensive internal investigation is not a mandatory component of a DPA, its use has become increasingly standard—in part, so that prosecutors can feel that they have gotten to the bottom of the conspiracy and revealed the truth.

Multiple reasons explain the sudden new popularity of this mechanism, but one key attraction is its logistical efficiency. Not having the manpower to investigate these cases anywhere near adequately, prosecutors can use the DPA to delegate the factual investigation to an allegedly independent law firm and then settle based on the facts that investigation disclosed. Of course, there is a catch to such outsourcing: this approach effectively allows the defendant to select its investigator (within some limits). In truth, these internal investigations were often quite thorough (and staggeringly expensive), but they seldom, if ever, discovered responsibility at higher levels within the corporation. Law firms specializing in internal investigations reaped extraordinary returns from this new line of business. Given the highly competitive nature of the legal industry and the bonanza that this new internal investigation line of business represented, one would be naïve to expect that a law firm that was selected by the defendant corporation (and that was charging prodigious fees for its services) would bite the hand that feeds it by implicating its client's senior executives—at least not if this law firm wanted to do business in the internal investigation marketplace again.

Many attribute the DPA's popularity to the Justice Department's embarrassment over its ultimately unsuccessful prosecution of Arthur Andersen (the auditor for both Enron and WorldCom).[11] Although that debacle no doubt was a factor (as will be discussed), DPAs were at least equally a cost-economizing strategy. In addition, DPAs offered further bonuses: they spared prosecutors from any risk of an embarrassing loss at trial, and they offered a speedy resolution that enabled prosecutors and regulators to declare an early victory (whereas a trial would potentially mean years of delay and then appeals). Early victories are important in dealing with Congress and the approaching budget cycle.

The only goal that the DPA did not achieve for prosecutors was the generation of meaningful deterrence. Here, many commentators have now agreed that DPAs resulted in a massive shortfall in deterrence. Nonetheless, bureaucracies favor arrangements that reduce cost and effort and allow them to claim credit. Today, based in large part on the research of Professor Brandon Garrett, the data suggest strongly that DPAs regularly permitted senior executives to escape prosecutions—and thus seemingly to buy immunity with their shareholders' money. In his book *Too Big to Jail: How Prosecutors Compromise with Corporations*, Professor Garrett has shown that major public corporations, despite repeated violations, were able to escape criminal prosecution through the use of DPAs—in effect, surviving as serial and unpunished recidivists. But even if DPAs amount to a relatively painless punishment that permits high-ranking executives to escape without penalty, and even if prosecutors know they will be criticized for relying on them, the problem remains: What is the alternative? How can the prosecution develop sufficient leverage to force the corporate entity to settle closer to the government's terms? That is our focus.

This brief reference to DPAs is intended to underscore a key and recurring theme for this book: logistics matter! Without denying that such critics as Jesse Eisinger make valid points, it is insufficient simply to call prosecutors too risk averse (or worse). Organizational crime and misconduct cannot be effectively addressed without designing a system that can investigate complex matters thoroughly and in a manner that neither compromises the integrity of the study nor imposes unacceptably high costs on the government.

Here, a word of caution must be added. The premise of this book is not that public corporations are corrupt and lawless. Indeed, American corporations appear considerably more law compliant than foreign corporations, and the United States invests far more on enforcement (even on a size-adjusted basis) than do comparable nations.[12] Rather, the premise is that complex organizations tend to persist in behaviors to which they have become accustomed (including, for example, money laundering for foreign clients). Draconian sanctions may change such behavior, but lesser penalties are often an acceptable cost of doing business. Under the current equilibrium, defense counsel have become skillful at minimizing reputational damage for their clients and in keeping penalties at a tolerable level.

That said, it is now time to provide a brief road map for this volume. We will begin with a capsule history of recent prosecutorial developments, beginning with the Arthur Andersen case in 2005, which forced federal prosecutors to reconsider criminal prosecutions of corporations and set the stage for new policies favoring DPAs. Then, we will examine several episodes during and after the 2008 crisis that contain lessons for the future. A sad low point in prosecutorial tolerance for egregious misconduct was reached in 2012 with the Justice Department's decision not to indict HSBC, a major international bank that had laundered money on a massive scale for Mexican drug cartels and Iranian terrorists alike.[13] After this episode and Attorney General Holder's awkward admission that some banks were "too big to prosecute,"[14] the public mood shifted, and the Obama administration became embarrassed by its prior leniency. Despite this shift and the public's demand for tougher enforcement, attempts by federal courts to hold prosecutors to higher standards have still failed, as appellate courts have denied lower courts any meaningful oversight over prosecutorial discretion.[15] Similarly, a much publicized policy shift by the Justice Department (known as the Yates Memorandum) that was intended to mandate more prosecutions of individuals has not yet resulted in measurable change.[16] Even in the face of a torrent of public criticism, prosecutorial practices have not been altered significantly, and the bureaucratic equilibrium seemingly remains stable.

The one thing that has changed (under President Trump) is that there is a declining rate of criminal corporate prosecutions. Mainly for this reason, there have been fewer DPAs recently. In this light, we will broaden our focus and look at the interplay of civil and criminal enforcement directed at public corporations. Prior critics, who have focused only on criminal prosecutions, have thereby ignored the much greater enforcement effort that is civil in character. Within this context, although the SEC has been the principal regulatory enforcer in cases of corporate wrongdoing, a host of other agencies are also active and sometimes in competition. But the pattern remains the same and is one in which civil fines and penalties are escalating enormously but without any apparent coordination or clear rationale.[17] Because (as later explained) these fines cannot be kept by the enforcement agency, they do not fund enforcement. Worse yet, enforcement actions against individuals remain more the exception than the rule. Efforts by federal judges to reject either deferred prosecution agreements or weak settlements by the SEC have been curbed by appellate courts.[18] No matter how hollow and empty the settlement, the district court is today required to accept it. This may sound outrageous, but it has become settled law, absent legislative change.[19]

This pattern of equivocal enforcement by both civil and criminal enforcers sets the stage for asking why it is so difficult to prosecute senior executives. At the outset, a basic distinction must be drawn between the 2008 crisis and earlier episodes (such as the savings and loan crisis of the 1980s) when bank executives were prosecuted en masse. One critical difference may be that the 2008 crisis involved regulatory crimes, but not traditional predatory crimes involving obvious personal gain or self-dealing (which was in fact at the core of many savings and loan failures). Another difference involves the size of the defendant corporation: savings and loans are relatively small and have thin management teams, while banks are greater in size by orders of magnitude and decision making is diffused within a much larger corporate hierarchy. Also, the empirical evidence suggests that if prosecutors did indict more senior executives, they would lose much more frequently. In this light, current policies that enable prosecutors to avoid individual prosecutions also protect prosecutors from embarrassment. Some will interpret this conclusion to confirm their view that prosecutors are excessively risk averse. But one can go further and recognize that, to prosecute individual executives successfully, the government needs an ally who can fund and assist its investigation. This book will suggest that federal prosecutors investigating major organizational misconduct will generally need the cooperation of the corporation before they can undertake successful individual prosecutions. Although prosecutorial culture favors a small tight-knit team of prosecutors taking on the much larger defendant, this lone wolf style cannot succeed in the contemporary environment. Just as the cavalry had to yield a century ago to tanks and a more mechanized attack, so too must the individual federal prosecutor forgo being a knight errant and join in a more coordinated plan of battle. That transition will, however, be resisted.

At this point, it is time to turn from description to prescription and outline possible reforms. Initially, we will consider the difficulties in achieving deterrence. To deter, economics insists that the expected penalty must exceed the expected gain, but this is hard to quantify or even estimate. A first question will be why it matters whether the organization or the executive is punished, as arguably both can be deterred. Here, economists sometimes argue that it is less costly to prosecute the firm than the individual.[20] But that analysis, it will be argued, misses much. Not only may it be impossible to deter the organization with financial penalties, but high penalties can cause externalities, as creditors, employees, and others closely connected to the corporation are injured. Politically, enforcement will be unsustainable if it requires penalties so high as to shut down plants, require layoffs, or curb corporate operations.

To be sure, this argument about externalities can prove too much; shareholders have to suffer if the firm is to be deterred. Nonetheless, other constituencies can be spared. This book will suggest the superiority of penalties that fall only on the firm's shareholders, not its employees, creditors, or others. Some have gone much further, arguing that corporate criminal liability should be abolished so that prosecutors would necessarily focus only on individuals. Such a policy, however, ignores the legitimate goals underlying a corporate prosecution. Better than anyone else, the corporation can identify the responsible employees and agents who planned and carried out the criminal conduct. Put simply, in the modern decentralized corporation, the responsible individuals are hard to identify and convict, unless their corporate employer cooperates against them. Only then can evidence and witnesses feasibly be assembled. Thus, an underrecognized purpose of corporate criminal liability is to create a threat aimed at the corporate entity that leads it to cooperate in the prosecutions of individuals (and particularly senior executives). It is a mistake then to pose an either/or choice between prosecuting the firm or the individual, as only joint prosecutions are likely to result in successful individual prosecutions in complex cases. Put bluntly, only if the corporate entity is threatened severely will it cooperate meaningfully against its executives.

Probably the greatest failure of current institutional arrangements is that the prosecutor today delegates the investigative function to a law firm chosen by the defendants. In a nutshell, that is how deferred prosecutions work. The result is predictable: a great deal of data is generated, but it tends to implicate only lower-level executives. Once, prosecutors did these investigations themselves, using the grand jury as their investigative tool, but in the internet era, when investigations sprawl around the globe and complex cases commonly involve millions of emails and tons of documents, this is no longer feasible. Thus, this book will propose means by which an independent investigation can be arranged and financed. But again this requires the cooperation of the corporation, and constitutional problems lurk here (as recent cases have shown[21]).

To prosecute individuals successfully, documents alone are not enough. "Flesh and blood" witnesses are needed to testify against the key defendants. To encourage such testimony, witnesses must be given incentives in the form of immunity or leniency. This is true in Mafia cases as well as in white collar cases. Although underlings and junior employees can sometimes be "flipped" and persuaded to testify against their superiors, this is most likely when they are motivated by a strong threat. The corporation needs to be motivated in the same manner, by giving the corporate entity strong incentives to turn over all evidence and cooperate in the prosecution of its senior executives. This requires that the corporation be threatened—much more than it is today. If a sufficient threat to the corporation is created, the corporation and its senior executives are forced to compete for the prosecutor's leniency in a zero-sum game. In such a world, either of the two—the corporation or the executives— could turn on the other. This is hard-nosed, even cruel, but desirable; the incentives for each to turn on the other should be deliberately maximized. This book will make a specific proposal to this end that it calls the *prisoner's dilemma strategy.*[22]

Other strategies have been proposed, including making senior executives strictly liable for their corporation's misdeeds or liable based only on a showing of negligence. In particular, Senator Elizabeth Warren has proposed highly controversial legislation that would adopt a respondeat superior standard under which the CEO would be liable for financial failures or illegal conduct by his or her company if either failure was attributable to the CEO's negligence.[23] This book will compare these and other strategies against its preferred strategy. It will conclude, however, that even if significant changes in substantive criminal law were adopted, their impact on the prosecutor's ability to prosecute individual executives successfully would likely be minimal.

Unsurprisingly, this book will conclude that there was disturbing underenforcement, both on the criminal side and by the SEC and other civil enforcers, following the 2008 crash. It will continue to be debated whether this was more attributable to political constraints, to risk aversion, or to the logistical challenge of identifying the most culpable decision makers within large organizations. But the issue for the future is not who was most at fault following 2008. Rather, it is how enforcement problems can be best addressed to minimize or mitigate the risk of another systemic failure. When we look at the most significant corporate scandals since the 2008 crisis (the most obvious nominees being Volkswagen's emissions scandal, Boeing's failure to recognize the problems with its 737 MAX airplane, and the opioid epidemic), we are witnessing not "one shot" corporate failures but persistent intentional misbehavior that flies in the face of government policies and regulations on the apparent premise that the government can be safely disregarded. That is the problem of underenforcement on which this book focuses.

Underenforcement, it argues, results chiefly from the logistical mismatch between the government's limited enforcement resources and the nearly limitless capacity of the large corporation to resist and delay. But this mismatch is greatly compounded because enforcement officials—both civil and criminal—have become convinced that the best policy for them is to trade leniency (through deferred prosecution agreements, prosecutorial declinations, and sentencing credits) for cooperation from the corporate defendant (chiefly through the conduct of an internal investigation). In all likelihood, an optimal enforcement policy should involve some mixture of carrots and sticks, but the key claim of this book is that today the terms of this trade unduly favor the defendants and leave the government with much too little. Worse yet, we are rapidly moving in the direction of an "all carrots and no sticks" policy. Not only is the business community pressing for such a policy that will save corporations from even being charged with a crime if they have a "robust" compliance plan, but academics have aided and abetted this transition by justifying the exchange of leniency for cooperation, without clearly recognizing the need for limits and conditions on this exchange.

Finally, one consequence of underenforcement needs special emphasis. In a society increasingly concerned with growing inequality, enforcement policy can foster growing legal inequality. The relative immunity of senior executives from legal punishment implies such legal inequality. Where once scandal and crisis triggered a punitive legal response, this reaction has become more muted since 2008. Continuing failure begins to call into question the legitimacy of our legal system. To paraphrase Anatole France, the law in its infinite majesty forbids the rich and the poor alike to steal bread, but it now arguably punishes fraud and deception only when committed by those at lower echelons or reckless outliers.

TWO

Scenes from the Crash

THIS CHAPTER WILL NOT attempt a comprehensive review of the 2008 crash. Such reviews are available elsewhere.[1] Instead, its goal is to sift through the evidence to find illustrations that show why the prosecutorial response to the crash was equivocal, inadequate, and possibly politically constrained. Unlike earlier market crashes, which produced waves of criminal prosecutions, the 2008 crash did not. Prosecutions were conspicuous by their absence. Those that occurred were generally of low-ranking employees, mortgage applicants, and a few unlucky persons who blundered their way into conviction. What explains this disparity? What were the obstacles to prosecution? Several episodes stand out.

The Arthur Andersen Debacle

The Department of Justice's attitude toward using the criminal sanction against public corporations changed abruptly following the Supreme Court's 2005 decision in *Arthur Andersen LLP v. United States*.[2] Embarrassed and placed on the defensive by the Court's unanimous reversal of Andersen's conviction, prosecutors needed to find a different approach—for legal, political, and logistical reasons.

By no means, however, did that decision show that Andersen was innocent or undeserving of criminal prosecution. Arthur Andersen had audited both Enron and WorldCom, the two biggest auditing scandals in U.S. history, and it was deeply involved in some other major contemporaneous accounting scandals.[3] Between 1997 and 2002, it had paid out more than $500 million to settle lawsuits, much more than any of its rival auditing firms.[4] In short, it was

15

hardly the unlucky scapegoat that a vengeful government chose to visit retribution upon; rather, it was the biggest risk taker.

The first sentence of the Court's opinion conveys the essential facts: "As Enron Corporation's financial difficulties became public in 2001, petitioner Arthur Andersen LLP, Enron's auditors, instructed its employees to destroy documents pursuant to its document retention policy."[5] At a minimum, that was reckless and probably culpable behavior, but the facts here need to be understood in more detail. In August 2001, Enron's CEO (Jeffrey Skilling) unexpectedly resigned, and a senior accountant at Enron (Sharon Watkins) turned whistle-blower and warned Ken Lay, the former CEO who had replaced Skilling, that Enron could "implode in a wave of accounting scandals."[6] She similarly notified the senior members of Andersen's engagement team that handled Enron. Then, on August 28, the *Wall Street Journal* ran a major story announcing that serious and continuing accounting improprieties had occurred at Enron.[7]

It was all downhill from there. In response, the SEC opened an informal investigation that same day. Andersen circled its wagons, formed a "crisis-response" team, and retained outside counsel to represent it. None of that was surprising or irregular. One member of that crisis-response team was Nancy Temple, an in-house counsel at Andersen. She clearly recognized, in her own words, that "some SEC investigation" was "highly probable,"[8] but from October 12 on, she sought repeatedly to "remind the engagement team of our document and retention policy"—which, of course, was a euphemism for reminding them of an Andersen policy of destroying all drafts and documents related to the Enron representation.[9]

Rightly or wrongly, such a policy is generally permissible—up until the government opens an investigation. On October 17, the SEC notified Enron that it was beginning an investigation, and on October 19, it forwarded a copy of that letter to Andersen. Nonetheless, on October 19 and 20, Temple continued to instruct the crisis-response team to "make sure to follow the [document] policy."[10] The shredding of documents appears to have continued until at least November 9, 2001, a day after the SEC served Enron and Andersen with subpoenas for records.

In contrast to its more equivocal behavior following the 2008 crisis, the Justice Department acted quickly, indicting both Andersen and an executive (David Duncan, the head of its Enron engagement team). Although the prosecution painted Nancy Temple as the principal villain who set the shredding in motion (and persisted in demanding it), she was not prosecuted. After a lengthy trial, the jury initially deadlocked and informed the court they could not reach a decision. Following standard procedure, the trial court delivered a "dynamite charge,"[11] and three days later, the jury convicted Andersen.

(Duncan had already pleaded guilty.) The Fifth Circuit affirmed,[12] but then the Supreme Court surprised many by granting certiorari.

Why? Andersen was hopelessly insolvent and had, by that point, almost no chance of economic survival. The Court's opinion justified granting certiorari by focusing on a conflict among the Circuits on the meaning of the particular obstruction-of-justice statute that the government had relied on.[13] That seemed a strange explanation for certiorari because the particular statute that the government had used (18 U.S.C. § 1512[b]) had been superseded for all practical purposes by a new criminal statute on obstruction of justice, which Congress had inserted into the Sarbanes-Oxley Act precisely in response to the conduct in Enron and WorldCom. Thus, because section 1512 was unlikely to be used again, there was no urgent need to resolve the Circuits' conflict. One is therefore logically led to infer that something else was bothering the Court and motivated its grant of certiorari.

What that factor was became clear in its decision. Section 1512(b) is a curiously drafted statute that reads:

> (b) Whoever knowingly uses intimidation, threatens, or corruptly persuades another person ... with intent to ...
> (a) cause or induce any person to——
>> (A) withhold testimony, or withhold a record, document or other object from an official proceeding;
>> (B) alter, destroy, mutilate or conceal an object with intent to impair the object's integrity or availability for use in an official proceeding; ...

There was little doubt that the crime's conduct elements had occurred (i.e., documents had been destroyed and thereby rendered unavailable for use in the Justice Department's investigation), but what level of intent did the prosecution have to prove? The Court found that the above statutory language required the prosecutor to show that the defendant had acted both "knowingly and corruptly" in persuading its employees to shred documents. The prosecution had argued (at least as plausibly) that section 1512(b) only required it to prove that the defendant acted "corruptly" when the defendant was accused of "persuading" another person to destroy documents. The significance of the Court's semantic union of "knowingly and corruptly" was (at least in the Court's mind) that it necessitated proof that a defendant was "conscious of wrongdoing."[14] Merely proving that the defendant had shredded documents that regulators wanted was not enough.

Because the trial court had instructed the jury that it could convict "even if the defendant honestly and sincerely believed that its conduct was lawful,"[15] the outcome at the Supreme Court was foreshadowed once the Court had determined the requisite level of intent. Further, the trial court's charge to the jury varied from the traditional formulation for such charges in that Circuit by stating that it was only necessary that Andersen have "impeded" the government's investigation, not that it have sought to dishonestly "subvert" or "undermine" the investigation.[16] To the Supreme Court, the critical difference here was that, although one can innocently "impede" an investigation, to "subvert" or "undermine" it linguistically requires a culpable intent.

That the Supreme Court was unanimous signaled that the Court believed the prosecution and the courts below were trivializing the mental element in crime—what the law calls mens rea.[17] In its view, the district court and the Fifth Circuit had rewritten section 1512(b) so as to eliminate any need for a requisite finding of dishonesty. Instead, all that was necessary was that the government's investigation be "impeded" (which could be seemingly satisfied if the investigation was simply delayed by the actions of a zealous defense counsel). To the Court, a showing of moral culpability was central to the long history of Anglo-American criminal law.[18]

Did this mean that the Court was acquitting Andersen or declaring it innocent? Not at all! The Court was simply holding that the jury instructions were erroneous and therefore the case would have to be retried, with the trial court giving appropriate instructions. Although the Justice Department could have retried its case against Andersen, it saw no good reason to do so. By 2005, Andersen was a corpse—dead and buried for all practical purposes.

But this distinction between requiring a retrial and finding the defendant innocent (or at least not guilty) was lost on the general public. From their simpler perspective, Andersen had been convicted, and then the conviction was overturned, leaving Andersen in seemingly the same position as an individual who had been executed while his appeal was pending but then had his conviction reversed posthumously. Indeed, this was exactly the message that the business community proclaimed: Andersen was a tragedy, they asserted, because an innocent defendant had perished. For the Department of Justice, this was a disaster and raised the danger of a hostile congressional reaction.

Would Andersen have still failed if it had not been indicted? The best answer is *probably*. Even before its indictment, its clients had begun to back away in large numbers, as any association with Andersen had become stigmatizing. Employees streamed out of Andersen before the verdict, apparently seeing the handwriting on the wall. Andersen had more than 85,000 employees in 2001 but was down to 3,000 in 2002 on its conviction.[19] Worse yet, the plaintiff's lawyers were waiting in the wings—like vultures. Eventually, their civil suits against Enron and others were settled for over $8 billion, and the class actions against WorldCom, which were then still at an early stage, settled for another $7 billion. Although Andersen paid little toward these settlements (because all realized it had nothing left), the plaintiff law firms compelled Andersen to agree that if it ever acquired any income or assets, it would promptly turn them over to benefit their class. In short, even though it never filed for bankruptcy, Andersen's assets were exhausted, and its partners were compelled to flee to make a good living elsewhere and escape personal liability.

Most importantly, the impact of Andersen's collapse fell disproportionately on those who were the most innocent. Not only were employees laid off, but Anderson's pensioners found that their pensions were not fully funded. In contrast, those Andersen partners who were not involved in the Enron representation could simply take their clients with them to another large auditing firm and only suffered the loss of their capital account at Andersen. But their employees were left at the mercy of the market. For a firm that depended on its reputational capital (as Andersen or any audit firm did), a criminal conviction implied a corporate death sentence—and one whose impact fell chiefly on the least culpable parties.

What produced all this destruction? Ironically, it was not the financial penalty, as the maximum fine that Andersen faced was only $500,000[20]—probably much less than its monthly legal bills from defense counsel. Rather, Andersen was uniquely vulnerable to the loss of its reputation. Although firms that did not deal with the public could suffer a conviction and survive, Andersen was in the unique business of providing assurances to investors and credibility to its clients. By the end, having Andersen as their auditor was as reassuring to investors as a certificate attesting to their management's honesty from Bernie Madoff.

So what are the lessons of the *Andersen* case? First, the use of the criminal sanction on the corporation can impose externalities on third parties (especially on employees and creditors). Corporate collapses from a conviction happen only rarely,[21] but Drexel Burnham is another example of a financial firm that also did not survive long after its conviction.[22] Financial firms seem more exposed to collapse, and similar "runs" did occur at a number of financial institutions during the 2008 crisis (Indy Mac, Washington Mutual, and, of course, AIG).[23] Most of these institutions were not accused of crimes, but a criminal prosecution would have likely sunk all of them.

This risk of postconviction insolvency is a factor that may cause courts to be unduly lenient in order not to force the defendant into bankruptcy. Even when insolvency is not an issue, high penalties can still fall on innocent third parties. If a "too big to fail" bank were subjected to an extremely punitive fine, it might be forced to curtail lending, lay off employees, or halt desirable activities. Some dismiss this problem as an inevitable cost that deserves no weight in public policy deliberations,[24] but that is ignoring the six-hundred-pound gorilla that is undeniably in the room. A balance needs to be struck. Later, in chapter 5, this book will explore alternative sanctions that are designed to fall on the corporation (and thus on its shareholders) but not on other constituencies (such as employees and creditors). The key point here is not just that we do not wish to punish the innocent but also that we cannot convince courts to be sufficiently punitive to deter effectively, unless we find a means by which to focus the incidence of the penalty so that it does not fall on the least culpable.

A second and more obvious impact of the *Andersen* case was to incline the Justice Department toward greater use of DPAs, because they were less likely to prompt a corporate collapse. The fear gnawing at regulators was that the indictment of a major bank could cause a run on the bank. Even if the likelihood of bank runs and Andersen-like collapses are remote, the business community pressed hard for greater use of DPAs (and even softer alternatives).[25] To be sure, the DPA was already part of the Justice Department's inventory well before Andersen's collapse, but its example propelled a marked shift to greater reliance on DPAs.[26]

Finally, *Andersen* contains an important lesson about judicial behavior: courts resist strict liability and try hard to preserve some requirement of mens rea as a precondition to criminal liability. Sometimes, they may twist the statutory language to achieve this result (and *Andersen* may have been such a case), but this is a recurrent phenomenon.[27] We will return to this theme when we consider current proposals for holding corporate executives to stricter or negligence-based standards. *Andersen*'s key message—that "consciousness of wrongdoing" is normally a precondition to criminal liability—may not be a constitutional requirement, but it is a judicial preference that courts will try hard to read into statutes.

The Bear Stearns Shocker

If the Arthur Andersen reversal cautioned senior policy makers at the Justice Department about indicting public corporations, that does not explain why they did not simply turn to individual prosecutions. Indeed, in 2008, even before the collapse of Lehman, prosecutors did make such an effort—and failed abysmally. How much this failure traumatized prosecutors and made them reluctant to bring similar cases can be debated, but clearly it was a factor, and the causes of this failure need to be understood.

In June 2007, as the housing market began to decline precipitously, two Bear Stearns hedge funds that had specialized in derivatives linked to real estate announced that the housing decline had placed them on the brink of insolvency.[28] Bear Stearns pledged a $3 billion loan (which later contributed to its own de facto insolvency), but the loan was not enough, and the two funds filed for bankruptcy on August 1, 2007.[29]

After a relatively quick investigation, the U.S. Attorney for the Eastern District of New York indicted the two senior managers of these two funds on June 19, 2008, on conspiracy and fraud charges, and the SEC sued them on the same day.[30] This prosecution occurred at a critical moment: after Bear Stearns itself had stumbled to the brink of insolvency (and been pushed by the Federal Reserve into a "shotgun marriage" with JPMorgan Chase in March 2008) but before the epic Lehman crisis in October 2008.[31]

Charging these two Bear Stearns managers—Ralph R. Cioffi and Matthew M. Tannin—required prosecutors to make a decision about tactics. The prosecution's basic claim was that the two defendants knew the hedge funds were nearly insolvent but repeatedly told their investors that all was going well.[32] The problem here was that to show that the two funds were already on the brink of bankruptcy could force the prosecution to use complex valuation models that would likely prove unfathomable to the jury. Also, the prosecution's burden was not simply to show that false statements were made but that defendants had "knowingly and willfully" made such statements—that is, with an intent to defraud.[33] For both these reasons, the prosecutors chose to focus on inconsistencies between the emails the two defendants exchanged between themselves and what they told investors. For example, in possibly the clearest example, Tannin, using his personal email, emailed Cioffi, through the personal email of the latter's wife, on April 22, 2007, to summarize how he saw the market. This circuitous routing alone was suspicious, but the message was devastatingly pessimistic: "The subprime market looks pretty damn ugly.... If we believe the [CDO report is] ANYWHERE CLOSE to accurate, I think we should close the funds now. The reason for this is that if [the CDO report] is correct, then the entire market is toast.... If AAA bonds are systematically downgraded, then there is simply no way for us to make money—ever."[34]

Two days later, the two defendants met with senior executives at Bear Stearns and told them they were confident and expected continued success.[35] A day later, they were even more confident, advising investors in a conference call: "So, from structural point of view, from an asset point of view, from a surveillance point of view, we're very comfortable with exactly where we are.... The structure of the fund has performed exactly the way it was designed to perform.... And there's no basis for thinking this is a big disaster."[36] These inconsistent statements certainly supported the prosecution's case that the defendants had made "knowingly and willful" misrepresentations. But they exposed the prosecution to a counterattack. Defense counsel responded that the prosecution was trying to hold the defendants criminally responsible for failing to predict a market crash that surprised virtually everyone. Having more resources and staff, defense counsel had searched the defendants' emails thoroughly and found other examples in which the defendants expressed confidence in the direction of the market. In fact, the two defendants appear to have alternated between deep depression and manic euphoria about the future of the market.

To be sure, the evidence contained other seemingly fraudulent statements; for example, the defendants had estimated that their subprime exposure amounted to only between 6 and 8 percent of their portfolios (but the actual figure was allegedly 60 percent).[37] Cioffi had also redeemed most of his own investment in the two funds at a late stage (without telling his investors), and he was thus indicted for insider trading as well.[38] But the jury saw the case as hanging on whether they truly knew the market was collapsing when they expressed confidence in April 2007.

After only two days of deliberations (a short time in a complex white collar case),[39] the jury came in with a verdict, acquitting both defendants on all counts.[40] As one juror explained to the press: "There was a reasonable doubt on every charge. We just didn't feel the case had been proven."[41] This abrupt outcome was a shock, a demoralizing blow to the solar plexus for the Justice Department and other U.S. Attorneys' offices, as all were awaiting an expected victory.

What were the lessons of this failure?

First, on the tactical level, the prosecution had relied too much on emails. For every "bad" email, there was another "good" or at least an ambiguous email.

Second, the prosecution presented no live witnesses that they had "flipped." Typically, in most criminal cases, there is an underling who testifies that the Mafia don or corporate CEO (as the case may be) was instructing them to cheat or commit a crime (and knew very well that they were defrauding victims). But in the Bear Stearns hedge fund cases, the prosecution offered no such testimony and relied only on documents and emails.

What then is the bottom line? Jesse Eisinger opines that the prosecutors had been "sloppy and hasty."[42] Perhaps, but the real irony here is that the one thing that these prosecutors were not was "chickenshit." They proceeded resolutely, convinced of the defendant's guilt, but possibly without the caution that other prosecutors show (which Eisinger generally deems cowardly).

Two other implications may be latent in the facts of this prosecution that we will encounter again. First, defense counsel usually have a logistical advantage. Here, even though defense counsel in this case were pressed for time, they had the financial resources to hire staff and investigate the entire record carefully, and this enabled them in this case to demonstrate that the prosecutors were only showing the jury one side of the emails. The defendants had been virtually manic-depressive in their shifting view of market conditions.

Second, juries may not care much about a regulatory violation, standing alone, at least as compared to a classic crime. Although the defendants in the

Bear Stearns case had understated their exposure to subprime mortgages, this did not show the jury that they were thieves and felons. A basic difference needs to be recognized between the conduct of Cioffi and Tannin and that of a more classic white collar offender (say, Bernie Madoff): Cioffi and Tannin were not embezzling money from investors (as Madoff was) but were trying to keep a sinking ship afloat. The victim that lost the most from their conduct was Bear Stearns itself, which made a $3 billion loan in an unsuccessful effort to save the two funds (based on Cioffi and Tannin's request). Without denying that the defendants' conduct was wrongful, their culpability was far from self-evident to the jury.

The bottom line was that the Bear Stearns hedge fund prosecution, which was supposed to initiate a tough, retributive policy toward those who had contributed to the 2008 crash, yielded only an abject failure and became the last criminal prosecution brought by the federal government against even mid-level officers at a Wall Street financial institution.

The Lehman Abdication

Lehman's bankruptcy in September 2008 implied that the firm itself would not be criminally prosecuted. Lehman was gone—an empty shell. If fines were imposed on it, they would only reduce the modest payout to creditors (and interfere with the faint hope of banking regulators that they could still find a buyer for Lehman somewhere).

But Lehman seemingly offered abundant opportunities for individual prosecutions. Indeed, Lehman was the functional equivalent to Enron, which was the star "villain" in the wave of scandals that followed a lesser market collapse in 2001 to 2002. But nothing happened to Lehman. Not only was no one indicted, but the SEC brought no actions against any senior Lehman executive. Only the plaintiff's bar sued (and they recovered a significant settlement, which suggests the SEC could have also settled an action favorably).[43]

Why did neither the Justice Department nor the SEC take action? There are three rival interpretations that each have their adherents: (1) there was no fraud; (2) political constraints caused both Justice and the SEC to hold back at a time when the federal government mainly wanted to stabilize Wall Street and restore the economy; and (3) Lehman's failure was just too large and complicated a phenomenon, and a thorough investigation would have imposed a logistical burden that neither Justice nor the SEC could have borne alone (particularly in view of other scandals they were then facing[44]).

Was There Fraud at Lehman?

Some view Lehman's failure as simply the natural result of an overly leveraged financial institution, which had failed to diversify and had concentrated all its bets on real estate, collapsing when the real estate market turned cyclically downward (as, sooner or later, it does). From this perspective, the only crime was that of stupidity.

But this overlooks that the market was closely watching Lehman's every statement and knew that Lehman was exposed because it had heavily concentrated its bets on real estate. For such a financial institution, a critical focus will be on its liquidity. Drexel Burnham had similarly failed a few years earlier when it could not roll over its commercial paper. That proved to be Lehman's undoing as well when it could not roll over its repos (a very short-term financial instrument). The sophisticated players were following Lehman's liquidity closely, but Lehman hid its problems skillfully.

Knowing the market's focus was on liquidity, Lehman reported that its liquidity pool was $34 billion at the end of the first quarter of 2008; then, it increased this figure to $45 billion by the end of the second quarter.[45] Finally, even on the doorsteps of bankruptcy, it gave the figure as $42 billion at the end of the third quarter.[46]

The problem with these estimates was that much of the money in this liquidity pool was not available to creditors but had been deposited with the principal clearing banks with whom Lehman did business (as a condition of their continuing to work with Lehman). Even if not formally pledged, these "comfort" funds would be under the control of these banks, which could set off Lehman's debts to them against these funds. According to Lehman's own internal estimate, something like $15 billion (out of a then $41 billion liquidity pool) had been so deposited as collateral with other banks.[47] In June 2008, Citigroup demanded and received another $2 billion in collateral, but this amount was also not subtracted from the liquidity pool.[48]

As the crisis deepened and investors became more anxious, Lehman's CEO, Richard Fuld, fired Erin Callan, Lehman's CFO, and replaced her with Ian Lowitt, who had been an investment banker and marketing star but was not a "numbers person." Lowitt confidently told investors on a June 16, 2008, conference call that Lehman had "significantly increased . . . our liquidity pool."[49] By the time Lehman filed its Form 10-Q for the second quarter, it had also pledged an additional $5.5 billion to JPMorgan Chase from this pool, but again this was not disclosed. Instead, Lehman disclosed only that it had "strengthened its liquidity position," and it added, even more questionably, that its liquidity pool was "unencumbered."[50] As Lehman's new CFO, Lowitt signed this second quarter Form 10-Q and certified its accuracy. Then, on September 10, 2008, five days before bankruptcy was declared, Lowitt told shareholders in a conference call that Lehman's liquidity "remains very strong."[51] Based on this evidence, Lowitt's legal neck was well into the noose, but shockingly prosecutors never even interviewed him. No one at Lehman was a more obvious target, at least for inquiry.

Another possible basis for at least a civil fraud action was Lehman's repeated use of an accounting gimmick that allowed Lehman to hide temporarily some of its debt (thereby improving its debt-to-equity ratio and reducing its apparent leverage). This stratagem has become known as Lehman's "Repo 105" gambit.

The gimmick works like this: At the close of the quarter, Lehman nominally would sell an asset to a bank or institutional investor, subject to an obligation on the part of Lehman to repurchase it. (This obligation to repurchase gives rise to the term *repo*.)[52] This arranged "sale" spared Lehman from having to acknowledge that its assets had declined in value and thus that Lehman's balance sheet was inflated (whereas a true sale at fair market value would reveal this). In substance, this transaction was really a short-term loan to Lehman, which was secured by the asset nominally "sold" to the counterparts (but in reality only parked with it as collateral). On an agreed date (generally only days later), Lehman would buy back the asset (with the investor receiving a small amount of interest for its de facto loan to Lehman). By doing this quarterly, Lehman could take the moneys it received and use them to pay down its outstanding debt on the last day of each quarter (but only temporarily). Of course, Lehman would then reborrow this amount to buy the asset back. The net effect was to allow Lehman on the last day of each quarter (when it reported its results) to remove billions in debt from its balance sheet (only to restore this amount days later). Yes, it was simply a gimmick to hide debt and improve its debt-to-equity ratio. According to Lehman's bankruptcy examiner, Lehman used Repo 105 transactions to move $50 billion off its balance sheet in the second quarter of 2008.[53] Needless to add, Lehman did not disclose its use of these Repo 105 transactions to the SEC, to its rating agencies, to its investors, or even to its own board.[54]

In fairness, neither of these fraud theories was a slam dunk. In the case of the failure to disclose the degree to which Lehman's liquidity pool was encumbered, defendants could reply that Lehman had the right to reclaim the funds that it deposited with its major clearing banks. Of course, if it had done so, those banks would have ceased to do business with Lehman (and it was doubtful that Lehman could find substitute banks). Arguably, Lowitt's misstatements could be characterized by defendants as the product of his being brand new on the job and not a "numbers person"; thus, it would be claimed that he did not have the requisite intent to defraud. Finally, the individual defendants might be able to rely on advice from Lehman's lawyers that more did not need to be disclosed.

In the case of the Repo 105 transactions, defendants could point to the fact that accounting rules permitted the characterization of these short-term loans as "sales." Also, accounting rules are confusing and opaque to a jury, and prosecutors might reasonably fear that a trial on accounting issues would become hopelessly arcane for a jury of laymen. Defendants could predictably assemble a host of accounting expert witnesses willing to testify on cue that Lehman's characterization of these transactions as sales was entirely appropriate.

Perhaps the most objective assessment of these questions was set forth in the exhaustive report of Lehman's bankruptcy examiner. Anton Valukas, a former U.S. Attorney for the Northern District of Illinois and the chairman of Jenner & Block, a major Chicago law firm, was appointed as bankruptcy examiner in January 2009. Using the full resources of his law firm, he conducted a diligent one-year study (as later discussed) and concluded that meritorious causes of action for fraud could be asserted for securities fraud against Lehman's officers.

Specifically, he made findings in early 2010 both on the issue of Lehman's overstated liquidity pool and its use of the Repo 105 transactions. At the outset, taking a moderate position, he conceded that the business decisions leading up to Lehman's failure "were largely within the protection of the business judgment rule."[55] But, he then added, "the decision not to disclose the effects of those judgments" gave rise to fraud claims that could lead a judge or jury to find Lehman's senior officers (including its last three CFOs) liable.[56]

Regarding the Repo 105 transactions, he described their "sole function as employed by Lehman" to have been "balance sheet manipulation."[57] He explained:

> In 2007–08, Lehman knew that net leverage numbers were critical to the rating agencies and to counterparty confidence. Its ability to deleverage by selling assets was severely limited by the illiquidity and depressed prices of the assets it had accumulated. Against this backdrop, Lehman turned to Repo 105 transactions to temporarily remove $50 billion of assets from its balance sheet at first and second quarter ends in 2008 so that it could report significantly lower net leverage numbers than reality. Lehman did so despite its understanding that none of its peers used similar accounting at that time to arrive at their leverage numbers to which Lehman would be compared.[58]

In short, this was not a "gimmick" that everyone used but instead one that no one else had ever attempted. Further, Valukas found it was material, even under Lehman's own definition of materiality,[59] because it "created a misleading portrayal of Lehman's true financial health."[60]

With respect to Lehman's overstated liquidity pool, Valukas was equally concise:

> Lehman did not publicly disclose that by June 2008 significant components of its reported liquidity pool had become difficult to monetize. As late as September 10, 2008, Lehman publicly announced that its liquidity pool was approximately $40 billion, but a substantial portion of that total was in fact encumbered or otherwise illiquid. . . . By September 12, two days after it reported a $41 billion liquidity pool, the pool actually contained less than $2 billion of readily monetizable assets.[61]

Lehman had lied about this pool for months and continued to lie until the very end. Although Valukas did not predict certain victory, he concluded that sufficient credible evidence existed to support a finding of fraud.[62] In fact, the Southern District had won a similar criminal case only a few years earlier that was based primarily on a financial institution's failure to disclose its eroding liquidity.[63]

Thus, the bottom line seems clear: there was sufficient evidence of fraud by senior Lehman officers that a reasonably aggressive prosecutor might have brought the case under normal circumstances.

Were Lehman and Its Officers Politically Protected?

If prosecutors could have pursued Lehman's senior officers but did not, does this imply that they were politically restrained? There is no direct evidence of this, but some circumstantial evidence points in this direction.

First, given the prominence and centrality of Lehman to the 2008 crash, it is surprising that the Justice Department in Washington never opened an investigation. In the Enron prosecution, the department formed a strike force, transferred many of its most experienced and able prosecutors to it, and did not allow individual U.S. attorneys' offices to compete with it. Instead, in the Lehman case, the investigation of Lehman was left to the U.S. attorneys in the Southern District and Eastern District of New York. Possibly still traumatized by its inability to secure any conviction in the Bear Stearns hedge fund case, the Eastern District dropped out quickly.[64] The Southern District did assign some personnel, but no serious investigation was undertaken. Many of the most prominent senior officers at Lehman were not even interviewed.[65] In his detailed study of the Lehman investigation, Jesse Eisinger identifies only one assistant U.S. attorney who regularly focused on Lehman (and even she was not working full time on the case).[66] Meanwhile, Valukas, as the bankruptcy examiner, had roughly 130 Jenner & Block attorneys working on their investigation of Lehman for over fourteen months.[67]

Possibly the Southern District's lack of interest in Lehman was because it thought the task was overwhelming and simply beyond its resources. Clearly, only the bankruptcy examiner caught on to the critical fact that Lehman's claimed liquidity pool was encumbered and not truly available in the event of a liquidity crisis. Thus, if we look only at the Southern District (and ignore the passivity of the Justice Department), one cannot easily decide whether the prosecution just missed it or whether an implicit understanding to avoid criminal prosecutions of senior financial executives had somehow been communicated within the department.

On the other hand, if we consider the response from both criminal prosecutors and the SEC, the total inaction on the part of regulators and prosecutors becomes more suspicious. Unlike prosecutors, the SEC, which has only civil authority, need not prove that a legal violation was "willful" but only that it was "reckless" (and in some cases, merely that it was negligent).[68] Although the SEC did interview Lehman's officers, it charged none of them, apparently believing that Lehman's collapse was only an error in business judgment. Thus, it ignored both Lehman's overstated liquidity pool and the Repo 105 transactions (which were designed to mislead and had no other business purpose). Interestingly, the two directors of the SEC's Division of Enforcement during this period left shortly after this decision, to return to private practice at major law firms that regularly represented the financial industry in securities cases.[69] In fairness, the SEC was overburdened, having filed a record number of enforcement actions in 2011 and 2012, and was under intense criticism for its failure to detect Bernie Madoff. Arguably, it thus needed to avoid any long-term commitment to a potentially costly case. Those arguments are not frivolous. Still, if the FBI had caught record numbers of petty gangsters in the 1930s but ignored Al Capone and John Dillinger, it too would have been criticized—and justly.

This failure to pursue Lehman does not stand alone. The Financial Crisis Inquiry Commission conducted an elaborate study of the 2008 crash and made a number of criminal referrals. None were acted upon and apparently not even seriously considered.[70] Foreign political leaders recurrently lobbied the Department of Justice to be lenient with their banks, lest the Justice Department provoke what they predicted would become a global financial disaster.[71] Lanny Breuer, then the head of the Criminal Division, told a Senate committee that, of course, he paid attention and gave serious consideration to predictions by foreign officials that a bank's prosecution would have "some huge economic effect."[72] Such predictions were recurrently made, and some of these foreign officials even claimed credit in their home countries when the Justice Department seemingly relented.

None of this proves a conspiracy to "go easy" on senior executives at financial institutions. Overworked agencies may shy away from large, complex cases with uncertain outlooks, particularly when they can anticipate strong resistance. Nonetheless, a culture may have become engrained at both the SEC and Justice, which saw it as irresponsible to pursue senior executives at major institutions when their firm had arguably failed because of a marketwide collapse (even if the firm had materially misrepresented its position). This "culture" might have been particularly shared by those officials at both agencies who planned to return to private practice via the "revolving door."

The most plausible alternative explanation to this "quiet conspiracy" hypothesis is that the evidence of fraud at Lehman did not emerge until too late. Although the bankruptcy examiner completed a diligent and expensive investigation that was well beyond the logistical capacity of either Justice or the SEC, this information emerged only after Justice and the SEC had allocated their troops elsewhere and could not recall them.

Does the Logistical Challenge Better Explain the Failure to Pursue Lehman's Officers?

Anton Valukas, as chairman of Jenner & Block, had access to most of his firm's lawyers. Once appointed bankruptcy examiner in January 2009, he involved roughly 130 of them in an investigation that continued for over fourteen months.[73] This team was broken into four units, and each pursued different aspects of the case. Organized, motivated, accustomed to such a pace, the Jenner & Block team produced a 2,200-page report in March 2010, for which Jenner & Block charged $53.5 million.[74] This was a real achievement, but it may have come too late to affect either Justice's or the SEC's own investigations, which had been assigned too little manpower. In any event, the cost and manpower expended on the Jenner & Block investigation were clearly beyond what either Justice or the SEC could afford out of their own budgets and limited staffs.

To be sure, bankruptcy examiners may sometimes engage in overkill (it happened in Enron also) because they know their costs will be paid by the bankruptcy court out of the firm's remaining assets. Law firms love to investigate every aspect of a case—especially when they are certain they can fully bill their time. But even if we were to assume that a fully adequate investigation, sufficient to uncover the critical facts, could have been done for much less than its $53.5 million price and would have taken only a much smaller number of attorneys, such an investigation was still well beyond the capacity of either agency to fund or undertake.

In normal times, the securities fraud unit in the Southern District U.S. attorney's office has between fifteen and twenty attorneys,[75] and they need to handle much more than only one investigation. Particularly in the 2008 to 2010 period, they had an abundance of high-profile cases that merited indictment, including the Bernard Madoff investigation and a series of insider trading prosecutions that soon made Preet Bharara famous.

In overview, the comparative advantage of a large law firm is that it can handle efficiently a major investigation, digesting tons of documents and searching millions of emails. That is something they do regularly, whether in a civil antitrust or securities case or in a major internal investigation for a corporate client. In contrast, assistant U.S. attorneys are used to working in small teams (three to four to a case, even for significant cases). Nor does a U.S. Attorney's Office have the same efficient structure as a modern law firm, where scores of paralegals can be used to assemble and summarize documents and "contract attorneys," hired on a short-term or temporary basis, can be employed to respond to any sudden need for manpower.

That leads to a blunt conclusion: although it is universally agreed that no bank should be "too big to jail," the reality may be that some are "too big to investigate"—at least if the investigation is to be conducted by a U.S. Attorney's Office acting alone. From a policy standpoint, this means that criminal prosecutors need to find someone else to conduct an investigation that in major cases will necessarily be both exhaustive and exhausting. To an unfortunate degree, prosecutors have solved this need by using DPAs that either contemplate an internal investigation or are conditioned on one being first completed. But in these cases, the corporate defendant chooses the law firm to investigate it, and the conflicts of interest are obvious. We will return to this theme, but one of the clearest lessons of Lehman is that the full truth emerged too late. The investigation came after prosecutors had made their fish-or-cut-bait decision on Lehman's executives. Prosecutors abandoned the case because, as of that critical moment, they knew too little.

Reasonable people can disagree about the sufficiency of the evidence of fraud at Lehman, and reasonable people can disagree about whether veiled signals were sent to discourage criminal prosecutions of senior bankers. But it is hard to disagree that Lehman needed a serious and timely investigation, which was done eventually but belatedly. Placing the cart before the horse, the decision not to pursue Lehman executives came before that investigation.

For our purposes, the relevant issue is not to explain definitively the Lehman debacle but to find ways to assure that it will not be repeated. Here, we have found a problem (the need for a full, objective, and timely investigation) that will recur in many cases of continuing corporate misconduct and has to be addressed.

The HSBC Negotiation and the Beginning of Public Outrage

Arthur Andersen, Lehman, the Bear Stearns hedge funds and a host of companies we have not discussed (including AIG, Citicorp, Countrywide Financial, etc.) were all companies that seemingly had engaged in "polite" fraud, hiding from the market the extent of their potential liabilities or riskiness. HSBC was different. It had worked hand in glove with Mexican drug cartels, Iranian terrorists, and other true criminals to launder funds through the United States in amounts that ran into the trillions of dollars. For the Mexican drug cartels, it was the bank of choice—so much so that these cartels specially designed wide boxes that they could just stuff (crammed with cash) into HSBC's overnight delivery windows.[76] When it moved millions around the world for Iranian terror groups, HSBC had to foresee the possibility that it was aiding and abetting future acts of terrorism.

Nor was HSBC a United States–based bank whose collapse would hurt U.S. citizens and possibly jeopardize other U.S. banks or elicit a wave of falling dominoes. Instead, although it was a British bank, it operated mainly in Asia. Its connections with the United States revolved around the need of its clients to convert their ill-gotten funds into dollars—the only international currency that was accepted everywhere. Finally, when the HSBC case came to the point when a decision on indictment had to be made, it was 2012, and the financial crisis had subsided. Panic was no longer in the air.

Prosecutors were essentially provided with their case against HSBC by an elaborate and lengthy report issued by the Senate Judiciary Committee after an extended investigation. Both because they were given their case on a platter and because HSBC had flouted money laundering rules for years and done so with contempt for U.S. regulators, lower-level Justice Department prosecutors pushed to indict HSBC.[77] But once again, senior officials at Justice equivocated. Lanny Breuer, head of the Criminal Division at Justice, conferred with U.S. bank regulators and then flew to England to consult regulators there. His concern was whether an indictment would destabilize the markets. In response, George Osborne, the United Kingdom's Chancellor of the Exchequer, engaged in heavy-handed lobbying, warning the Federal Reserve and the secretary of the Treasury that bringing criminal charges against HSBC could lead to a "global financial disaster."[78]

Why could an indictment have had this effect? A credible explanation was never seriously attempted. Still, the threat worked, and Justice was persuaded to accept one more DPA. To be sure, this was a state-of-the-art DPA, with the fines and forfeitures totaling $1.9 billion.[79] For window dressing, some HSBC officers did step aside, and a corporate monitor was appointed. But neither

HSBC nor any officer was indicted. The monitor reported in 2015 that HSBC was "too slow" in its efforts to improve its internal controls. Unrepentant and unchanged, HSBC had dodged the bullet.

Today, years later, there is little point in emphasizing that the Justice Department's decision seemed weak-kneed, overly deferential, and even cowardly. But three other aspects of this case are very relevant to our purposes.

First, although HSBC can be cited as an illustration of Jesse Eisinger's contention that prosecutors are "chickenshit," it is probably a better illustration that political influence works. If a British official can lobby the head of the Criminal Division not to indict a bank that was a true recidivist, think how much more influential domestic officials, belonging to the same political party and administration, can be. Moreover, by the time HSBC escaped criminal prosecution, the markets had largely stabilized. The HSBC case thus tends to corroborate (but not, by itself, prove) the hypothesis that the Justice Department's behavior was influenced by political pressure not to indict.

Second, the HSBC case marks a key inflection point. Although the Justice Department may have thought it was just doing what it had done before with respect to large banks, it encountered a much more hostile reception this time, both from the public and the press. Attorney General Eric Holder compounded this problem when he told a Senate committee in March 2013 (just three months after the HSBC settlement): "I am concerned that the size of some of these institutions becomes so large that it does become difficult for us to prosecute them when we are hit with indications that if you do prosecute—if you do bring a criminal charge—it will have a negative impact on the national economy, perhaps even the world economy."[80] Holder had not quite said that banks were too big to jail, but it sounded that way to the press.[81] His comments provoked a political firestorm, and he spent the rest of his days in office stressing that no entity was too big to jail.

Third, the HSBC case attracted attention and drew a then record fine because its eager participation in money laundering was detailed in a 340-page report prepared by the Senate's Permanent Subcommittee on Investigation.[82] Once again, a detailed study made a difference, and once again, embarrassment worked, making HSBC more than willing to pay record fines. Absent the Senate report, the case might have attracted little attention, and the fines would likely have been an order of magnitude lower.

After HSBC, the phrase "too big to jail" entered the public domain and became a political watchword. But the next major media development came from out of the blue and appeared in a most unlikely publication for a political broadside, *The New York Review of Books*. In January 2014, *The New York Review of Books* prominently ran an essay by Southern District Judge Jed Rakoff with the very topical title "The Financial Crisis: Why Have No High-Level Executives Been Prosecuted?"[83] Not only was the title provocative, but it ran with a famous nineteenth-century cartoon by Thomas Nast of the Tweed Ring and Tammany Hall, a cartoon that placed all the politicians of that era in a circle, each pointing to the next as the person responsible for some scandal. The implication was that, once again, no one would take responsibility, but collusion was in progress. Together, the article and cartoon caused a sensation. Rakoff was already well known as an independent and activist judge because of earlier battles in 2010 and 2011 that he had fought (and lost) with the SEC over the latter's standard form of settlement (which does not require the defendant to make any admission).[84] But *The New York Review* article went beyond any specific case and described a general pattern. It is hard to overestimate the impact of a respected federal judge saying effectively that the criminal justice system was not working and that the federal government was pulling its punches in the case of the big banks. If Rakoff was already a hero to liberals, he now became an icon.

What Rakoff actually said in *The New York Review* was carefully guarded. He began by stating that he had "no opinion about whether criminal fraud was committed in any given instance" connected to the 2008 crisis,[85] thus protecting himself from disqualification for bias in future cases that might come before him. But he did note "the prevailing view . . . that the crisis was in material respects the product of intentional fraud."[86] If that were true, he added, it was hard to understand the lack of prosecutions, which could amount to "one of the more egregious failures of the criminal justice system in many years."[87]

Then, he shifted into high gear and rejected the Justice Department's claims that high-level fraud was too difficult to prove in most cases. In the course of so doing, he made the point that, even if some firms (very few, he thought) were too big to jail, this rationale for nonprosecution simply did not apply to executives: "No one that I know of has ever contended that a big financial institution would collapse if one or more of its high-level executives were prosecuted, as opposed to the institution itself."[88] This may have been obvious, but it resonated with the public. Then, Rakoff turned to a subtler point: individual prosecutors may prefer the easier case, such as an insider trading prosecution, that can be resolved much more quickly and that produces a personal benefit for the prosecutor (namely, a high-profile conviction that enhances the prosecutor's reputation).[89] Few prosecutors wanted to invest years in a complex investigation that might ultimately produce no prosecution.

Shifting to policy, Rakoff argued that the better policy would be for prosecutors to shift back from a focus on companies to a focus on individuals. They needed to "go up the ladder" within the organization, flipping low-level participants so that they would testify against higher executives.[90] His bottom line was that the "future deterrent value of successfully prosecuting individuals far outweighs" the benefits of a corporate prosecution (which largely resulted in enhanced compliance measures that to his mind were "often little more than window-dressing").[91]

All of this resonated with the public, the press, and much of legal academia. As a former Southern District of New York prosecutor himself, Rakoff had great credibility. Economists were less persuaded, arguing that bubbles do not have masterminds that plan them the way that a Mafia don plans a drug network. They saw instead a wave of "irrational exuberance" that overtook the housing market.[92] But some law professors raised a more legal concern: namely, that it was harder to prosecute high-ranking executives than Judge Rakoff argued. In particular, Professor Daniel Richman argued that prosecutorial resources were sufficiently strained that it would seldom be possible to achieve more than a handful of high-ranking prosecutions.[93] Flipping lower-echelon personnel to testify against their bosses works in some cases (such as insider trading) but less well when the superior only has a general understanding of the context (such as that mortgage underwriting standards have fallen).[94] Deterrence gains, Richman argued, would be a "function of prosecution frequency."[95] Unless there was a means of achieving frequent convictions, the likely outcome would be only that "a few heads would roll when the market takes a dive and the public seeks retribution."[96] If, as most social scientists believe, the likelihood of detection is far more important to deterrence than the severity of the sanction,[97] then prosecutorial success in a few convictions might still leave most (or at least many) utility-maximizing corporate executives willing to take the risk and commit the crime. In short, the government had to win repeatedly to generate deterrence.

We will return to all these themes: that market crashes may not involve fraud, that it may be difficult to ascribe sufficient knowledge to senior executives to establish criminal liability under existing legal standards, and that isolated convictions may accomplish little. For the moment, however, Judge Rakoff opened an important debate, and he motivated other judges (and eventually even the Justice Department) to view such practices as the DPA more skeptically. But, as we next will see, the incipient revolt that he sparked was quickly snuffed out by appellate courts.

The Judicial Revolt (and Its Suppression)

The 2008 crash soon placed federal district court judges in tension with the SEC and the Department of Justice. The issue with respect to both was whether the trial judge had any discretion when a settlement was presented to the court. Could the judge say, "This is so weak and vague as to be meaningless, and I will not approve it"?

Here, again, Judge Rakoff was the leading figure. In 2011, he refused to approve two settlements proposed to him by the SEC and two major banks (Bank of America and Citigroup). In the *Bank of America* case, he was concerned that the bank's disclosures in its proxy statements relating to its acquisition of Merrill Lynch omitted material information about the extraordinary bonus compensation that Merrill Lynch executives would receive, even though Merrill had collapsed. When he rejected the initial settlement, the parties negotiated some limited admissions and additional disclosure, and Judge Rakoff grudgingly approved the settlement.[98] A full-scale confrontation was thus avoided—for the time.

Then, in the *Citigroup* case,[99] an SEC settlement again came before Judge Rakoff, who again rejected it. This time, the settling parties decided that they had to take on Judge Rakoff. In this case, the SEC, following its standard practice, had filed (1) a complaint accusing the defendant, Citigroup Global Markets Inc., of a substantial securities fraud involving the bank's dumping "some dubious assets on misinformed investors"[100] and simultaneously (2) a proposed consent judgment to which the bank consented. Although the bank was not accused of fraud, but only of negligence, the SEC simultaneously sued a bank officer and seemingly accused him of fraud.[101] Citigroup was let off lightly in this respect, but it was required to disgorge $160 million in profits (plus an additional $30 million in interest thereon) and to pay the SEC a civil penalty of $95 million. Nonetheless, Judge Rakoff was again bothered by the failure of Citigroup to make any admission. This, of course, protected Citigroup from follow-on securities class actions brought by the plaintiff's bar that would have sought to hold the bank liable based simply on its admissions to the SEC.[102]

For Judge Rakoff, this implied, however, that he was being asked to enjoin and fine Citigroup simply based on the SEC's allegations without any evidence or even the defendant's admission. To his mind, judges could not do that. As a result, he concluded: "The Court is forced to conclude that a proposed Consent Judgment that asks the Court to impose substantial injunctive relief, enforced by the Court's own contempt power, on the basis of allegations unsupported by any proven or acknowledged facts whatsoever, is neither reasonable, nor fair, nor adequate, nor in the public interest."[103] This dispute could possibly have still been negotiated if, as in the prior *Bank of America* case, the defendants made some modest admissions and Rakoff had relented. But the SEC was indignant. They were unwilling to let a federal judge review the adequacy of their settlements or even refuse to grant an injunction. This was a fight over who controlled this turf: the SEC or the courts. If they could not negotiate easy settlements, the SEC may have feared they could not manage their caseload.

The SEC thus appealed, and the Second Circuit vacated Judge Rakoff's order and instructed him that he had virtually no discretion with respect to an

SEC settlement.[104] In short, he had to approve it. For the Second Circuit, the wisdom and propriety of the SEC's "neither admit nor deny" policy was a matter for the executive branch and not judicially reviewable. Less well explained, however, was why the executive branch (in the form of the SEC) could insist that an Article III judge had to grant an injunction simply at its request.

Rakoff's battle with the SEC involved civil actions, but the same issue arises with respect to DPAs. Can a federal judge resist or disapprove such a settlement? In 2015, this issue surfaced when U.S. district Judge Richard J. Leon rejected a DPA that the Justice Department had negotiated with Fokker Services BV, a Dutch company, finding that the settlement was so weak as to be "grossly disproportionate to the gravity" of the behavior.[105] He added that accepting the DPA "would undermine the public's confidence in the administration of justice and promote disrespect for the law for it to see a defendant prosecuted so anemically for engaging in such egregious conduct for such a sustained period of time."[106] Strong words indeed!

But they did not persuade the circuit court. Just as the Second Circuit had done in the *Citigroup* case, the DC Circuit vacated Judge Leon's order, saying that it amounted to an unwarranted impairment of the powers of another branch of government.[107] In both cases then, the core holding of these circuit courts was that, under the "separation of powers" doctrine, the charging power belongs to the executive branch, and the prosecutor's decisions in exercising that power are not judicially reviewable.[108] Nor do these cases stand alone. Most recently, in 2017, the issue surfaced in a new way. Judge John Gleeson of the Eastern District of New York sought to exercise supervisory power over the DPA between the Justice Department and HSBC Bank USA, which had been filed before him. The DPA had provided for a monitor (who eventually found HSBC's progress toward implementing internal controls to be "slow"). Judge Gleeson first ordered the monitor to prepare an annual report and then, on a request from the public, decided to unseal the report. This was a considerably lesser intrusion than rejecting the settlement itself. Nonetheless, HSBC and the government appealed the district court's unsealing of the report—and won in the Second Circuit.[109] Again, the Second Circuit found that the district court had impermissibly encroached on the executive branch and had no authority to supervise the implementation of a DPA.[110] One judge in a concurring opinion did, however, express anxiety, suggesting that "it is time for Congress to revisit the issue of deferred and non-prosecution agreements."[111]

Despite this call for some judicial oversight, the combined impact of the *Fokker Services* and *HSBC Bank* decisions plus the reversal of Judge Rakoff in the *Citigroup* decision strongly suggest that appellate courts will continue to defer to prosecutors with respect to DPAs and will resist attempts by trial courts to supervise them. Although Congress could conceivably intervene, no movement in this direction is apparent, and Congress seems too polarized to act aggressively. Nonetheless, although Judge Rakoff and his colleagues lost their respective battles, they won the war in the public's mind. The SEC's prestige was damaged, and the Justice Department's leniency toward executives was becoming a political liability.

A Shift in the Wind: The Yates Memorandum

Politics can produce change. By the end of the Obama administration, the Justice Department had been deeply embarrassed by its seeming inability to convict higher-level executives and by Attorney General Holder's ambiguous comments about "too big to jail." Facing an upcoming election in which this could be a liability, the Justice Department modified its official policy in late 2015 to stress the need for individual accountability. Deputy Attorney General Sally Quillian Yates issued a statement to all U.S. Attorneys that limited the credit that corporations could receive for cooperation with the government (and hence their eligibility for a DPA).[112] To qualify for such credit in the future, the corporation would have to satisfy a number of conditions, of which the key and "threshold requirement" was that "the company must completely disclose to the Department all relevant facts about individual misconduct."[113] This was deliberately framed (and publicly described by Justice) as an "all-or-nothing rule"; that is, either the corporation had to disclose all that it knew about the involvement of all corporate executives and employees in the misconduct, or the corporation could not qualify. Known as the Yates Memorandum, this policy also prohibited any deferred prosecution agreement or other corporation resolution from containing any provision protecting any individual from criminal or civil liability. In short, a DPA could not confer immunity on corporate officers or employees.

Much ink has been spilled discussing whether the Yates Memorandum actually changed practices. On this issue, there is no consensus, but it remains difficult to identify many senior executives who have been prosecuted in the wake of the Yates Memorandum. The Justice Department is a very decentralized agency, and individual U.S. Attorneys are like powerful barons in a medieval kingdom. They can often ignore policies established in Washington, at least so long as they have the support of the senator who effectively selected them. Overall, little effort is made by the Justice Department to monitor them.

Still, for the criminal defense bar, the Yates Memorandum implied that corporate defense counsel would have to search for all documents (and emails) relating to the involvement of individual executives. They protested that they were being made agents of the prosecution,[114] and eventually, under President Trump, they won a relaxation of the Yates Memorandum's most critical provision.[115] At a minimum, the Yates Memorandum shows that the Justice

Department was aware that the public mood had changed. If a U.S. Attorney settled with the corporation, the Attorney had to be prepared for criticism from the press and the public. But the key problem remained: How could the prosecution, with a limited staff and budget, digest an immense volume of information and identify the critical decision makers? Bankruptcy examiners, using a hundred or more attorney and billing fees in the multimillion-dollar range, might do this, but not a staff of five or six prosecutors (who had other cases to try as well).

A Final Scorecard

Everyone has heard the generalization that no bank CEO went to prison after 2008. This is largely true but still misleading.[116] A more important statistic is this: between 2002 and 2016, the Justice Department entered into 419 deferred prosecution and nonprosecution agreements, as opposed to only 18 in the preceding ten years.[117] Meanwhile, the number of corporations indicted and criminally prosecuted fell significantly.[118] Clearly, this was a massive shift in prosecutorial behavior.

What happened in these DPAs? Professor Brandon Garrett has found that, between 2001 and 2014, individuals were criminally charged in only 34 percent of these cases in which companies received DPAs.[119] This period (2001–2014) covers both the period before the *Arthur Andersen* case and the period before the 2008 crash. Thus, the post-*Andersen* and postcrash rate of indictment of individuals may have been even lower. The immediate point, however, is that this statistic shows a consistent pattern that cannot be explained solely by the alleged power and influence of Wall Street banks or the prosecutors' fear of prolonging financial instability by pursuing them. The pattern is both deeper and longer. The most plausible explanation for this pattern is that federal prosecutors do not prosecute most eligible individuals in cases of corporate misbehavior either because they lack the manpower and resources to take on a large number of individual prosecutions or (as later discussed) they fear they would lose a significant percentage of these possible cases.

Another finding by Professor Garrett merits similar attention. Looking at the small number of individuals who were charged, he finds: "Of those individuals charged, most were not higher-up officers ... but rather middle managers of one kind or another and also some quite low individuals."[120] Thus, not only are few charged, but those that were did not qualify as senior executives. Why? It could be that internal investigations were biased or limited because counsel sought to protect the corporate managers that hired them. Or it could be that it is just genuinely difficult to make a case against the corporation's top executives because "smoking guns" that implicate them turn out to be few and far between. On an ongoing basis, midlevel managers have little incentive to tell their supervisors that there are serious problems or risks in their line of business; they would rather claim they are doing a great job and deserve bonuses. As a result, bad news travels upward slowly and incompletely in the corporate hierarchy. That too can explain why evidence of senior misconduct is hard to find.

In any event, this pattern transcends the special case of Wall Street executives and the 2008 crash. Other more recent scandals (including at Volkswagen, General Motors, and Boeing) are reviewed later and seem to reflect the same pattern. Only in the opioid investigation have there been some (but not yet many) exceptions.

Of course, in 2015 (after the period described above), the Justice Department adopted the Yates Memorandum. Clearly, the Justice Department has learned to talk the talk of individual accountability. But whether it will also walk the walk of individual accountability is more doubtful. As chapter 3 next discusses, corporate criminal prosecutions have declined sharply during the Trump administration, and even fewer of these corporate prosecutions are accompanied by individual prosecutions of corporate executives.

To sum up, the Yates Memorandum is not yet having a pervasive impact. The problem is not just that the Yates Memorandum may have been primarily an exercise in better public relations (and did not reflect a desire to make a major change). Even if it was sincerely intended to change policy, such a shift to a policy of individual accountability requires the Justice Department to address logistical and manpower problems that understandably led it to rely on DPAs and internal investigations directed by the company. To date, no serious attempt to solve these problems is discernible.

THREE

Postcrash Developments

THE CRASH OF 2008 is now over a decade back in our rearview mirror. Much has happened since then. This chapter will survey several postcrash scandals: in particular, Volkswagen, General Motors, Boeing, and the opioid crisis have attracted national attention. Alone, the opioid crisis shows U.S. Attorneys sometimes behaving in a new fashion that stresses individual accountability (and that is a very recent development). This chapter will then turn to a closer examination of the settlement agreements used to resolve allegations of corporate misconduct. Increasingly, defense counsel are disdaining DPAs and instead seeking nonprosecution agreements under which nothing is filed with the court and no public record is created. Both sides see advantages in this approach (which eliminates the judge, who can sometimes be bothersome for both sides), but transparency suffers, and courts are excluded from even a remote monitoring role.

Next, this chapter will examine what has happened under the Trump administration. The Trump administration has backed away from both the Yates Memorandum and corporate prosecutions generally, and it has expanded the leniency accorded to corporations who adopt a compliance plan. Finally, this chapter will assess a new problem that has arisen with internal investigations: namely, that if prosecutors begin to direct or substantially influence the investigation, they may trigger constitutional protections that could defeat (or at least complicate) the internal investigation. All in all, this will bring us up to the present.

Recent Scandals and Investigations

Several major and unrelated scandals have followed the 2008 crash. The brief reviews that follow are less about the scandals themselves than the prosecutorial responses to them: Whom did they indict? How did they gain information? Why didn't they do more?

"Dieselgate" (the Volkswagen Emission Scandal)

This scandal broke in September 2015, when the Environmental Protection Agency (EPA) issued a notice of violation of the Clean Air Act to the Volkswagen Group. Based on information discovered by environmental researchers outside the federal government, the EPA found that Volkswagen had deliberately programmed its diesel engines to activate their emission controls only during laboratory testing. As a result, Volkswagen cars equipped with a "defeat device" emitted up to forty times more nitrogen oxide under actual driving conditions than under laboratory testing conditions. At least 500,000 Volkswagen cars in the United States were so equipped (in model years 2009 to 2015), while worldwide about 11 million vehicles employed this device.

As frauds go, this may have set the record for intentionality and wide-ranging scope. Nor was it particularly hard to investigate, as engineering staffs could be interviewed to learn who had designed and installed the device and who had authorized it. Volkswagen's CEO, Martin Winterkorn, was forced to resign in 2015 within days of the story first breaking, and Volkswagen's stock price fell by a third. In January 2017, Volkswagen pleaded guilty to a variety of fraud charges and received a $2.8 billion criminal fine.[1] Larry Thompson, a former chief of the Criminal Division at Justice and the author of the much cited Thompson Memorandum on DPAs, was appointed a monitor by the sentencing judge to oversee Volkswagen's regulatory compliance practices for at least three years. All in all, as criminal cases go, this was a pretty fast pace.

How did the prosecutors gather information? Much of what they learned came from a lengthy internal investigation conducted for Volkswagen by the American law firm Jones Day. This study found that Volkswagen's engineers had developed the defeat device after they had realized that Volkswagen could not possibly pass U.S. emissions standards.

Earlier in August 2015 (prior to the EPA's notice of violation but after the disparity between the testing data and on-the-road data for Volkswagens had been noted), a Volkswagen employee confided to the EPA that Volkswagen had long used the defeat device, and this was confirmed by Volkswagen executives in a conference call from Germany on September 3, 2015.[2] This admission was apparently provoked by the EPA's threat that it would withhold model approval for Volkswagen's and Audi's 2016 model year cars.

In short, the prosecutors uncovered relatively little information on their own. Caught red-handed, Volkswagen essentially confessed to a U.S. regulatory agency (which had a stranglehold on it because of the agency's ability to disapprove the 2016 model year cars). Then, it hired a law firm to write up the details in a formal statement. Eventually, three years later in 2018, federal prosecutors did indict Winterkorn, the former CEO, but they were well aware that he was immune from extradition to the United States under German law so long as he remained in Germany. Having been fired by Volkswagen and facing likely prosecution in Germany, he was a disgraced figure that no one sought to protect. Otherwise, prosecutors indicted basically midlevel managers in the United States.[3]

The point here is not to criticize the federal prosecutors (who were based in Detroit, where Volkswagen was headquartered in the United States, and had limited staff) but to recognize that prosecutors were handed a ready-made case on the proverbial silver platter by civil regulators. That Volkswagen's CEO was also indicted was an arguable improvement over the earlier bank cases (most notably, HSBC and BNP Paribas), but Winterkorn had no supporters. The brazen character of Volkswagen's fraud had shocked everyone.

The General Motors Ignition Investigation

Beginning in February 2014, General Motors (GM) began to recall certain models of its cars, eventually recalling nearly 30 million cars worldwide, because of a faulty ignition switch that could shut off its engine during driving. This could both cause a loss of control and prevent airbags from inflating. Eventually, some 124 deaths were attributed to this flaw, and these victims were paid compensation.[4]

Most importantly, the flaw seems to have been known within the GM hierarchy for over a decade. No evidence has been uncovered indicating a conspiracy to suppress this information, but the quantity and quality of the evidence found depends on the depth of the investigation undertaken. GM did commission an investigation into why the recalls were delayed and hired Anton Valukas, the same attorney who prepared the bankruptcy examiner's report in Lehman, to prepare a report. His report, completed very quickly and announced in June 2015, found that a number of problems had caused delays but that "a critical factor in GM personnel's delay in fixing the switch was their failure to understand, quite simply, how the car was built."[5]

All in all, this was certainly plausible. Negligence happens. But remember that Valukas's client this time was the defendant (GM), not a more objective third party (such as a bankruptcy court). That may make a big difference.

Based in part on the Valukas report, General Motors entered into a deferred prosecution agreement with the Justice Department on September 17, 2015, under which GM admitted that "from in or about the Spring of 2012 through in or about February 2014, GM failed to disclose a deadly safety defect to its U.S. regulator." Further, "it also falsely represented to consumers that vehicles containing the defect posed no safety concern." Pursuant to its DPA, GM forfeited $900 million to the United States (and it paid another $600 million to victims of these accidents[6]).

Where are we left? The line between negligence and reckless or knowing awareness is probably the most difficult line that the criminal law has to face. No conclusion is here expressed, but the information that the prosecution relied on came from the defendant's experts. Nor did the prosecution have other means by which to gather information from a giant corporation about its activities over a decade or more. This same pattern characterized the Volkswagen case as well, where Jones Day prepared the report. Both law firms are highly regarded, but the process would be healthier and more objective if the internal investigation was freed from these conflicts.

The Opioid Crisis

In contrast to the prosecution's relative passivity in the Volkswagen and General Motors investigations, federal prosecutors have recently been much more aggressive in a series of actions taken against the distributors and producers of opioids. But this is a new development. When the first major opioids case was brought in 2007 against Purdue Pharma Inc., the maker of OxyContin, federal prosecutors reached a plea bargain under which Purdue Pharma and three of its top executives acknowledged guilt, but no jail time was imposed.[7] Rather than Purdue Pharma pleading guilty (which would have had collateral consequences), a corporate affiliate of Purdue Pharma was substituted, which pleaded guilty and agreed to pay $600 million in fines and other payments. The three executives pleaded guilty to misdemeanor charges and paid a total of $34.5 million in fines (some of which was indemnified by Purdue). This accommodation seems characteristic of that era, even if it was an improvement over the standard pattern of not prosecuting individual officers at all.

Beginning in late 2016, however, prosecutors began to play by different rules, first indicting executives at Insys Therapeutics Inc. on racketeering charges[8] and then filing a superseding indictment in 2017 to include John N. Kapoor, the controlling shareholder of Insys and formerly an opioids billionaire. All were convicted on all charges in May 2019, and Kapoor received a stiff sentence of five and a half years, despite his advanced age.[9] Also in 2019, prosecutors indicted and settled drug-trafficking charges with Rochester Drug

Co-Operative, a major opioids distributor, and further indicted two of its senior officers.[10]

This is activism. Contrary to past practice, even when the corporation entered into a settlement, senior executives were still indicted and did not receive a pass. This change in behavior can possibly be explained as a response to the Yates Memorandum (as these prosecutions did follow it), but there are at least three other factors that may better account for this new pattern.

First, these were smaller firms with controlling shareholders. Decision making was thus less diffuse, and policies could be traced to their source. This same characteristic also distinguished small savings and loan banks (whose officers were frequently prosecuted in the 1980s and 1990s) from giant investment banks (where neither the bank nor its officers were prosecuted following the 2008 crash).

Second, the alleged crimes were generally not regulatory crimes but behavior akin to drug trafficking, as pharmaceutical firms flooded rural regions with extraordinary levels of opioids, stocking well-known drug mills and promoting high-potency, addictive drugs for unapproved uses.

Third, the public, the press, and now prosecutors have all recognized that hundreds of thousands of Americans have died as a result of opioid drug overdoses.[11] To be sure, the 2008 crash impoverished an equally large number of victims or left them unemployed. But the sins and errors of 2008 largely sounded in negligence, whereas the behavior of the drug companies in the opioid crisis resembled a Mafia family establishing a national drug network—except that the pharma companies were far more efficient and made much more money.

Perhaps the response to the opioid crisis provides some grounds for optimism. Particularly in the Insys Therapeutics prosecution, prosecutors made their case by flipping executives to turn on their seniors. Still, one must remember that these were small companies with direct reporting lines and senior executives who were heavily involved in operational decision making. Proving these same charges against senior executives at a Pfizer or a Johnson & Johnson would likely be far more difficult and roughly comparable to prosecuting the top executives at Lehman or another large investment bank. That has not yet happened.

The New World of Internal Investigations

By now, it has been repeatedly stressed that prosecutors rarely have much information (at least at the outset of an investigation) about what happened within a public corporation. Because of budgetary and manpower limitations, they often need to rely on an investigation conducted by the corporation itself, which hires an at least nominally independent outside law firm. What has not yet been explained, however, is the enormous and growing cost of such an investigation.

As long as eight years ago, Peter Henning, the White Collar Watch columnist at the *New York Times*, estimated: "When a corporation is caught in a governmental investigation, the legal fees can quickly exceed $100 million—and that's before the lawsuits even begin."[12] That was in 2012 (and he may have underestimated even then).[13]

Internal investigations have become the largest new source of business for major U.S. law firms. They are to the last decade what the mergers and acquisitions business was to the 1980s—a source of enormous new revenue over which these firms competed intensely. The scale of these investigations is best shown by a landmark investigation conducted by Siemens AG, a German conglomerate, which was raided by German prosecutors in 2006 over allegations that it had bribed governments and potential customers around the globe. In response to this approaching prosecution, the Siemens board of directors undertook a broad and global internal investigation aimed at discovering the scope of the corrupt payments made.[14] It hired Debevoise and Plimpton LLP, a prominent New York firm, and the Big Four accounting firm of Deloitte LLP; together, they jointly undertook a two-year investigation.

That investigation grew and snowballed. By the time it was completed, it had spanned thirty-four countries, involved 1,750 interviews of witnesses and over 300 attorneys working for Siemens, and resulted in the collection of 100 million documents (of which 24 million were produced to the U.S. Department of Justice).[15] The cost of this investigation to Siemens has been estimated at around €650 million (with €204 million going to Debevoise and €349 million going to Deloitte).[16] Ultimately, Siemens paid fines of €1 billion to the Department of Justice and German authorities.[17] Thus, the direct cost of the investigation came to roughly two-thirds of the then record penalty.

Now think what this meant to the prosecutors (both in Germany and the United States). The scale of this investigation was wholly beyond their ability to duplicate or even monitor closely. Unable to match it, the prosecutors were compelled to rely on it. The significance of this point was not lost on corporate defendants. As expensive as these investigations were, they shifted control of investigative fact gathering to the defendant and its agents. In effect, prosecutors are outsourcing the investigative stage of criminal enforcement to defendants. The danger, of course, is that this delegation may spare at least the highest level of corporate executives from adverse findings about them in the eventual report by the outside law firm.

Of course, not just any firm would be permitted to conduct this investigation. It is necessary to have a partner or partners with substantial experience as a prosecutor or an enforcement official (usually at the SEC). Debevoise &

Plimpton won the Siemens assignment in part because their investigation would be led by Mary Jo White, the former U.S. attorney for the Southern District of New York (and later chairman of the SEC under President Obama). But law firms know very well how to compete, and soon other prestigious law firms established highly comparable and competitive departments. The Paul Weiss firm has been particularly successful in this line of work (and internal investigations are now a respected professional line of business to which current federal prosecutors can aspire to enter once they eventually leave low-paid governmental service).

Although no one would suggest that respected professionals would hide, destroy, or ignore documents that turn up in the course of their investigation, the relevant question is what inferences they will draw. Will they deem it necessary to conduct a lengthy interview with the CEO or the CFO simply because some lower-level officer in Europe or Asia made a casual remark in an email or other document that he was keeping U.S. headquarters advised? At this point, it is necessary to underline the obvious: these are lucrative assignments that may yield over $100 million to their law firm, and the best law firms compete intensely for these assignments.

To be sure, the prosecutors could veto the choice of a law firm that has an obvious conflict of interest (such as being the corporation's regular outside counsel). But for the prosecutors, it is awkward to seek to discourage the selection of a top-ranked law firm with no obvious conflict of interest simply because it is not perceived to be as aggressive as some other law firm. This might seem to be questioning the professional ethics of the lawyers so chosen. Also, the sheer cost of such an investigation is another factor that makes it difficult to resist the corporation's choice of counsel. If the corporation will be spending many millions of dollars on the investigation, it can insist that it deserves to be able to hire a firm in which it has confidence (as, after all, the investigation is initially intended to inform its board of directors). The lawyers conducting those investigations must be skilled diplomats, able to appear aggressive to prosecutors but cautious and understanding to the defendant who hired them.

Two new developments relating to internal investigations complicate the problem even further. First, the Trump administration has modified the Yates Memorandum in an important respect. As noted earlier, the Yates Memorandum took a deliberately all-or-nothing position: to receive credit for cooperation (which includes qualifying for a DPA), the corporation had to identify every individual involved in the misconduct. In a November 29, 2018, speech Deputy Attorney General Rod J. Rosenstein relaxed and modified this policy, expressly ending its all-or-nothing character.[18] As he stated, "Our revised policy ... makes clear that any company seeking cooperation credit in criminal cases must identify every individual who was *substantially* involved in or responsible for the criminal conduct."[19] Numerous corporate law firms circulated memos to clients, emphasizing and applauding this change.

How important is this revision? To the ear of the corporate lawyer, Rosenstein's focus "on the individuals who play significant roles in setting a company on a course of criminal conduct" (as he phrased it elsewhere in this speech) would not include a CEO or CFO who learned about it after the fact. Thus, if a CEO asked some midlevel official to serve as a liaison with lower levels and the liaison reports back about unlawful payments on an after-the-fact basis, one can view the CEO as less than "significantly involved" where he played no role in initially authorizing or "setting a company on a course of criminal conduct." Yes, this may be a rationalization, but it would allow the attorneys running the investigation to say nothing about the knowledge of high-level executives.

According to Brandon Garrett, it is only in about one-third of the cases in which a public company received a DPA that any individual was prosecuted.[20] Although generally someone knows about and authorizes the misconduct, higher-ranking executives have escaped identification in most internal investigations and, in the future, may be even more protected because they can be viewed as not being "significantly" or "substantially" involved. No claim is here made that this was the intent of the Rosenstein revision, but realism suggests that this may be its impact in many cases where law firms are struggling to please both the prosecutor and the corporate client.

A second major development in the law of internal investigations is the 2019 federal court decision in *United States v. Connolly*.[21] The case grows out of an investigation launched by the Commodity Futures Trading Commission (CFTC) in 2008 into the possible manipulation of LIBOR (the London Interbank Offering Rate) by three financial firms (Barclays PLC, UBS Group AG, and Deutsche Bank). Notified that it was being investigated, Deutsche Bank retained Paul Weiss in 2010. The CFTC then advised Deutsche Bank that it expected the bank to cooperate fully and conduct a full "external review" of Deutsche's involvement in possible LIBOR manipulation. As the CFTC made clear, such a review was necessary if the bank was to receive "cooperation credit." According to the senior Paul Weiss partner heading this investigation (himself a former senior SEC enforcement official), Deutsche Bank's participation was less than "voluntary"; the consequences of noncooperation were unacceptably Draconian to the bank, which could potentially be barred from the United States.

As a result, the court found that

for five years, Deutsche Bank and its outside counsel coordinated extensively with the three Government agencies—the SEC, the CFTC, and eventually the United States Department of Justice ("DOJ")—that were looking into LIBOR manipulation. Indeed, it is apparent that the Government was kept abreast of developments on a regular basis, and that the federal agencies gave considerable discretion to the investigating Paul Weiss attorneys, both about what to do and about how to do it.[22]

Arguably, this is exactly how an adequate investigation should work. These agencies directed Paul Weiss to interview certain specified employees (and also those whom Paul Weiss found had worked closely with these employees). It was understood that employees who refused to be interviewed (or who did not answer fully) would be terminated by Deutsche Bank.

After an elaborate inquiry, Paul Weiss prepared a final report in 2015 (which it called a "white paper"), summarizing its investigation. Overall, this five-year investigation involved some 200 interviews of more than fifty bank employees, reviewed over 158 million electronic documents, and listened to some 850,000 audio files. Along the way, there were some 230 phone calls and 30 in-person meetings between Paul Weiss and government officials.[23] Paul Weiss reported that Deutsche Bank had fully cooperated, and the Justice Department allowed it to enter a DPA under which Deutsche Bank paid $775 million in criminal penalties.

Although Deutsche Bank got what it wanted (at considerable cost[24]), one of its traders—Gavin Black—was indicted and convicted. On appeal, he asserted that his interview testimony to Paul Weiss had been compelled by the threat of his dismissal. Ordinarily, this threat would not have made his testimony inadmissible because a private employer can tell an employee to "talk or walk." The Fifth Amendment does not apply to private persons, only to the state. Still, if the government threatens to fire you if you do not waive your privilege against self-incrimination, then a famous Supreme Court decision— *Garrity v. New Jersey*[25]—holds that such compelled testimony is inadmissible. Also, even if this testimony is not used at trial against the defendant, any leads that the government obtains from this testimony are deemed "fruit of the poisonous tree" and can also necessitate a reversal.[26] It was this latter theory that the defendant principally stressed in seeking reversal of his conviction.

The government was shocked in *Connolly* by the court's finding that "the United States outsourced its investigation to Deutsche Bank and its lawyers."[27] The implication here is that if prosecutors maintain close contacts with a corporation's internal investigation, the investigation can be attributed to the government, thereby making the prosecution constitutionally vulnerable. One of the factors that the court relied upon in reaching this conclusion was that prosecutors did very little in the way of conducting their own investigation. Is that strange? Not at all! Given that this internal investigation was described by both Paul Weiss and Deutsche Bank as the most expensive they had ever undertaken,[28] it was plainly beyond the capacity of the Justice Department to undertake (either in terms of manpower used or financial cost).

Nor does it seem efficient for the law to encourage dual and parallel investigations by both the prosecutors and the corporation. But such an unfortunate "separate but equal" standard may be what the *Connolly* decision eventually encourages. Consider the government's dilemma: If it stays remote from the investigation, offering no instructions and never directing that specific interviews be conducted, the consequence may be a lame investigation that does not penetrate very deeply (but will still cost the corporation sky-high legal fees, as the law firm has to run up the hours to give the impression that no stone was left unturned). Conversely, if the government does monitor closely and request that specific persons be interviewed, this may trigger constitutional provisions that make a subsequent prosecution much more problematic. To be sure, the government could ask the corporation not to terminate employees who refuse to waive the privilege against self-incrimination, and this may solve the *Garrity v. New Jersey* problem of coerced testimony. The corporation might still terminate such nontestifying employees and claim it did so on its own initiative. But this would trigger fact-intensive hearings in most cases, and it is probably not worth the effort.

All that is clear here is that prosecutors would have been unlikely to convict the defendant (Gavin Black) in *Connolly* without the Paul Weiss investigation, as his involvement was not known to prosecutors at the outset. If we want internal investigations to produce information that is of true value, the prosecutors need to have an important role in supervising them. Later, some possible options will be considered (including having the prosecutors hire the outside law firm and direct the investigation but with the corporation paying the cost of the investigation as a condition of eligibility for a DPA). Conversely, defense counsel argue passionately that this is an abuse that tramples on the defendant's constitutional rights.[29] For the moment, however, all that needs to be concluded is that how to structure "internal" investigations is a critical and unresolved issue (with risks on all sides). Also clear is that the one approach that cannot work is to ask prosecutors to do the investigation entirely on their own.

The Evolution of Deferred Prosecution Agreements

In the interval between 2002 and the fall of 2016, the Justice Department entered into 419 settlement agreements with corporations that can be described as either deferred prosecution agreements or nonprosecution agreements (NPAs).[30] This was in contrast to only 18 such agreements in the prior ten years.[31] Obviously, this was a major transition in prosecutorial policy, and Professor Brandon Garrett has properly focused on it.[32]

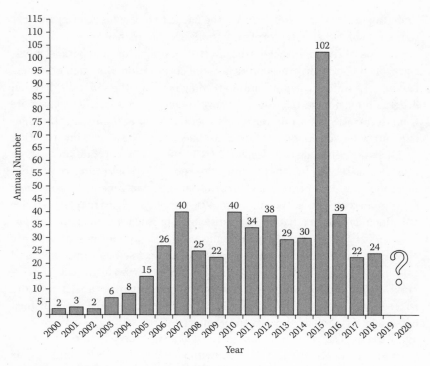

FIGURE 1 The Curious Spike: Deferred Prosecution and Nonprosecution Agreements, 2008 to 2018

But the world did not stop in 2014 (the date of his important book). Since then, there have been other developments as captured in figure 1.[33]

As shown in figure 1, compiled by the Gibson Dunn law firm, these settlement agreements peaked at 102 in 2015 and then fell dramatically to 39, 22, and 24 in the years 2016 through 2018, respectively. This decline in DPAs began just as Deputy Attorney General Sally Yates announced a return to individual accountability in her famous memo (issued in late 2015).[34] Prosecutors may have realized that use of a DPA was likely to lead to press and public criticism. Possibly also, this decline reflected a lesser interest on the part of the Trump administration in prosecuting corporate crime at all.[35] But before we assume that corporate settlement agreements are today less important, we need to understand that the total payments made by corporations pursuant to them came to $8.1 billion in 2018, a number exceeded only by the $9 billion record paid in 2012.[36] In short, the total number of DPAs has declined, but the penalties have skyrocketed. Also, DPAs have recently been used primarily in the case of financial institutions.[37] For such firms, a plea of guilty or a criminal conviction may have unacceptable collateral consequences.[38]

A second transition in these settlements is also important. In 2018 (the last year for which data are available), there were twenty-four such corporate settlements (DPAs and NPAs). Of these, thirteen were NPAs and only eleven were DPAs.[39] What is the difference? Deferred prosecution agreements are filed in court and assigned to a specific judge. Almost always, they are public documents and contain significant admissions or at least an acceptance of responsibility. Nonprosecution agreements are only contracts (or understandings) between the defendant and the prosecutors: if the defendant abides by the terms of the agreement, no charges will be filed. These agreements are not filed in court and, with some exceptions for specific categories, are generally not made public.[40] Thus, they spare the corporation public humiliation and at least some reputational loss. Also, their private status ensures that no pesky federal judge can make disparaging public characterizations about them (or even learn of them).

Why do prosecutors agree to these seemingly less punitive settlements? One reason may be logistics: they simply do not have the manpower and resources to insist on more. In this light, nonprosecution agreements may reflect the greater leverage of defense counsel. But there is another reason: prosecutors also may want to escape judicial supervision, in particular because judicial skepticism about the value of the settlement reflects even more harshly on them. The increase in nonprosecution agreements probably also reflects competition among law firms. Arguably, a nonprosecution agreement represents a greater achievement by defense counsel. The defendant has escaped the glare of sunlight, and the prosecution has agreed to drop the case (of course, after payment of a typically substantial fine). The client is obviously happier avoiding prosecution than being placed on probation (even if the fine is the same in either case).

A third disposition that is even more favorable to the defendant has recently come into use: *declinations with disgorgement.* Here, the prosecutor declines to prosecute (although there will often be a repayment of defendant's gains, if any, to the victims). As of early 2019, there have been twelve such declinations under the Foreign Corrupt Practices Act, with three such dispositions in 2018.[41] From the defendant's standpoint, it sounds far better that the prosecutors declined the case than that they worked out a plea bargain. Although such a disposition suggests that the evidence was weak, that is often not the real motivation underlying these cases. As the Justice Department has explained, a declination is granted in "a case that would have been prosecuted or criminally resolved except for the company's voluntary disclosure, full cooperation, remediation, and payment of disgorgement, forfeiture and/or restitution."[42] These then are frequently cases in which the corporation has turned in its employees (lower-ranking ones to be sure).

This same general policy has recently been followed in a parallel respect. In early 2018, the Justice Department announced a policy of declining criminal charges against corporations accused of foreign bribery (in violation of the Foreign Corrupt Practices Act) if they cooperate fully.[43] In both cases, the Justice Department is offering a carrot to firms who disclose before prosecutors are hot on their trail. As will be argued later, such an incentive is necessary, as the Justice Department will need to pay for meaningful cooperation by the firm; the real issue is how to combine carrots *and* sticks to reach a closer to optimal outcome.

One last observation: in the transition from deferred prosecutions to nonprosecution agreements, we are seeing a loss of transparency. The public may learn that the defendant settled and paid a fine, but they are less likely to learn the details of the alleged misconduct and who was involved. Nor is the defendant as likely to admit or accept responsibility. The question that thus surfaces is whether there should be a minimal level of disclosure when the prosecutor resolves criminal charges. We will return to that theme as well.

The Impact of Trump

To no one's real surprise, the Trump administration has relaxed federal criminal enforcement directed at corporations. To give a simple comparison, in its last twenty months, the Obama administration imposed $14.15 billion in total corporate penalties (prosecuting some seventy-one financial institutions and an additional thirty-four public corporations). In contrast, during the first twenty months of the Trump administration, the total penalties imposed on financial institutions and public corporations were only $3.4 billion (with seventeen financial institutions and thirteen public corporations being prosecuted).[44] These are declines on the order of 75 percent or more. Some of this was predictable and understandable, because cases emanating from the 2008 crash were ending, but the decision to relax the Yates Memorandum and a related decision to deemphasize the use of corporate monitors in deferred prosecution agreements[45] suggests that we are returning to the old status quo.

President Trump entered office in 2017. In that year there were twenty-five deferred and nonprosecution agreements, but only ten of these also involved accompanying individual prosecutions. In 2018, these numbers fell to twenty-one deferred and nonprosecution agreements, but only five had accompanying individual prosecutions.[46] The implication is that the Yates Memorandum is being given little or no weight—either because its policy is disfavored or, more likely, because bureaucracies (including the Justice Department) revert to the practices that require the least effort and encounter the least resistance. If so, the future appears to be one in which corporations will be fined for criminal misconduct, but executives are likely to be prosecuted only if they blunder badly.

In 2019, the Trump Justice Department announced another significant relaxation. Since 1993, the Antitrust Division had enforced a tough policy under which it would give no credit for corporate compliance plans in price-fixing and cartel cases. Instead, to receive credit, the corporation had to turn itself in, disclose the identities of the other members of the cartel, and cooperate with the Antitrust Division in all respects—and only the first corporation to turn itself in received any credit. The second such corporation could thus be very disappointed. But the benefit to the first corporation was substantial, as the first corporation and its employees would receive complete immunity if the corporation confessed before the government was hot on its trail. The result was to create a competition to snitch and inform.

This policy worked, and companies did use it, but it was resented within the business community. In July 2019, the Antitrust Division relaxed its policy, so now any member of this cartel or price-fixing conspiracy could receive a charging and sentencing if it had a credible compliance plan.[47] Complete immunity will still require that the corporation turn itself in, but even the ringleader of the conspiracy could escape with only a misdemeanor charge if it had a credible compliance plan (which, as usual, would have failed in this instance).

One could pause here to assess whether excessive credit is being given to corporate compliance plans, which prosecutors have little ability to contest.[48] But the bigger point is that the proven effectiveness of the Antitrust Division's immunity-for-confession policy is now undercut. Hypothetically, if a corporation discovers today that it is a participant in a cartel or price-fixing conspiracy, it has multiple options: (1) it can confess; (2) it can rely on its compliance plan and possibly invest in making it appear more formidable; or (3) it can persist and hope not to be caught. Some combination of (2) and (3) seems likely to predominate. No longer must the corporation fear (at least to the same extent) that a rival conspirator will confess before it does, because now that will only imply the loss of the difference between complete immunity and the sentencing and charging credit under the compliance plan. In the past, corporations turned themselves in to the Antitrust Division because it meant an all-or-nothing difference in the leniency that they received. In the future, the incentive to self-report will be diminished.

PART 2

Analysis: What Policy Levers Could Work?

Introduction to Part 2

PART 2 SHIFTS FROM DESCRIPTION to policy analysis. How can we better generate deterrence? What tools have not been used? Chapter 4 starts by arguing that fines imposed on the corporate entity generate far less deterrence than is generally imagined. In the wake of the announcement of a fine, the corporation's stock price usually rises significantly, suggesting that the threat of a fine will not compel the corporation to cooperate.

In response, several proposals are made: First, prosecutors need to create a "prisoner's dilemma" so that both the entity and potential individual defendants must fear that if they do not confess and cooperate (and the other does), they will be dealt with harshly and the other leniently. This is intended to create a competition to cooperate.

Second, control over the corporation's internal investigation must be taken out of the hands of management and given to a committee of the board, and the prosecution needs to be involved both in the selection of the counsel conducting the investigation and the conduct of the actual investigation. But constitutional problems lurk here.

Third, because high fines do not deter well, a better answer is the *equity fine* (a fine in stock), whose impact would not fall on creditors, employees, or other nonculpable constituencies. This minimizes the externalities associated with very punitive fines and allows the court to impose a greater penalty. This in turn should spur greater corporate cooperation.

Finally, chapter 6 makes a controversial proposal: because civil enforcement agencies lack the staff, budget, or experience to handle a "big" case, which typically involves massive discovery, they should retain private counsel that has such experience. Such private counsel would need to be closely supervised by the agency's senior counsel, but if they were compensated on a contingent fee basis, the cost to taxpayers would be negligible (because the defendant is effectively paying their fee).

FOUR

The Difficulties with Deterrence

WE HAVE SEEN THAT individuals in corporate criminal cases are prosecuted far less frequently than the corporate entity.[1] The Yates Memorandum sought to change this by insisting on individual accountability. Although it was a political success that attracted broad support, the pattern since then has changed little. Curiously, there has been a marked increase in the size of corporate penalties but no increase (and even a small decline) in the number of individual prosecutions.[2] Apparently, the Department of Justice does not practice what it preaches in terms of the Yates Memorandum or whom it pursues. Instead, prior practices persist (a standard pattern in bureaucracies).

But why does this matter? Although most of us intuitively believe that sending an individual to prison generates far more deterrence than a corporate prosecution, hard proof is lacking. Some economists argue that deterrence can be achieved at a far lower social cost by sanctioning only the corporate entity,[3] but probably more economists consider the decision whether to pursue the entity or its executives to be simply a pragmatic choice between strategic substitutes, neither of which is inherently superior.[4]

Fair enough. Let us assume for the moment that the choice between pursuing the individual executive versus the corporate entity should be made pragmatically, based on which option will yield greater deterrence. The next step for most law-and-economics scholars is to point out that the corporate entity can be incentivized by the state to monitor its employees and turn over those who have engaged in or authorized unlawful conduct.[5] In their view, the incentive that should best motivate the corporate entity is leniency—both in sentencing and charging decisions. Underlying this reasoning is the strong likelihood that the corporation has a major comparative advantage over the government in investigating the corporation's own employees. This seems undeniable. Less constrained by due process or other legal restrictions and better positioned to investigate, the corporate can act quickly and demand obedience from its employees. While the government is compelled to seek a search warrant to obtain documents and is denied by the Fifth Amendment the ability to compel testimony from individual defendants, the corporation is not similarly restrained. It can demand documents and read its own email system (which the employee has probably regularly used), because neither the Fourth nor Fifth Amendments apply when the corporation questions its own employees. Thus, because in most American states the employee can be fired at will by its employer, the corporate employer can bluntly tell its employee to "talk or walk." That is, if the employee does not cooperate and answer questions, the employee can be dismissed.

Given this, the exchange of leniency to the corporate defendant in return for its efforts at monitoring and compliance makes sense to law-and-economics scholars. These arguments have enabled the business community to lobby successfully for a sentencing structure under which the corporate defendant ordinarily receives (1) substantial sentencing credits for having established a compliance plan designed to prevent violations of law and (2) a deferred prosecution agreement, even where its criminal acts can be proven.

Nonetheless, this chapter submits that a policy of trading leniency for corporate cooperation has not worked well. That the corporation could provide valuable services to the prosecution in return for leniency does not mean that it typically does so. Too often, only the corporation (and not the state) gets the benefits of the bargain. Too often, the government obtains only a nominally enforced compliance plan, while the internal investigation undertaken by the corporation in return for a deferred prosecution agreement turns up only a few low-ranking employees. Time and again, defendant corporations receive substantial sentencing credit for a compliance plan that was a dismal failure and that missed misconduct that continued for years.

If so, should we fall back on a policy of severe corporate penalties? That also is a flawed prescription for two principal reasons: (1) the prosecution needs the corporation to conduct an investigation that it cannot feasibly undertake itself; and (2) the problem with a Draconian policy of very high corporate penalties is that to truly cancel the expected gain, penalties would often have to be staggeringly high—to the point that they would trigger high externalities (as later discussed in this chapter). Also, we must recognize the implications of the *Arthur Andersen* case. Even if bankruptcy is not triggered (and it was not in the *Andersen* case), large penalties can injure employees, pensioners, creditors, and local communities that depend on the corporate defendant. One might be so tough-minded as to conclude that this is the necessary cost of adequate deterrence. But these constituencies can be vocal, and sentencing judges, who will always hear defense counsel predict disaster if a high penalty is imposed, are seldom that tough-minded. Hence, because of the coalitions that can form to resist high penalties, penalties inadequate to deter (even if seemingly set at record levels) are the usual outcome when prosecutors focus on the entity only.

The Economic Perspective

Economists long left the field of criminal law to criminologists—until the publication in 1968 of Gary Becker's famous article "Crime and Punishment: An Economic Approach."[6] Becker stood criminology on its head and assumed that the rational actor will commit a crime unless the expected penalty exceeded the expected gain. The "expected penalty" was in his mind simply the product of the likely penalty times the probability of apprehension and conviction. Moral inhibitions on the part of the defendant and the fear of reputational loss were largely ignored.

Although criminologists, since Cesare Beccaria in the eighteenth century, had viewed the risk of apprehension as far more important than the severity of the penalty, Becker saw no basis for this conjecture. As economists were quick to argue in his wake, public policy could most easily seek to increase deterrence simply by raising penalty levels. In principle, the certainty/severity trade-off could be manipulated so that a low probability of apprehension could be offset by a more severe penalty. Because enforcement is costly, it was more efficient to raise penalty levels than to seek to catch more offenders. To economists' intent on cost minimization, the optimal enforcement policy thus became combining high severity with limited investment in detection and conviction. One could safely anticipate that at least a few defendants would be caught for any crime, and hard-nosed economists saw these few as the sacrificial lambs through whom adequate deterrence could be generated.

A second implication of the Becker model was that, because incarceration was costly, it was more efficient to rely on monetary sanctions (whether called fines, restitution, or disgorgement). Thus, incarceration was to be reserved for those who could not afford to pay an adequate penalty that canceled out the expected benefit. Hence, the rich could escape jail if they could pay the expected penalty. A related implication for at least some economists was that it was cheaper to fine the entity than to pursue the individual (who seldom could pay an adequate fine and thus had to be incarcerated). Incarceration implied costs for the state (jails require guards) and also imposed costs on innocent third parties (spouses, children, family, and others who relied on the defendant), costs that could be avoided if financial penalties were preferred.

A final indirect implication of this model involved the use of penalty discounts. Logically, public policy should seek to incentivize the entity to monitor its employees to prevent crime through the use of internal controls. To be sure, if penalty levels were high enough, the corporate entity would already be naturally incentivized to monitor, but very high penalty levels again raised the risk of bankruptcy and other externalities. The shadow of the *Arthur Anderson* case loomed over criminal justice policy planning in this era. Thus, it was easier (and politically more popular) to create a sanctioning structure that offered corporations large penalty discounts for self-reporting or for internal compliance systems that were thought to reduce the risk of employee malfeasance. In the 1990s, the U.S. Sentencing Commission did precisely this, even though ironically this discount would only be earned in cases where this compliance system had failed. For the economically minded policy analyst, it made sense that the corporation should be "bribed" by the criminal justice system through sentencing discounts to erect an adequate compliance system.

One twist on this idea of using penalty discounts to motivate law compliance involved the deferred prosecution agreement. Although even in these cases a sizable fine was usually imposed as part of the deal, the financial penalty would be accompanied by various internal controls, governance reforms, and possibly an outside monitor to prevent recidivism. All these features justified and necessitated some discount in the penalty level so that the corporation would voluntarily choose to appoint the monitor, install the internal controls, adopt the governance reforms, and so on. As the deferred prosecution agreement developed, it regularly came to require a full-scale internal investigation by an outside counsel chosen or approved by the defendant that would examine the causes and extent of the corporation's misconduct, possibly also identifying individuals who were involved in the misconduct. This innovation pleased all those immediately involved in the process: prosecutors realized that a defendant-funded investigation was imperfect, but it was far better than nothing, because prosecutors lacked the resources to proceed on their own; defense counsel loved it because they were enriched, as was the bar that conducted internal investigations; and it satisfied judges (who wanted some effort made to get to the bottom of things, as they knew very little when all they saw was an indictment and a deferred prosecution plea agreement).

The law-and-economics wing of academia largely supported these developments, believing that penalty discounts were necessary to encourage companies to install costly internal controls.[7] For some, it constituted the best justification for corporate criminal liability.[8] Others in this camp still resisted corporate criminal liability for fear that it inevitably leads to overdeterrence and excessive risk aversion.[9] They were at least right that relative risk aversion is a key variable. In general, most observers and practitioners believe that corporate managers and employees will be more risk averse than the corporate entity for a number of reasons (including that they fear prison more than a fine). A key economic reason for this difference in risk aversion is that share-holders are generally protected by limited liability (so that shareholders will not bear the full penalty imposed if the fine were high enough to place the corporate entity into bankruptcy). Shareholders are also generally diversified, such that a high penalty on the corporation falls less painfully on them. Managers enjoy no similar shield and are not diversified. (They hold only one job.) Nor can they be indemnified for jail time. What this simple point ultimately means is that we can place higher penalties on managers than we can on shareholders (who can only be made to bear a penalty up to their investment in the firm). This in turn generates a powerful argument for preferring individual over entity liability, because individuals can be compelled to internalize a greater penalty through jail time.

Some economists do have doubts about the current policy toward corporate leniency and penalty discounts. They argue that if discounts induce substantially greater investment in internal controls and such controls do detect more corporate misbehavior, the increased penalties that result from more convictions could overwhelm the penalty discounts.[10] Although indeterminacy thus results at the theoretical level, an obvious implication at the practical level is that the corporation may deliberately design imperfect internal control systems that are designed to earn the discount but not detect future violations. This incentive for sham compliance also carries over to the problem of internal investigations conducted for the corporation by an independent outside counsel pursuant to a deferred prosecution agreement or other plea bargain. If the corporation is assumed to be a rational actor, it logically wants a report that implicates few of its managers but shows sufficient study and investigation so that prosecutors cannot reject it.

Although it is possible to disagree with the Becker model on a variety of grounds, the immediately relevant point is that, even if one fully accepts it, it is still likely that a policy of focusing financial penalties on the corporate entity will prove inadequate to deter, as next discussed.

Why Do Financial Penalties Fail?

The old answer to this question was simple and dispositive. Financial penalties for corporate misbehavior used to be set at ridiculously low levels, such that they would not deter even if there were a 100 percent likelihood of apprehension.[11] Largely, this was a consequence of inflation, which trivialized penalties set decades before in legislation.

Still, an antiquated penalty structure cannot explain everything. In his study of deferred prosecution agreements, Brandon Garrett found that in the 255 cases he studied between 2001 and 2012, nearly half of the cases (47 percent)

included no criminal fine.[12] Often in these cases, civil sanctions and/or restitution were paid to some regulatory agency, but the prosecution did not feel
it necessary to demand their own financial sanction (even though criminal
misconduct is normally seen as more serious than a civil violation). Moreover,
when fines were paid, they were usually at the bottom of the sentencing guide-
line range.[13] Only in a very few high-profile cases did he find high fines imposed.[14] One suspects that, in tough negotiations, prosecutors surrendered on
the amount of the fine to get the admission of liability.

The low level of fines began to change when the U.S. Sentencing Commission introduced its organizational sentencing guidelines, which took effect in
1991. Although these guidelines specified ranges that at the top end could exceed several billion dollars, the Sentencing Commission emphasized the carrot at least as much as the stick. A large credit was authorized for self-reporting
the crime, but very few corporations have qualified for this credit.[15] The Sentencing Commission also authorized a significant credit if the corporation accepted responsibility and cooperated fully. To this latter incentive, companies
have responded with alacrity. Most companies that are caught in a criminal
case cooperate (51 percent in 2012), but few self-report (only 3 percent in
2012).[16] In short, corporations want the sentencing credit, if caught, but not
enough to turn themselves in. Even if they "cooperated," they still did not turn
in high-ranking executives. (We can infer this because so few high-ranking
executives were prosecuted.) Arguably, corporations do not need to do so—
so long as the internal investigation by outside counsel turned up no culprits
within U.S. jurisdiction. All this suggests that corporations, as defendants,
take the course of least resistance, but it also shows that corporations do respond to and will exploit the incentives that they are provided (at least if they
can do so without much effort or risk).

Now that fine levels have increased (and actual corporate sentences show
this), we need to recognize that there is a totally independent reason for why
fines may fail to deter: it is not that they are low but that their expected value
falls way below the expected gain from the crime. Here, we need to consider
this comparison on two levels: (1) the actual gain versus the actual penalty
and (2) the actual penalty versus the expected penalty.

First, if the actual fine falls below the actual gain, then Becker's key economic criterion is by definition not satisfied (because the risk of apprehension is always less than 100 percent). Much anecdotal evidence suggests that
actual fines do not typically exceed the gain in regulatory cases. Take, for example, the sentencing of BNP Paribas. In 2015, it paid nearly $4 billion to
prosecutors and an additional $5 billion to regulators and local prosecutors.[17]
The total payment ($8.9 billion) was the largest criminal fine paid in such a
case as of that point.[18] It might have been higher but for the intervention of
French government officials, who publicly warned that a higher fine "could

spark a systemic crisis, endangering the wider financial system."[19] Yet even if this was a record fine, did it exceed the expected gain? A *Wall Street Journal* study reported that for every $1.00 of alleged violations engaged in by BNP Paribas, the bank paid only $0.27–$0.30 in penalties.[20] Even more convincing is the fact that on announcement of this record penalty, "BNP Paribas shares jumped over 3% in Tuesday morning trading" (just after the announcement of the fine).[21]

A similar example is supplied by Standard Chartered, another large bank, which also pleaded guilty to similar charges for violating Iranian sanctions at roughly the same time. According to Brandon Garrett, Standard Chartered admitted to processing over $240 billion in illegal transactions with Iranian clients, resulting in almost $7 billion in pretax profits. What did it pay? Only $674 million in combined criminal and civil penalties![22] Even this amount is not the "expected penalty" because if we assume hypothetically that the likelihood of apprehension was only 50 percent, then, under the Becker model, the penalty would have to be raised from $7 billion to $14 billion in order to produce an expected penalty that canceled the expected gain. If we assume only a 25 percent risk of detection, the expected penalty would have to be $28 billion. Either amount would bankrupt virtually any bank—and this frames a critical problem to which we will return: How can we make the deterrence calculation work?

Of course, these anecdotal examples could be outliers or otherwise unrepresentative cases. But they are not! Brandon Garrett computed the ratio between the fines for public companies prosecuted between 2001 and 2012 and their market capitalization and found that these fines averaged only 0.04 percent of the corporation's market capitalization, while the total payments (fines, restitution, disgorgement, etc.) paid to the government came to only 0.09 percent of market capitalization.[23] Although these ratios between the fine imposed and the defendant's market capitalization do not tell us if the Becker criterion has been satisfied (because we do not know the size of either the expected gain or the expected penalty), they do tell us that these fines are sufficiently small that they can be absorbed as a cost of doing business and need not greatly concern a management that might prefer to ignore them.

More generally, a distinctive characteristic of much corporate crime is that we cannot determine the expected gain. In the case of ordinary street crime, we know the amount of money the bank robber stole or the "street value" of the cocaine that the drug dealer possessed. But in the case of regulatory crime, the value of outflanking the regulation is much harder to estimate.

Let's take two well-known examples. Probably the most startling corporate crime of the last decade was Volkswagen's decision to install defeat devices in its autos that turned off their emission controls, except when they were being tested. Even the most hard-boiled corporate veterans were shocked by this. "What were they thinking?" was the standard question. "How long did they think they could get away with that?" But these reactions ignore that Volkswagen was caught in a desperate bind. It had staked its company's future on a "clean diesel" strategy, but it was facing the reality that it could never comply with California's newly enhanced air quality standards. And the EPA's standards were also being increased. Volkswagen thus faced the loss of its entire American market, because it could only sell its cars in the United States if it could satisfy those air quality standards. The loss here had to be well up in the billions of dollars. So Volkswagen cheated. This misconduct may have been imprudent and highly culpable, but it was not irrational given Volkswagen's predicament.

Another example can be taken from the ongoing opioid epidemic. The most criticized pharmaceutical company has been Purdue Pharma Inc., which was the first firm to market OxyContin (in early 1996). In 2007, it pleaded guilty in federal court to the felony charge of "misbranding"—essentially, pushing their high-potency, highly addictive drug as a remedy for lower grades of chronic pain (instead of just for the end-of-life cancer pain that it had been originally approved to alleviate). This violated FDA rules, but Purdue had discovered a huge market for chronic pain relief. Overall, it is estimated to have sold over $25 billion in OxyContin tablets (and thus caused countless deaths). Federal agencies have estimated that the deaths from overdoses of opioid prescription drugs have exceeded 200,000 as of 2017. What fine did Purdue pay? Answer: roughly $600 million in 2007 (and no Purdue executive went to prison). Perhaps unsurprisingly, Purdue kept on marketing OxyContin for moderate chronic pain. One reason for their persistence may have been that the expected penalty here fell way below the expected gain from selling opioids to an already heavily addicted audience.

If we know little about the expected gain in corporate cases, we probably know even less about the expected penalty. The actual penalty has to be reduced by the risk of apprehension. If the risk is only 25 percent, the expected penalty becomes 25 percent of the actual penalty. Estimates here are highly unreliable, but the paucity of corporate prosecutions seems more likely to imply a low rate of apprehension than a low rate of criminal misbehavior.

To be sure, penalties in corporate cases rose significantly after 2015, but not enough. For example, in 2019, Facebook was fined $5 billion by the FTC in a civil case, and sweeping regulatory controls were also imposed.[24] Facebook had already publicly reserved $3 billion for expected FTC sanctions, so the $5 billion penalty that was actually imposed likely exceeded the market's expectation (particularly given that the prior record FTC penalty had been only a $22.5 million penalty imposed on Google in 2012).[25] What happened this time?

On July 12, 2019 (the day of the FTC's announcement), Facebook's stock rose 1.8 percent.[26] If this penalty had exceeded the gain, we might expect Facebook's market price to fall, as it would be less able to engage in some profitable practices. Instead, when the stock price rises, it looks more like the expected penalty was not high enough to change those practices. Further, if we assume a 50 percent (or lower) chance of apprehension, the actual penalty would have to be increased to a level that few corporations could feasibly pay.

Still, even if we cannot reliably measure the expected gain and expected penalty in most cases, there may be a second-best way of estimating the impact of a penalty. An eye-opening statistic emerges if we examine the stock market reaction to the announcement of even record fines. In response to the fine's announcement, the stock market price of the defendant corporation has generally gone up (often significantly) and seldom down to any significant degree. Thus, the earlier-noted BNP Paribas case (where its stock price went up 3 percent) is not unique but is fairly representative. To see this pattern in closer detail, the cases shown in table 1, which each involve very high penalties, are collectively assessed in a larger data sample.

As illustrated in table 1, the stock market price of a defendant public corporation has generally gone up in response to the fine's announcement. To investigate this intuition further, a sample was constructed of the twenty-five largest fines imposed on corporations that traded on a U.S. stock exchange, and an event study was run of the stock price reaction, using the market model.[27] The results of this event study confirm the initial intuition and indicate positive and statistically significant abnormal returns of 1.45 percent on the day of the fine's announcement and a cumulative abnormal return (CAR) of 2.5 percent beginning one day following the announcement and rising to 4.3 percent at the end of the event window.[28] Counterintuitive as it may be, the stock price goes up on announcement, even in the case of the largest fines.

Visually, this is evident in figure 2, which shows the abnormal return peaking on the date of the public announcement, and the CAR peaking on the following day through the end of the event window.

Because the CAR statistic reflects the cumulative abnormal return through the entire event window, it naturally becomes larger and more significant toward the close of the event window.

What does this pattern imply? Here, one must be careful. By no means can we infer that shareholders were happy about the fine (and other possible sanctions). Nor does it prove that the expected penalty was less than the expected gain; both those values remain mysteries. But it does strongly imply that shareholders believed the defendant corporation made out better than they had expected. That the penalty was less than expected is not necessarily proof of underdeterrence, but it is highly consistent with it, particularly when this

TABLE 1 An Event Study of Market Reaction to the Announcement of Corporate Fines

Company	Year	Cumulative Total Return	Change in Stock Market Price on Date of Announcement (+ or −)	Cumulative Abnormal Return (CAR): Event Window +/− 8 days	Cumulative Abnormal Return (CAR): Event Window +/− 15 days	Total Fine (in dollars)
Anadarko Petroleum Corporation	2014	17%	+	23%	29%	1,250,000,000
Bank of America	2012	9%	+	9%	21%	11,800,000,000
Teva Pharmaceutical Industries LTD	2016	5%	+	8%	−8%	519,000,000
Citigroup Inc.	2014	6%	+	7%	8%	7,000,000,000
Barclays PLC	2015	8%	+	7%	5%	2,400,000,000
UBS Group AG	2015	6%	+	6%	14%	545,000,000
Royal Bank of Scotland	2015	4%	+	6%	6%	669,000,000
The Goldman Sachs Group Inc.	2016	7%	+	5%	8%	5,000,000,000
Wells Fargo and Company	2018	3%	+	4%	6%	2,100,000,000
Bank of America	2014	6%	+	4%	10%	16,650,000,000
Citigroup Inc.	2015	3%	+	2%	10%	1,267,000,000
Eli Lilly and Co.	2009	−4%	0	2%	3%	1,415,000,000
Allergan PLC	2010	4%	+	0%	0%	600,000,000
JPMorgan Chase Bank NA	2013	0%	+	0%	−1%	13,000,000,000
BP Exploration and Production Inc.	2012	−1%	+	−1%	−1%	4,000,000,000
Credit Suisse	2014	−2%	−	−3%	1%	2,600,000,000
GlaxoSmithKline LLC	2012	−2%	+	−3%	1%	3,000,000,000
Deutsche Bank AG	2015	−10%	+	−6%	−3%	2,500,000,000

pattern is nearly uniform. In the foregoing cases, shareholders had faced a range of uncertainty, but the actual outcome almost always elicited a positive market response, suggesting that the actual penalty was less severe than the market had expected. If an informed market expects a harsher penalty, that suggests underenforcement is a pervasive pattern.

If these were record penalties (as some were), what else can explain this pattern? A few alternative answers are plausible.

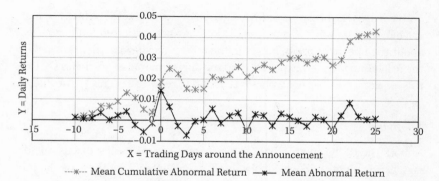

FIGURE 2 Abnormal Return around the Announcement of a Fine

Reputational Loss Avoided

One possible hypothesis is that a plea agreement spared the defendant corporation a public trial at which the evidence could have been lurid and humiliating. Thus, a plea or a deferred prosecution agreement averted reputational damage, and the market was pleased. Indeed, it may be a major shortcoming of the Becker model that it gives too little attention to reputation, as empirical research shows that reputational damage in the white collar context can be very costly.[29] But this answer only works if the resolution of the case is announced on the same date as the fine (and not earlier).

Collateral Civil Consequences

Another possibility is that a deferred prosecution agreement reduced the prospective civil liability the defendant faced (because there was no criminal conviction that could prevent the corporation from defending itself in these follow-on civil cases). This involves the legal doctrine of *offensive collateral estoppel*, which may prevent a defendant convicted of a crime from denying guilt in a subsequent civil proceeding.[30] Again, this explanation depends on the deferred prosecution agreement being announced with the fine (which is common but not universal).

The Value of Peace

Whether the case is resolved through a settlement or culminates in a sentencing, that event marks the end of the ordeal for a corporation in a high-profile case. It means that management's time will no longer be diverted, and they can get back to running the business. That could justify some positive market reaction. But this hypothesis should not be pushed too far. If the announcement both resolves the litigation or investigation and announces the fine, the market may well be relieved that the dispute has been resolved (and cares less about the fine amount). If, however, the matter has been earlier resolved (or the resolution is widely expected) and the only remaining question is the fine, this explanation does not work, as the market response is only to the fine.

Lobbying

In both the HSBC and the BNP Paribas cases, as was earlier discussed, foreign governments publicly lobbied for a lesser sentence for these banks, and to some degree, they succeeded. This could similarly happen in domestic cases as lobbyists and political officials warn the Department of Justice of the economic consequences of severe punishment. Such lobbying will be less public and more discreet in domestic cases to avoid triggering a political backlash. Such practices could potentially account for last-minute reductions in the penalty that surprised the market favorably, but this pattern is fully consistent with the claim that underenforcement is the norm in cases of misconduct by major corporations.

Whatever the explanation one prefers, this pattern of a positive market reaction to the announcement of a sanction illustrates what this book calls the problem of underenforcement: namely, the federal criminal justice system's tendency to pull its punches, imposing lesser sanctions than had been feared or that were necessary to deter. The market is an unbiased judge of what was expected, and a persistent pattern of lesser punishment than expected is consistent with underenforcement.

From a policy perspective, the immediate relevance of this evidence is that a system that imposes penalties only on the corporate entity will likely not deter adequately; chiefly, this is because even the actual penalty (which is always greater than the much smaller expected penalty) often does not exceed the actual gain. This actual penalty would need to be further discounted by the substantial risk of nonapprehension before we could conclude that the expected penalty exceeded the expected gain.

The unavoidable policy implication then is that corporate prosecutions need to be supplemented by individual prosecutions in order to generate minimally adequate deterrence. If we rely only on corporate sanctions (as the Department of Justice still largely does), the confounding conclusion that follows from this pattern is that corporate penalties would need to be increased to an extreme point at which these penalties would impose unacceptably painful externalities on the nonculpable before they could adequately deter. After all, JPMorgan Chase was fined $13 billion (for relatively modest misconduct compared to that of other banks in the period leading up to 2008). How much higher can penalties go? Politically, significant further increases are not politically sustainable. The bottom line here is that the only way that we can escape this underenforcement problem is by relying more on individual prosecutions to at least supplement corporate prosecutions.

This pattern leads to a final observation: Professor Garrett was surprised at the high rate of recidivism that he found among large public corporations. Even after receiving deferred prosecution agreements, they violated the law again and again.[31] But this pattern of high recidivism is fundamentally congruent with this pattern of underenforcement. The defendant corporation may suffer some reputational damage, may experience some interference with its internal governance, and may bear a hefty fine, but in the short run, it usually and quickly decides to cooperate with the prosecution and accept responsibility in order to gain a sentencing credit. That also evidences underenforcement (as it would predictably resist harsher penalties). Nonetheless, this seemingly repentant corporation often reappears in the criminal justice system only a few years later. Why? Very probably because crime still pays.

Penalties on Corporate Officers?

To this point, evidence has been assembled that is profoundly pessimistic in its implications: nothing seems to work! However, empirical research does point to one strategy that does work: fines on corporate officers. Some states impose civil fines on corporate officers who engage in aggressive tax avoidance. A recent empirical study comparing this system to fines imposed on the corporation for the same behavior reached two conclusions: (1) nothing showed that fines imposed on the corporation changed anything, and (2) fines imposed on corporate officers significantly reduced tax evasion.[32] Little distinguishes tax evasion from securities fraud or antitrust violations. If this tactic works in one context, it should work in others.

Why Do Prosecutors Resist Individual Prosecutions for Regulatory Crime?

The public clearly wants prosecutions of individual executives alongside their corporate employer, and the Yates Memorandum called for such a change. Yet, as of 2018, despite the Yates Memorandum, there were very few such individual prosecutions, and their number actually declined in 2018.[33]

What explains this reluctance? There is no single answer, but the following account for much of the phenomenon:

1. Both the acquittal rate and the rate of defendants going to trial go up as prosecutors indict individuals in regulatory cases, particularly those cases in which the individual defendant was pursuing no personal gain but was acting as the corporation's agent;

2. Prosecutors prefer to bring "sexier" cases against individuals who have a public identity or who have allegedly engaged in highly publicized misconduct. (This category includes insider trading cases and also cases against lurid misbehavior, such as that alleged against a Jeffrey Epstein or a Harvey Weinstein.); and

3. Above all, there is the problem of scale; a small prosecutorial team must take on a giant organization in which there may be dozens of actors who behaved with varying degrees of culpability. At the outset, the prosecution has relatively little detailed knowledge, must face a much larger and more experienced legal team, and the only feasible way that the prosecutorial team can generally assemble detailed knowledge at an acceptable cost (in time, money, and effort) is to agree to an internal investigation by an "independent" counsel chosen (or at least approved) by the corporate defendant. Typically, this requires that the parties enter into some form of deferred prosecution agreement, and the internal investigation rarely implicates higher executives at the main headquarters.

Each of these cases deserves a more detailed consideration.

The Impact on the Acquittal Rate

Corporations are much easier to prosecute than individuals. Under federal law, the prosecutor normally need prove only that some employee or agent, acting with an intent to benefit the corporation (at least in part), engaged in the forbidden behavior. When we turn to an individual defendant, the prosecution may need to show what the defendant knew and when the defendant knew it; in addition, the prosecution may need to prove that the defendant acted "willfully" (which under some statutes can be a higher standard requiring considerably more than knowledge of one's action).

In federal criminal prosecutions, the guilty plea rate has recently ranged between 95 percent and 97 percent.[34] Any sudden increase in defendants going to trial would burden prosecutors and constitute a serious management problem for U.S. attorneys. Yet, in Professor Garrett's study of individuals prosecuted between 2001 and 2014 in connection with deferred prosecution agreements, he found that the rate of defendants going to trial was slightly over 10 percent.[35] That is at least double the usual rate in other types of prosecutions.[36]

Even more disturbing to prosecutors is the increase in the acquittal rate. In Garrett's study of 414 such cases, the prosecution lost in 15 percent of these cases in which the defendant went to trial.[37] To show the contrast, in fiscal 2013, in white collar criminal prosecutions, federal prosecutors lost (either by way of dismissals by the court or by acquittals) only 7 percent of their cases.[38] A 15 percent acquittal rate thus doubles that rate; it is not only bad from a management point of view but demoralizing for the staff. A young prosecutor may have worked two years (or more) to develop this case, only to see it go down the drain when the jury acquits. Just like pitchers in baseball, the prosecutor treasures a winning (and possibly undefeated) record.

Today, prosecutors tend to resist such individual cases, either based on a proper exercise of prosecutorial discretion or because they are in James Comey's much-quoted phrase "chickenshit."[39] Yes, there is a problem here with their risk aversion. Nonetheless, if prosecutors were compelled to follow the Yates Memorandum, this 15 percent rate could increase to a much higher level—maybe even double. For prosecutors with careerist motives, a trial record with no defeats is a marketable credential, possibly enabling them to move later to lucrative law partnerships at major firms. The bottom line is that the Yates Memorandum is likely to be resisted by many prosecutors.

The "Sex Appeal" of Cases

An insider trading case has great appeal for prosecutors. It will typically receive press coverage and often attract television cameras. Even though prosecutors cannot give interviews, the words they utter in court will likely be quoted by the press. Once again, this publicity may translate into enhanced marketability for the prosecutor who wins.

Also, the acquittal rate varies with the type of case. Securities fraud cases are almost hard to lose. In 2012, for example, there were 231 guilty verdicts in securities fraud cases—and only 1 acquittal and 13 dismissals.[40] Obviously, this factor also makes insider trading cases more popular with prosecutors than a complex tax fraud or a purely regulatory violation.

Finally, an insider trading case is typically modest in size and basically manageable, with fewer moving parts. The prosecutor's job is usually to establish the chain of information. Whom did the insider tip, and whom did that tippee pass the information onto? This is simpler than establishing (in cases never brought) whether General Motors' ignition was known to be unsafe or what Boeing knew about its 737 MAX model.

Still, if insider trading cases are easier to bring, they are like other organizational cases in one respect: prosecutors find it difficult to go up the organizational ladder to the top. For example, although prosecutors in the Southern

District were able to convict several traders at SAC Capital Advisors for insider trading, they were not able to make a criminal case against the chief executive and founder of that firm, Steven A. Cohen, even though he was in regular contact with these traders.[41] Ultimately, after much bargaining, the firm paid $1.8 billion in criminal fines, but its billionaire founder escaped liability and remains a prominent figure in the New York sports world.

From the perspective of younger prosecutors, the question is whether they are willing to be assigned to a massive investigation of a bank's failure (Lehman) or its mistreatment of customers (Wells Fargo), which may still result, after two to three years, in a decision that there was no indictable crime. Or would they prefer an exciting insider trading case where the evidence of a crime is strong and a high-profile trial within a year is likely. The answer seems obvious. Moreover, because they are talented and in demand, young prosecutors can usually go elsewhere if they do not like how they are being used.

Nonetheless, even if the preferences of individual prosecutors are clear, the needs of society may be different: a criminal conviction of executives at a Lehman or a Wells Fargo might deter senior executives across the financial industry, while one more conviction of a hedge fund trader for insider trading adds only modest marginal deterrence. Phrased differently, how many convictions for insider trading are needed before the law of diminishing returns becomes applicable and reduces the value of further convictions? At one recent point, the Southern District was 85–0 in the insider trading cases it prosecuted,[42] but well-known commentators have suggested that the U.S. attorney for the Southern District failed the public by concentrating only on insider trading and passing with respect to misconduct that injured far more Americans.[43]

To sum up, what is fun for the prosecutor is not necessarily optimal for society.

The Problem of Scale

In a street crime case, the prosecutor has a simple goal: proving who shot, robbed, or raped the victim (and who else was involved). In a large white collar case, the first issue is whether there was a violation at all. Were prices fixed through collusion or just conscious parallelism (which is not unlawful)? Was material information willfully withheld from an SEC filing? Did senior executives know of (and tolerate) a serious safety defect in their best-selling auto, airplane, or pharmaceutical product? After that hurdle, the next barrier is no less daunting: What executives with decision-making authority knew of the problem (and when)?

This second problem is vastly compounded by the decentralized structure of the modern public corporation. Decision making is diffused through various levels and divisions.[44] The president of a division may have operational responsibility, but financial decision making may be allocated to a chief financial officer one level above him, who holds control over all substantial investments and expenditures. Rarely is the firm's chief executive involved in operational decisions. That is, CEOs have been convicted for fraudulent financial statements (as they were in Enron and WorldCom) because they must sign and certify those statements but very seldom for product defects, design problems, or injuries to workers.[45] This difficulty in identifying who really made the decision has long been the standard justification given for why executives were not prosecuted when the corporation was; the defense is that the prosecution could simply not establish with confidence who actually made the decision.

Consider then the problem that prosecutors face if they wanted to investigate a large corporation that has experienced multiple airplane crashes or many deaths from its opioid drug. Unless prosecutors are lucky and are informed by a whistle-blower (which does happen with increasing frequency), they are essentially chipping at a large iceberg with small ice picks. They can subpoena all emails from targeted executives, but reading those emails (even using advanced computer search technology) will require the extended time of multiple persons. Remember next that, even at a large U.S. Attorney's office (such as the Southern District of New York), the population of a given subdivision (say, the Securities Fraud Office) is likely no more than twenty attorneys. And they already have a full caseload. To be sure, these attorneys can seek to rely on the FBI and other agencies, but these people are seldom trained in securities, antitrust, or other technical law.

Next, the investigation may be global. Assume that the government believes that XYZ Corp., a U.S. company, has paid bribes to obtain defense contracts or weapon sales in five or six different countries (two in South America, two in Eastern Europe, and one in Africa). This violates the Foreign Corrupt Practices Act, and such conduct is frequently prosecuted. But there is little possibility that the U.S. Attorney can send personnel to all these countries or deal with the multiple languages involved. Still, for its own reasons, the corporation may well want to settle with Justice and the SEC, and it proposes a deferred prosecution agreement and an internal investigation conducted by a highly regarded New York law firm. If you are the U.S. Attorney who has to make the manpower allocation decision and you cannot give a dozen attorneys for two years to this case, do you see a better alternative?

In fairness, federal prosecutors have learned to work with foreign criminal prosecutors, but the likelihood is low that foreign governments will extradite their citizens to the United States. Absent the ability to compel the foreign individuals who were on the scene to testify, it is often difficult to learn who in the United States authorized them. Again, the deferred prosecution agreement may seem the only feasible alternative, and as a result the investigation of such a case is effectively outsourced to a private law firm.

An Evaluation

This chapter has raised the theme of underenforcement: namely, that prosecutors regularly (and maybe unknowingly) let large corporations off too lightly, even when they are imposing record penalties. There are possible responses to this claim: First, it can be argued that the civil penalties imposed for corporate misconduct often exceed the criminal penalties, and the sum of the two may be adequate to deter. Although this is conceivable, it seems unlikely to be generally true. If it were generally true that the combination of criminal and civil penalties was adequate to deter, the high rate of corporate recidivism that Garrett and others have emphasized would be inexplicable.

Consider here the extraordinary gains and losses involved in some recent cases. In the Volkswagen case, the company was faced with the loss of its American market if it could not claim to be in compliance with American emissions standards (and it was not close). This means that it faced the loss of a significant part of its market capitalization. Similarly, the pharmaceutical companies that encouraged the sale of opioids for chronic pain from non-life-threatening illnesses would have faced the loss of the majority of their market if they had ceased to promote these dubious sales. In such cases, legal penalties again would have to be staggeringly high to make the expected penalty exceed the expected gain from the criminal behavior. Again, this would raise the problem of externalities, as employees, creditors, and others would suffer if penalties were raised to an extreme level. Once more, this buttresses the conclusion that adequate deterrence requires a focus on the individual executive.

Arguably, this same point can be made about senior executives as well. Although senior executives are rarely indicted, it might be argued that they are often fired, hit with civil penalties, or forced to settle class actions as a result of their misconduct. The facts, however, are to the contrary. Although executives are sometimes fired because of a scandal (think of Wells Fargo and several recent sexual harassment cases), executives rarely face salary reductions or other economic penalties as a result of corporate criminal behavior. Indeed, executive compensation actually increases after a deferred prosecution agreement.[46] Although class actions may name corporate executives as defendants, these class actions are almost always settled out of the company's directors-and-officers insurance (without any significant payment by the executive).[47] Corporate indemnification is also available to pick up any possible balance.

Is this problem unsolvable? This book's answer: not at all! But an adequate answer requires that we think more strategically than criminal law scholarship usually does. This book's fundamental response is that adequate deterrence depends on focusing criminal enforcement much more on the individual than the entity. The confounding problem, however, is that individual prosecutions are difficult to bring.

That complication requires us to redefine the problem and recognize that it is very difficult to prosecute executives—unless the law and prosecutors aggressively encourage someone to turn them in. The prosecutor must have an ally that provides the evidence. This is possible in various ways. In some cases, it could be a whistle-blower or even a rival firm that turns in its former co-conspirators in an effort to obtain leniency. But the party most able to turn the executive in to prosecutors is the principal: the corporation that employs the executive. Generally, the corporate principal has the most knowledge about the agent's behavior but little incentive to disclose it. Today, the corporation need not turn in its agents because it can already receive a sentencing credit simply for token "cooperation" and "accepting responsibility." Existing incentives are insufficient to encourage much more. The next step is critical: if potential corporate penalties were raised and deferred prosecutions and sentencing credits required full cooperation (meaning that the corporate entity needed to identify the individuals responsible for the crime and turned over all evidence in the corporation's possession), then this enhanced incentive might generate valuable, rather than sham, cooperation (in order that the corporation escape the threatened penalty). This proposal will be more fully sketched out in the next chapter.

At this point, we can conclude this chapter by focusing on what the true rationale for corporate criminal liability should be. Usually, the debate over this issue (which has continued for decades) involves critics of corporate liability emphasizing that the corporation is a fictional entity (or, in more economic terms, merely a "nexus of contracts") that is incapable of the intent required by the criminal law. Accordingly, retributive justifications for punishment do not sensibly apply to it. Proponents of corporate criminal liability respond that it is pragmatically useful. Although these proponents hope that the corporation can be deterred by penalties, they may be overconfident, because, particularly in major cases, it is often unlikely that the expected cost exceeds the expected gain.

What then can corporate criminal liability truly achieve? Three goals seem realistic.

First, in cases where no executive or agent can be reliably identified, it can serve as the residual risk bearer. This will not work very well in the case of public corporations with diversified shareholders (because they will feel little economic pain, and they will be protected by limited liability even when the ownership is not diffuse), but corporate liability at least promotes greater transparency.

Second, the corporation can be motivated to monitor its employees through the use of the best available internal controls. This will work well when the criminal conduct is in the employee's interest but not necessarily in the corporation's interest. In these cases, the misconduct can be an "agency cost"— that is, the responsible employee is opportunistically misbehaving. The corporation already has an incentive to catch this employee, but higher corporate penalties enhance that incentive.

Third, the corporation can be motivated to turn in all responsible employees after the violation is detected by prosecutors. This is the variable that has been the most ignored.

The important point here is that corporate criminal liability is a means to an end, rather than an end in itself. The end that should be sought is to induce the corporation to monitor its employees (and thus prevent crime) and to turn responsible employees into the prosecution when a crime occurs (thus deterring executives for the future, once this pattern becomes evident). Pursued consistently, this strategy can enable us to identify and prosecute individuals who would otherwise escape. To understand this point, we should start with the recognition that it takes far less of a legal threat to cause the corporation (once detected) to turn in its culpable agents than to cause the corporation to behave lawfully in the first place (at least when the crime is profitable). Once detected, the corporation is no longer deciding whether to violate the law but how to minimize its punishment. To deter the corporation at the outset, we need to make the expected penalty exceed the expected gain, but to motivate the corporation to turn in responsible officers, the incentive offered by the prosecution (usually a penalty discount) need only exceed the costs of losing the employee and of possibly damaging corporate morale. This is a much more feasible goal.

If we can motivate the corporation, as principal, to turn in its agents, we have a strategy for making individual prosecutions work that could generate adequate deterrence. To be sure, there are issues and complexities in designing such a system, but unless prosecutors have an ally who is motivated to assist them, prosecutors have little chance of winning the big case on their own.

FIVE

The Prisoner's Dilemma Strategy

IN THE STANDARD CRIMINAL investigation of an organization, the prosecutor starts at the bottom and tries to flip lower-echelon personnel, offering them leniency in return for their testimony and cooperation against their superiors. This is never easy. The Godfather, for example, does not communicate directly with his hitmen or drug dealers but deliberately stays remote and isolated. Still, it may be even more difficult in the setting of the large public corporation. The top of the hierarchy is remote, both physically and in terms of the frequency of communications, from the lower echelons. In addition, decisions are more fragmented; public corporations have operational, design, marketing, financial, and legal dimensions, which require the participation and consent of different actors. The more the levels, the harder the strategy becomes of flipping those at the bottom to implicate those at the top.

Still, there is an alternative to the traditional strategy of working from the bottom up. This is to work from the top down. If the prosecution could make the corporation an "offer that it couldn't refuse"—one that would involve the threat of economic pain far beyond what is today imposed on the corporation—then, subject to such a threat, the corporation might cooperate against the highest-ranking senior executives who did coordinate or approve the conduct that produced the crime. This top-down strategy would require that great pressure be placed on the corporation (and the last section of this chapter will focus on how that could be done), but the point of this pressure is to compel cooperation by the corporation, because, if the corporation were so motivated, it could usually identify those responsible for the misconduct.

A further critical element to this strategy is that a corresponding offer could also be made to the firm's executives: Cooperate and tell us all you know before someone else does, and you will receive leniency. But wait too long (until after someone else cooperates first), and you may forfeit that opportunity (or, at the least, receive much less leniency). This tactic maximizes the pressure because each executive now is uncertain as to whether the superior strategy is to hold out and resist or to cooperate and betray his or her colleagues. And he or she faces time pressure, because the first to talk will reap the largest gain.

At this point, we have begun to describe a choice that resembles the classic "prisoner's dilemma" of standard game theory.[1] It is therefore useful to take a step back and examine that problem.

The Prisoner's Dilemma

The prisoner's dilemma is the standard example of a game in which rational individuals do not cooperate, even though it would be in their best interests to do so. Put differently, individuals in this position have a strong incentive to make a choice that represents a less than optimal outcome for all the individuals as a whole. And that is why it provides a useful model for policy planning.

As the prisoner's dilemma is usually specified, two members of the same gang are arrested and imprisoned (so that they cannot communicate with each other). The authorities do not have sufficient evidence yet to convict either, and so they offer a deal to each prisoner: If the prisoner will confess, he can plead guilty to a misdemeanor and receive a one-year sentence. If one prisoner does not confess but the other prisoner does, the nonconfessing prisoner will be indicted for a felony and receive a three-year sentence. If, however, they both hold out and do not confess, neither will be convicted. The various outcomes are described in figure 3.

Clearly, both A and B do better if both do not confess (for them, that is the optimal outcome), but both are subject to the worst possible outcome if one prisoner does not confess and the other prisoner does (and thereby betrays the first prisoner by confessing). Also, if both confess, the total penalty (1 plus 1) is less than the total penalty if one confesses and the other does not (3 plus 1). Under these circumstances, the standard assumption is that both will confess to avoid the worst possible outcome.

Now, let us assume that we are dealing with a corporate defendant and an unknown (but relatively small) number of senior executives. The prosecution's offer is now communicated to both the corporation and senior executives that those who cooperate fully will receive leniency (probably in the form of a deferred prosecution agreement). But if the corporation does not cooperate (including by funding an investigation conducted by counsel selected by the U.S. Attorney, as described later in this chapter), it can anticipate an extreme penalty (as later also described). To be sure, if all hold out and resist, it remains possible that the prosecution will fail. But the more the executives given this

	Does Not Confess	Confesses
Prisoner A: Confesses	A = 1 B = 3	A = 1 B = 1
Prisoner A: Does Not Confess	A = 0 B = 0	A = 3 B = 1

PRISONER A (rows) / PRISONER B (columns)

FIGURE 3 The Prisoner's Dilemma

offer of leniency, the greater the prospect that at least one risk-averse executive will crack and defect.

Implementation

The corporate setting largely mirrors the standard prisoner's dilemma problem, with one major difference: the defendants in our corporate setting can communicate. They will possibly agree to resist (although this conduct could constitute the additional crime of obstruction of justice). But there is also another difference: multiple executives probably have sufficient knowledge to cooperate, confess, and assure the conviction of the corporation. We can also manipulate our incentives—for example, by offering complete immunity for the first to defect and lesser credit for those who cooperate later. Complete immunity could also be given to the corporation for identifying its responsible executives (and, as we will soon see, the Antitrust Division of the Department of Justice does exactly this for the first to cooperate).

The corporation, however, faces a different decision calculus. It will not be able to obtain a deferred prosecution agreement unless it agrees to conduct an internal investigation using a counsel selected by the prosecution. Department of Justice policy could explicitly limit deferred prosecution agreements to cases where there is an adequate and independent investigation. If the corporation refuses to fund an investigation, the U.S. attorney would announce publicly that the corporation had failed to cooperate (which is likely to cause some reputational damage).

What will the corporation decide? It may depend on who makes the decision for the corporation. If the CEO controls this decision, he or she may decline the request for the corporation to fund the investigation because it could uncover misconduct by the CEO or his or her colleagues. However, if it were a condition of deferred prosecution agreements that the negotiations between the prosecutors and the corporation had to be conducted for the corporation by an independent committee of its directors (most likely its audit committee) on the grounds that its senior executives were conflicted, that could make a significant difference. Such an independent committee might decide that it was better to cooperate and turn evidence over to the prosecutors about its senior executives' involvement than for the company to bear a very harsh penalty. The members of this committee might even tell themselves (with considerable logic) that it was their fiduciary duty to so cooperate. At the outset however, such a committee of directors would know little, if anything, about the possible involvement of senior executives in any misconduct. Thus, the immediate question for the committee would really be whether to authorize and fund an investigation by counsel selected by the prosecutors. If this investigation turned up evidence, it would automatically be in the prosecutors' possession (and there would be no need to turn it over). Ideally, this committee of directors would be represented by its own independent counsel (and not the corporation's regular counsel).

If this procedure were followed and an investigation were commenced at the corporation's expense, the corporation's senior executives might individually reconsider their prior decisions as to whether to cooperate. They might see the decision to start such an investigation as making it more likely that incriminating facts would come out and decide that it was better to cooperate than to miss their chance at leniency by waiting too long. Presumably, a twelfth-hour decision by executives to cooperate after the investigation had already uncovered "smoking guns" would win them very little in terms of reduced charges and sentencing credits.

To restate, the key idea here is to place the corporation and its executives into a competition for leniency. Uncertainty (which is here maximized) often makes individuals more risk averse and thus willing to cooperate with the prosecution. To earn significant leniency, the executives would have to cooperate and confess not long after this investigation had begun. Between the corporation and the executive, the game should be nearly zero sum; that is, both cannot escape liability.

To be sure, it is possible that the executives would refuse to cooperate or even to be interviewed. As discussed in the next chapter, this might give the board the necessary justification to terminate them (or, at the least, suspend all bonuses and incentive compensation). Once the prosecution knew which executives were not cooperating, prosecutors could on their own call these executives before the grand jury. Although these executives could assert the Fifth Amendment, this is easier said than done by senior officers of a publicly traded corporation who exist in a fishbowl of constant disclosure—and this embarrassment might again influence their decision whether to cooperate.

The Experience with Leniency Incentives

Is there any precedent for this hard-nosed effort to force cooperation by denying leniency to those who do not cooperate fully? The short answer is yes; indeed, the Antitrust Division has done something very similar since at least 1993. In that year, the Antitrust Division recognized that cartels were secretive, conspiracies were hard to detect, and earlier leniency policies had not created a sufficient incentive.[2] Under its revised policy (as adopted in 1993), any member of a cartel could approach the government, confess, and (with some conditions) thereby earn complete immunity for itself (and for its officers, directors, and employees as well)—at least so long as the corporation admitted its misconduct before the prosecution was hot on its trail. As originally implemented, only one corporation in the cartel could receive this credit, thereby incentivizing a race to the prosecutor's door and creating a near zero-sum game.[3] The second to confess would be very disappointed.

What was the impact of this expanded leniency policy? In 2005, the deputy assistant attorney general responsible for it noted that the new policy had produced an immediate "surge in amnesty applications," which as of 2005 had risen to "roughly two per month."[4] A large empirical literature has investigated the impact of leniency programs, and the "general conclusion of this body of work is that leniency programs make collusion more difficult."[5] By now, a number of European countries have adopted similar programs. Much about the special case of cartel enforcement remains in debate, but it seems beyond argument that corporations do respond to a leniency incentive. Faced with a choice between holding out (and hoping not to be detected) and seeking amnesty, many corporations apply for amnesty (and thereby enrage their coconspirators who feel betrayed).

From a public policy perspective, this is a policy innovation that causes collusion to give way to rational defection (as the other coconspirators will face both civil and criminal liability). Rational defection is exactly the behavior that the law should seek to encourage.

There may be limits on how far we wish to push a leniency program. Impressed by the Antitrust Division's Corporate Leniency Program, Congress passed the Antitrust Criminal Penalty Enhancement and Reform Act in 2004, which permits a corporation that qualifies for leniency to avoid paying treble damages in private follow-on lawsuits. This may be too sweeping a proposal to endorse for all forms of corporate misconduct. But, at a minimum, it is clear that the use of leniency as a policy lever has been more aggressively pursued in some contexts than is being proposed here. What is proposed here has two essential elements: (1) the corporation should receive a major leniency credit for turning over evidence on senior corporate executives and for agreeing to fund (and cooperate with) an independent internal investigation; and (2) a significant difference in the leniency credit should be structured between the first executive to cooperate and later executives. Otherwise, all may wait and then attempt to follow on the coattails of the first executive to cooperate.

Making the Investigation Independent

Perhaps the most disconcerting feature associated with the deferred prosecution agreement is that the internal investigation that constitutes the factual foundation for the negotiations between prosecutors and defense counsel is conducted by an outside counsel largely selected by defense counsel. In effect, the prosecution outsources its investigatory function to the defendant. We should not be surprised when such investigations rarely implicate the company's highest-ranking executives in criminal misconduct. For many of the most prestigious U.S. law firms, the conduct of internal investigations has become immensely lucrative, and they are locked in intense competition to win such assignments. Inevitably, this means that they cannot afford a reputation as "aggressive" or "suspicious"—which is precisely what society wants investigators to be. This is not to say that the counsel conducting these investigations are corrupt lackeys. Rather, these counsel must be consummate diplomats, convincing both the prosecution that they have been thorough and house counsel that they will demand credible evidence to support any conclusions about culpability. But they are compromised.

Add to this pattern the fact that the total cost of a corporate internal investigation can sometimes exceed $100 million,[6] and a difficult question must be faced: Is it realistic to expect a corporation to accept the prosecution's choice of counsel for this very sensitive and expensive undertaking? Why should it agree to spend millions to fund an investigation by a counsel that it suspects may be quick on the trigger or too ready to infer guilt on ambiguous evidence?

The answer to this question may depend on a variety of factors: (1) How much does the defendant corporation need a deferred prosecution agreement? (2) How harsh could the sanction be if the corporation were instead indicted and convicted? (3) Who will the prosecution select as its lead counsel for this investigation? (4) How likely is it that whistle-blowers or executives cooperating to avoid their own indictment will arm the prosecution with sufficient evidence to indict? (5) How much will it cost?

As an initial reform, suppose the Department of Justice issued a follow-up directive to the Yates Memorandum that required any deferred prosecution agreement to be negotiated by the prosecutors with an independent committee of the board represented by an independent counsel (i.e., not the corporation's regular counsel). Arguably, an independent board committee might be less resistant to an investigation led by the prosecution's choice of counsel. The CEO might also be less concerned if the CEO was convinced he was sufficiently remote from the misconduct and had never known of it. Or maybe the corporation desperately needed the deferred prosecution agreement (either because an indictment would be unthinkably dangerous for it or because it feared the collateral consequences in terms of civil liability if it were convicted[7]). Today, these concerns about the consequences of conviction may not loom large, but they could in a post–Trump administration.

If one can imagine a corporation willing to submit to a rigorous investigation by a truly independent counsel in order to earn a deferred prosecution agreement, the next question becomes: Can the prosecution select the counsel to lead this investigation or direct its activities? This is a complex question with constitutional dimensions, which must be approached carefully. Let's therefore take a simpler question first: Who does the government want leading this investigation? Choosing a prestigious and experienced law firm sounds sensible, but it might give the investigation to precisely those firms with an apparent track record of never leading their investigation to the top of the corporate hierarchy. These firms have historically worked only on the defense side of the aisle and might not be energetic in serving as in effect counsel for the prosecution. The most natural choice for the government would be a lawyer of unimpeachable integrity—such as a Robert Mueller, who could then select the lawyers to assist him. But there are simply not enough Robert Muellers to go around.

Another plausible source of counsel for such an investigation would be the plaintiff's bar. Although these firms are not experienced in corporate internal investigations, they have experience in a related activity. They investigate, prepare, and draft class actions against corporations, and to do this successfully, they must tell a convincing and persuasive story. In the case of securities class actions (which are today hitting record levels), plaintiff's counsel know that their action will be dismissed by the court unless they can plead facts at the outset (and without formal discovery) that give rise to a "strong inference of fraud."[8] To meet this mandatory standard, plaintiff's counsel have learned to hire private investigators (often former FBI or other law enforcement agency veterans) to interview the defendant corporation's employees and others so that counsel can plead a complaint that satisfies the requisite "strong inference of fraud" standard. Often, they succeed.

Without doubt, counsel experienced in investigating corporate misconduct could be found. Conceivably, former federal prosecutors could form new law firms to specialize in such investigations (if the practice of such independent investigations became established). The problem, however, is that it is difficult to imagine a public corporation consenting to be investigated by a plaintiff's securities law firm—unless it was desperate to obtain a deferred prosecution agreement. The antagonism between them runs deep. That leaves one other possibility: a few firms have made a unique career of representing both plaintiffs and defendants in class action cases. These firms—Boies Schiller Flexner, LLP, is a leading example[9]—might be more acceptable, but they would, of course, be highly expensive.

All this suggests that some negotiation over the ground rules would be necessary. At a minimum, the corporation would insist that the prosecution's choice of counsel (1) not be a firm from the plaintiff's bar (as defined) and (2) agree that it would not serve as plaintiff's counsel in any follow-on litigation against the company or sue it in any other litigation for a defined period. The government might submit a list of law firms and allow the defendants to either select off that list or veto one or two (with the government then making the final selection). That would still leave the prosecution with its choice of counsel. Nonetheless, the plausibility of the defendant corporation allowing the government effectively to choose the counsel for the investigation remains in doubt. This prospect may only be likely if the prosecution can threaten the defendant with penalties that truly scare it—a theme to which we will return shortly.

Characterizing the Internal Investigation: Private or Public?

One of the advantages of a private investigation is that the usual restraints on the prosecution do not apply to the corporation's own internal investigation. The corporation can tell the employee to "talk or walk"—that is, the employee must answer its questions or face termination. The Fifth Amendment's privilege against self-incrimination simply does not apply to such a private inquiry. But if the prosecution either chooses the counsel or directs the investigation, it is likely that courts will view such de facto control as making the investigation "attributable" to the government, and then the Fifth Amendment will apply. Thus, any compelled waiver of the privilege (based on even an implied threat of dismissal) will be invalid and will render the testimony inadmissible. Worse yet, any evidence (or other information) gained even indirectly through such compulsion may be deemed "fruit of the poisonous tree" and also made inadmissible.[10] Thus, for example, if the employee subject to such compulsion provides information identifying a third party (not employed by the corporation) and this person does provide damaging information as a result, even this unrelated information provided by the third party may also be deemed inadmissible "fruit of the poisonous tree," because the original source was unconstitutionally compelled.

This dilemma is vividly illustrated by a recent case, *United States v. Connolly*, in which the court found that, even where the defendant selected the counsel for the investigation, the frequent contacts between that counsel (the Paul Weiss firm) and the prosecutors could also trigger this doctrine.[11] In 2008, the Commodities Futures Trading Commission opened an investigation into the manipulation of LIBOR trading by several banks and eventually expanded its investigation to include Deutsche Bank. Deutsche Bank retained the Paul Weiss firm to conduct an internal investigation, and the CFTC bluntly informed the bank and Paul Weiss that it wanted access to all testimony and documents produced in that investigation. Failure to comply, it indicated, would mean that Deutsche Bank would not be eligible for a negotiated resolution.[12]

Deutsche Bank decided to comply fully, and Paul Weiss conducted a nearly five-year investigation, during which it held some two hundred interviews with bank employees, reviewed over 159 million electronic documents, and listened to hundreds of thousands of hours of audio tapes.[13] Both Deutsche Bank and Paul Weiss reported that this was the largest, most intensive investigation that either had ever conducted.[14] It was also an investigation clearly beyond the capacity of the Department of Justice. As a result, Deutsche Bank did obtain a deferred prosecution agreement pursuant to which it paid a $775 million fine and appointed a corporate monitor for three years; in addition, a Deutsche Bank subsidiary pleaded guilty to wire fraud.

Paul Weiss was not instructed by the government as to whom to question, but it did regularly "download" all the testimony it received with the various agencies that came to participate in this investigation. Although corporate employees were not expressly threatened with dismissal if they failed to testify, the senior Paul Weiss partner conducting the investigation testified that there was "no doubt" that dismissal would follow if an employee refused to cooperate.[15]

Eventually, one employee—Gavin Black, a relatively low-level Deutsche Bank trader—was indicted and convicted for participating in a conspiracy to manipulate LIBOR. He appealed on the ground that Justice had obtained critical evidence based on his compelled testimony, with such evidence being "fruit of the poisonous tree." Although the district court denied his motion on technical grounds,[16] the court clearly held that the investigation was "attributable" to the government so that the Fifth Amendment applied. In particular, the court relied on the fact that the government had not conducted its own independent parallel investigation but had just relied on Paul Weiss's work.[17]

This is a curious, even perverse, argument. Almost by definition, the government cannot conduct two hundred interviews, review 158 million documents, or listen to hundreds of thousands of hours of tapes. The whole purpose of a deferred prosecution agreement is to induce the corporation to conduct a serious investigation. Here, it did (although we do not know if it could have gone higher into the corporate hierarchy). If we use as our standard to determine the applicability of the Fifth Amendment whether the government conducted an independent parallel investigation, we will only create an incentive for the government to erect a Potemkin village—a minimal investigation that satisfies the court but that cannot approach the seriousness of the private internal investigation. Such duplication serves no legitimate purpose.

Connolly's holding that an investigation in which the government participates significantly triggers the Fifth Amendment is likely to be followed, and as a result the government faces a difficult choice between two imperfect options: (1) it can take the position that the investigation was not conducted by it, either by not engaging with the corporation's counsel during the conduct of its investigation or by relying on cosmetics, such as conducting a minimal parallel investigation; or (2) it can treat the investigation as its own, direct it closely, but advise all potential witnesses that they will not be terminated or penalized by the corporation if they decline to testify. If the government chooses the first option, the risk is that the investigation will not go as deep or pursue leads or clues that point upward into the corporate hierarchy. Counsel leading the investigation will be reluctant to risk alienating senior management, unless counsel is pushed and prodded by the government. Alternatively, if the government accepts that the investigation is attributable to it, then testimony cannot be compelled. Employees cannot be told that they will be terminated if they do not cooperate, and defense counsel for the individuals so interviewed may advise them not to testify. To be sure, the corporation conducting the internal investigation may request testimony from employees and may even imply that it will look unfavorably on a failure to cooperate. But harsher sanctions would threaten the admissibility and use of the information so gathered.

If prosecutors choose the counsel conducting the investigation (and they did not in *Connolly*), it will probably be necessary for prosecutors to accept that the investigation will be deemed to be their investigation. This means that corporate employees will have the right to claim the Fifth Amendment privilege, and prosecutors will have to be very careful in requesting testimony from employees to make clear that the corporation will not sanction them for a refusal to testify. Quite possibly, many (and perhaps most) defense counsel will still advise their clients that they should not testify. Indeed, they may seek to organize all defense counsel to resist in this fashion. But such noncooperation has its own costs. The prosecution can call such recalcitrant witnesses before the grand jury (where the witness can certainly claim the Fifth Amendment privilege, but this may be considerably more unpleasant than testifying in the private investigation). Also, the employee who refuses to testify or cooperate may forgo future promotions or bonuses. Still, even if many do not testify, the prosecution gains an investigation of greater depth and breadth than it can conduct itself.

The bottom line here involves an uncertain tradeoff. Under *Connolly*, significant participation by the prosecution in a private corporate internal investigation will raise a litigable issue as to whether the individual defendant's Fifth Amendment privilege was violated. Yet, if the prosecution stays out of this process and remains on the sidelines, the likelihood grows that defense counsel will yield to the corporation's preferences and not pursue leads or ambiguous evidence leading to the top of the corporation. Sometimes, the better option for prosecution may be to accept the investigation's public character from the outset but then not seek to compel testimony from employees in this investigation. At the least, such a corporate internal investigation can start the inquiry, even if it does not provide sufficient value to justify a deferred prosecution agreement.

Ultimately, the best option for prosecutors may be an intermediate one: prosecutors could indicate that they preferred that class counsel came from a small list of law firms they had cultivated and worked with, but they would not insist on any specified firm (or that the choice come from off their list). Thus, they would not choose the counsel, so as to make counsel their agent. But if prosecutors later refused to accept the findings of this investigation and declined to enter into a deferred prosecution agreement, the corporation would have wasted millions and achieved little. The next corporation to face a similar choice might learn to listen more intently to the prosecution's preferences. By declining to grant a deferred prosecution agreement in one case, the prosecution sends a message to all future defendants to cooperate better in the next cases.

What Threat Will Deter?
The Case for the Equity Fine

We have seen that the market's response to the announcement of multibillion-dollar penalties on Facebook, BNP Paribas, and other corporations was only to move their stock prices upward. Although this hardly suggests that these penalties yielded adequate deterrence, the question remains: What penalty or threat might work to induce the corporation to conduct and fund an internal investigation, using counsel approved by the prosecution?

Let us start with a simple example and then move to a broader theory. Financial institutions probably fear—more than anything else—that they might be indicted for money laundering. Some banks, such as HSBC, have been clearly guilty of this offense; in HSBC's case, it funneled billions of dollars from Mexican drug cartels into New York banks. Yet no bank appears ever to have been indicted for money laundering.[18] Why not? Corporate counsel have successfully convinced prosecutors, time after time, that such a charge would be too drastic because it could potentially cause a loss of the bank's license to engage in banking. Under federal law, if a bank is convicted of money laundering, the comptroller of the currency is obligated to initiate proceedings to determine whether to terminate "all rights, privileges and franchises of the bank"—in effect, to put it out of business.[19] But the comptroller is not required to do more than initiate a hearing; forfeiture of the license is not automatic. Nonetheless, with this Draconian but unlikely consequence in view, defense counsel have persuaded prosecutors to charge banks only with violations of the Bank Secrecy Act, typically ones that only involve a failure to install adequate internal controls. Alternatively, prosecutors have settled (as they did in *Connolly*) for a guilty plea by a corporate subsidiary. Either way, particularly if the matter is resolved through a deferred prosecution agreement, the prerequisite conviction of the parent to trigger these proceedings is missing.[20] This explains in large part why banks in particular need a deferred prosecution agreement.

Does this mean that we should generally indict banks for money laundering? Not necessarily! Indeed, that response would seem normally disproportionate. The threat of charter revocation is similar to a nuclear weapon that no one dares use because of the havoc it might cause. Left of center groups sometimes call for its use, but the threat remains remote.[21]

A better policy would be to advise the bank that it would be so indicted on a money laundering charge unless it agreed to a new, stiffer form of deferred prosecution agreement that involved an independent investigation conducted by counsel of the prosecution's choice. Our goal here is not to compel forfeiture of the bank's license or to force it out of business but to obtain evidence that would lead to conviction of senior bank personnel. Again, our basic approach should be to treat corporate liability not as an end in itself but as a means to an end. Here, that end is to place the corporation in a serious prisoner's dilemma vis-à-vis its executives in order to force each to implicate the other. Ultimately, even if the bank cooperated, it would still likely bear a large fine, but the lion's share of the deterrence generated would come from convicting executives.

The foregoing is but one example of an enhanced threat that might work to induce cooperation. Other regulated industries (e.g., broker dealers, insurance companies, and investment advisors) are also subject to similar forfeiture provisions if firms in them are convicted of a crime.

Of course, most firms do not face this risk, and that compels us to consider the problem of corporate deterrence on a more general level. This book has repeatedly argued that existing monetary penalties do not adequately deter. This does not mean that some much more severe monetary penalty would not deter, but courts would be highly reluctant to levy such a penalty because of the externalities they would impose on nonculpable persons (e.g., employees, creditors, local communities—all of whom would suffer). Simply stated, this is the trade-off: high penalties seem not to deter, but the extraordinary penalties that might deter would hurt the innocent.

But there is a way around this dilemma: find a penalty that does not fall on the least culpable. Deterrence requires that someone feel the pain of sanctions. But there is no legitimate reason to make lower-echelon employees, creditors, consumers, or local communities bear this burden if a way to exempt them can be found. Above all, these constituencies are powerless to act and cannot change the corporation's behavior (even if they were motivated). Only shareholders, executives, and directors can change that behavior. Hence, the optimal corporate sanction should be one that is felt by shareholders (who, of course, include executives and directors), but not by these other constituencies.

A means to this end is possible. As this author has argued elsewhere,[22] if very severe corporate penalties were imposed in stock rather than cash, their impact would fall almost exclusively on shareholders (who would be diluted), but not on creditors, employees, or other nonculpable constituencies. From the standpoint of creditors, for example, it does not matter if the underlying equity of the corporation were divided into 10 million shares or 12.5 million shares. The corporation would still have the same cash flow. The impact then on a corporation with 100 million shares outstanding of a hypothetical equity fine of 20 million shares would fall on the shareholders, diluting their respective interest but not harming others. For example, the riskiness of the corporation's debt should not increase, so bond prices need not move. Similarly, employees will be hurt by a severe cash fine, as employee cutbacks would become likely, but employees can be indifferent to the number of shares outstanding (unless they hold stock or options in the company, which suggests that they are executives).

Some will say that such a punitive fine is unfair to shareholders. It is severe, but deterrence requires that someone somewhere suffer. Shareholders tend to be diversified and indexed, so no one stock is critical to their portfolio.

Executives are less diversified and so will feel a stock penalty more. Unlike shareholders, employees hold only one job and may not be able to find another easily. Bondholders are probably also diversified investors, but they have little, if any, ability to influence corporate policy (while shareholders can react to a severe penalty by seeking to oust management). As a result, shareholders make the best cost bearer when high penalties need to be visited on the corporate entity.

Because the equity fine is designed to be punitive, it should not be used in cases of lesser severity. But in cases where the defendant company has defied the law over an extended period (think of a company like Volkswagen), the court could order the defendant company to issue such number of shares as equals a specified percentage of its outstanding stock (say, 20 percent) to a state-administered victim compensation fund. An equivalent cash fine on Volkswagen would likely have meant bankruptcy and certainly massive layoffs (and economic shock for at least the German economy).

The equity fine would be implemented by an injunction issued by the sentencing court to the relevant corporate officers to prepare and deliver the necessary share certificates. Resistance (other than through appeals) would be treated as contempt. Under existing exemptions under the federal securities laws, the shares would be exempt from registration if certain easily satisfied procedures are followed.[23]

Who should be sentenced to an equity fine? Obviously, not most corporations, even for serious offenses. Lesser penalties could suffice. But some corporations persist in misconduct, because they do not believe they can be threatened with penalties severe enough to deter them. Several persons have suggested to this author the example of Pacific Gas and Electric. As a utility, it had a natural monopoly, and it appears to have had little incentive to invest in new equipment. Aged equipment, poorly managed forests, and possibly climate change all led to a series of forest fires that destroyed entire towns. The *Wall Street Journal* has reported that PG&E's "electrical equipment has sparked more than a fire a day on average since 2014," including four hundred in 2018 with over one hundred persons dying.[24] But still, PG&E resisted change, and eventually it filed for bankruptcy. Cash fines against it would simply have been borne by customers or stockholders, neither of whom could likely replace its management, and cash fines would have depleted its ability to pay the tort creditors injured in the fires it caused. But an equity fine could have deterred and destabilized its management, without depleting PG&E's assets.

As it has turned out, PG&E has settled with these creditors for $13.5 billion, which it will pay to a victim compensation trust fund in cash and stock.[25] Stock had to be used because PG&E did not have (and probably could not raise) $13.5 billion in cash.

Yet this is exactly what the equity fine could similarly achieve (and without the defendant corporation having any veto power). If an equity fine in stock were imposed on PG&E, its cash flow would remain the same (and could fund to some degree payments to its tort creditors); more importantly, the proceeds from the sale of the company's stock would go to a victim compensation fund that would pay its tort creditors.

How would this system work? The simplest approach would be for the court to order the defendant corporation to transfer the shares to a trustee who would auction them off, possibly in several installments over an extended period, with the proceeds going to a victim compensation fund. If insufficient victims could be identified who were injured by the defendant's conduct, the excess could go to a broader compensation fund.

As a safeguard, the defendant corporation would be precluded from repurchasing its shares for a defined period. This is necessary, as otherwise stock repurchases could place the corporation in the same overly leveraged position that a cash fine would have caused. If the corporation had outstanding multiple classes of common stock (probably because of the use of a dual-class, supervoting stock), the court could exact the penalty in the supervoting stock. Conceivably, this could threaten corporate control, but that simply adds to the equity fine's deterrent value.

Needless to add, this proposal would require legislation, and such legislation would be bitterly resisted by corporations and shareholders. In the short run, this proposal thus may have little chance of adoption. Nonetheless, this author has recently received inquiries from state regulators in the United States who are interested in adopting the equity fine (or something like it). They have encountered large corporations that seem to be uniquely resistant to deterrence and that persist in the same misconduct over a decade or more.

Even apart from the case of any specific company, another market crash could so alienate the public that they would favor Draconian measures. Or the election of a "progressive" president and a Democratic Congress could break the current political stalemate. Indeed, Senator Elizabeth Warren has proposed changes in the personal criminal liability of executives (which are discussed in chapter 8) that are considerably more radical than this proposal.

The final advantage of the equity fine is that it could coerce corporate defendants into seeking plea bargains by turning in culpable executives in order to avoid its application.

A Summary

This chapter has made some complicated arguments, and a quick summary is useful. Empirically, there is little reason to believe that our contemporary system of fines deters large corporations, at least when the potential gains are substantial. Not only are the fines a trivial percentage of market capitalization (around 0.01 percent or less), but even in the case of record fines, the defendant's stock price goes up on the date of the penalty's announcement. Nor can this problem be solved by insisting on higher cash fines. The externalities that such megafines would cause make such a program politically unrealistic; labor and capital would link arms to fight such penalties.

This assessment has two policy implications: First, it is necessary (and certainly more realistic) to focus on the individual executive. But such a focus requires that prosecutors enlist the corporation as a cooperating ally. As much as the corporation may not want to inform on its employees, it wants even less to be convicted when serious sanctions are threatened. The law can make cooperation the path of least resistance for the corporation. Second, to the extent we need to deter the corporate entity, different threats (such as the equity fine or even the remote threat of charter revocation) should be utilized, particularly when they do not fall on nonshareholder constituencies. Such threats would be only rarely employed, but their impact should cause the corporate entity to inform on its agents and employees and cooperate with the prosecution. When both the corporation and its executives can be incentivized to inform on the other—a strategy here called the prisoner's dilemma—then the odds shift in favor of law enforcement in the big case. Both sides need to be offered leniency for cooperation, but the first to cooperate should receive the lion's share of that credit.

On the procedural level, the prospect of leniency should lead the corporation to cooperate with and fund a significant internal investigation conducted by truly independent counsel. But leniency should not come cheap (as it does today). When the corporation self-reports criminal behavior (a rare event today) or when the investigation is deep and thorough and implicates supervisory officials (and not just low-level employers), leniency is appropriate. To be sure, a full-scale investigation is not necessary in every case, but it is much needed in major cases where today prosecutors may learn relatively little about what happened within the large organization. Ultimately, transparency and deterrence are independent goals, and both are advanced by this proposal.

SIX

Civil Agency Enforcement
An Overview

CIVIL ENFORCEMENT DWARFS CRIMINAL ENFORCEMENT, whether in terms of manpower allocated, aggregate damages collected, or number of actions brought. Thus, this may seem a late point to introduce the topic of public enforcement by federal agencies. In truth, both criminal and civil enforcement have the same basic objectives: deterrence, compensation, and prevention (although civil enforcement focuses much more on compensation). Both may also have the same tendency to focus more on the entity than the individual executive (although civil enforcement by agencies can disbar or suspend the individual).[1] More importantly, the last decade has seen an extraordinary, even hyperbolic, increase in the magnitude of the penalties imposed on public corporations. Finally, in both contexts, there has been the same debate over whether public enforcement has been too soft and equivocal, and the focus of this chapter will be on reforms that respond to that critique.

To keep our topic manageable, this chapter will concentrate on enforcement actions directed at financial institutions (where there is more data), but its implications and recommendations apply broadly to all large corporations. Within this context of financial institutions, informed critics on both the Left and the Right acknowledge that civil enforcement overshadows criminal enforcement (although they draw very different conclusions from this fact). Both sides also recognize that civil enforcement has recently concentrated on the financial services industry to a much greater extent than in the past. To illustrate, in April 2019, Better Markets, a nonprofit advocacy organization that is distinctly left of center, issued a special report titled *Wall Street's Six Biggest Bailed-Out Banks*, which announced in outraged tones that, over the last two decades, the six largest banks in the United States had been the subject of more than 350 "major legal actions" that had imposed approximately $182 billion in sanctions and settlements.[2] For just six banks, that is a very large number indeed, and Better Markets characterized this as an "ongoing crime spree." Conversely, in June 2018, the Committee on Capital Markets Regulation, a nonprofit research and advocacy organization that is distinctly right of center, similarly released a report entitled *Rationalizing Enforcement in the U.S. Financial System*, which focused on "financial system-related enforcement" actions.[3] Unsurprisingly, it found that the total number of enforcement actions brought by federal enforcement authorities against financial institutions had risen significantly after the 2008 crash, peaking in 2010 (when some 2,208 actions were brought) and then receding to a lower number in 2016 (1,363 actions) that was still substantially higher than precrash levels.[4] Unlike Better Markets, its tone expressed anxiety more than outrage. More importantly, it reported that the total amount of monetary sanctions imposed in financial system-related enforcement actions by administrative agencies had soared, increasingly more than tenfold in a few years, and then receding only modestly.

Figure 4 summarizes the committee's findings and shows a dramatic change in penalty levels.[5]

Rarely does one see so sharp a cliff differentiate past versus present practice. In 2000, the total monetary penalties imposed by public agencies against financial institutions were less than $1 billion. Even in 2010, after the 2008 crash had hit, aggregate penalties still came only to $5.2 billion. Only later did penalties soar into the stratosphere, hitting $37.1 billion in 2012 and topping out at $45.5 billion in 2014, before declining to $19 billion in 2016.[6] This delay in recoveries until a 2014 peak probably reflects the time it took to litigate or negotiate settlements.[7] In any event, the total recoveries in these cases differ by an order of magnitude from prior periods, as just the years 2012–2016 show a total of $158.9 billion in penalties being imposed—just by administrative agencies and just against financial institutions.[8]

The policy question here is, of course, are these sanctions accomplishing enough (or anything)? Are they truly deterring? The Better Markets report concludes that existing penalties have not worked well, while the Committee on Capital Markets Regulation suggests that they may be excessive. Both sides can marshal evidence, and interpretation is a subjective business. Still, the fines imposed by administrative agencies are even more subject to the critique discussed in the preceding chapters that fines do not deter large corporations adequately. In the case of civil enforcement, the penalties imposed by administrative agencies are unlikely to cause the stigma and reputational loss that judicially imposed fines at a criminal sentencing do. The almost ceremonial imposition of punishment at sentencing carries more weight with the public and receives more attention in the media (and banks have long feared the

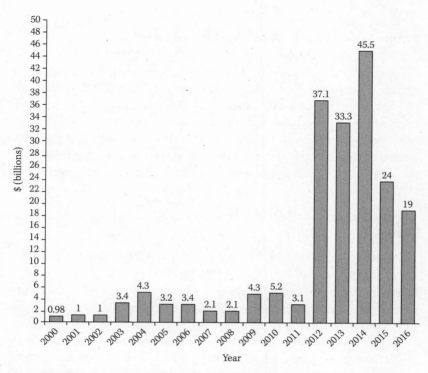

FIGURE 4 The Escalation in Financial Enforcement (Aggregate Total Monetary Sanctions Imposed on Financial Firms, 2000 to 2016)

danger of a "run on the bank" after such an event). Even more obviously, the prospect of jail time being imposed on executives is wholly absent from the civil enforcement system. Hence, it seems intuitively obvious to infer that civil penalties are less likely than criminal penalties to generate adequate deterrence.

By no means does this suggest that we should write off the civil enforcement system as irrelevant. Civil enforcers can also sue individual executives, and the resources devoted to civil enforcement by public agencies are enormous. For some agencies, enforcement is their primary activity. Also, most public corporations (particularly financial institutions) know that they have to cooperate, coexist, and reach mutual understandings with their regulators (because they are closely regulated entities and need regulatory approvals on a continuing basis). But large fines or penalties, imposed only on the corporate entity, may simply be absorbed as a cost of doing business, particularly by giant banks that arguably hold oligopolistic power. If so, how do we increase the impact and efficiency of civil enforcement by public agencies (including the Department of Justice)?

Public Enforcement: Who Does It and How?

Let's begin with a quick overview of public enforcement by administrative agencies with respect to the financial industry. Excluded for the time being will be private enforcement by litigants in class and other representative actions. Although many have examined individual contexts (such as securities or antitrust enforcement), few have considered the general topic of public enforcement through civil and administrative actions by public agencies. Such an analysis best begins by noting four key features of public enforcement in this context:

1. Enforcement is fragmented, with a significant number of agencies having overlapping jurisdiction.

2. Agencies coordinate among themselves relatively poorly with respect to enforcement policy (in part because they compete for credit).

3. Where the recovery in these actions goes is surprisingly uncertain and undisclosed, even though the general rule is that public fines must go to the U.S. Treasury. Other alternative recipients include victims, whistle-blowers, and the agencies themselves (to cover the costs of enforcement). But at both the federal and state level, little effort has been made by policy makers to integrate deterrence and victim compensation or to use penalties to fund agency enforcement.

4. Public enforcement agencies are overworked, resource constrained, and must negotiate settlements against a backdrop where it is obvious to all that, for logistical reasons, the agency can only carry a few cases to trial.

Each of these features needs further analysis.

Fragmentation

Some eleven federal enforcement agencies (and a couple more state agencies) regularly supervise and litigate against U.S. financial institutions. Alphabetically, these include the Consumer Financial Protection Bureau, the Commodity Futures Trading Commission, the Department of Justice, the Federal Reserve Board, the Federal Deposit Insurance Corporation, the Financial Crimes Network, the National Credit Union Administration, the Office of the Controller of the Currency, the Office of Foreign Assets Control, and the Securities Exchange Commission. Another agency (the Office of Thrift Supervision) was formerly a major player, but it was abolished by the Dodd-Frank Act, based on Congress's determination that it had become ineffective. Of these agencies, the most important in terms of enforcement activity is the

SEC.[9] On the state level, the New York State Department of Financial Services stands out for its activism, but the "blue sky" securities regulators of California, Massachusetts, and New York are also frequently active. As a result, overlapping jurisdiction is common, and sometimes after a matter appears to have been resolved, still another agency surfaces, even years later, to reopen the issue to the surprise of all who settled earlier.[10]

Just the length of the above list of agencies tells you that coordination among these agencies is more the exception than the rule. Indeed, some of these federal agencies are known for their "sharp elbows," and a competition to control cases breaks out from time to time. Within the business community, a strongly held view exists that overlapping jurisdiction implies multiple actions by multiple agencies, all dealing with the same underlying conduct and hence resulting in "piling on."[11] In short, the business community believes that the competition for credit leads to penalties that are duplicative and excessive.

If fragmentation is a problem, what should be done? One option would be greater centralization on the federal level with possibly a federal oversight agency playing the role of a traffic cop that could preclude excessive duplication or "piling on." Yet any proposal for greater coordination to avoid such duplication would be highly controversial. If there were a federal "czar of enforcement," the danger arises that a strong-minded administration could stifle the views and independence of the more aggressive of its agencies (even though in theory these agencies are established by Congress to be beyond White House control).[12] Some agencies have a long tradition of independence (such as the SEC and the Fed), but they might be dominated or at least constrained by such a czar.

Thus, while coordination is desirable, supervision by a centralized overseer is a much more problematic proposal (although it would certainly find support within the business community). The safest initial step might be a formalized council of the major enforcement agencies, where each director of an enforcement division of an agency that regularly brought enforcement actions would have a seat; monthly meetings would facilitate information sharing and policy formulation. Such a body could also fund research and might be, itself, funded out of penalties collected by these agencies. Such a body—here called the WGEA, for Working Group of Enforcement Agencies—would parallel earlier bodies that were formed to place financial regulatory agencies into closer contact. Eventually, they matured into the Financial Stability Oversight Council (FSOC), which the Dodd-Frank Act created to ensure comprehensive monitoring of the stability of the U.S. financial system. Conceivably, that could happen here also.

Where Does the Money Go? Where Should It Go?

Under the Appropriations Clause of the U.S. Constitution, money may not be withdrawn from the U.S. Treasury or spent by a federal agency without congressional authorization.[13] This provision was intended by the Constitution's framers to protect Congress's ability to exercise its "power of the purse" (a power that the House of Commons had traditionally used to control the English monarchy). The net result of this provision is that federal enforcement authorities cannot constitutionally spend money that they have collected from penalty assessments unless expressly authorized to do so by Congress. Indeed, the 1982 Miscellaneous Receipt Act requires that "an official or agency of the Government receiving money for the Government from any source shall deposit the money in the Treasury as soon as practicable."[14]

But Congress has acted to create exceptions from this obligation. One justification for such a relaxation is that many persons (including those fined) cannot or will not pay their debts to the government and must be sued in often costly litigation. Take, for example, the SEC, which in 2015 collected only $2.4 billion of the $4.2 billion it claims the SEC was entitled to be paid (or 57 percent).[15] In fact, over its three most recent fiscal years ended in 2017, it was also paid only 57 percent.[16] The Commodity Futures Trading Commission did even less well, collecting only 50 percent of the civil fines ordered against its enforcement targets over the last decade.[17] Typically, these agencies refer these outstanding debts to the Department of Justice and ask it to sue on their behalf. In fiscal 2016, Justice disclosed that it had received over $17 billion in such referrals.[18] As a result, Congress has authorized the Department of Justice to create and withhold from fines and other penalties a 3 percent deduction that goes to its "3 percent fund" to cover its costs of enforcement.[19] As we will see, the scope of this authorization is ambiguous, but this precedent may deserve to be expanded.

Why should we care about those technical details? Deterrence, of course, suffers if fines are not collected. For some defendants (with securities brokers being the best example), leaving the securities industry is an alternative to paying the fine. The ability to make such a choice, however, undercuts deterrence.

Beyond this point, these shortfalls also compound the next problem to be examined: To what extent could this money be paid to victims? Using fines and penalties to compensate victims, instead of paying them to the Treasury, is an attractive policy, which may enable the regulator to gain increased public support and may engender greater confidence among citizens in the fairness of the financial system. Both the SEC and the Consumer Financial Protection Bureau have victim compensation funds authorized by Congress. The SEC's "Fair Funds" policy dates back to 1990 when Congress authorized the SEC to collect disgorged ill-gotten gains in enforcement actions and distribute them to investors.[20] After a further congressional extension of this power in the Sarbanes-Oxley Act in 2002, the Dodd-Frank Act in 2010 broadly empowered the SEC to create a distribution fund (known as a "fair fund") to which even civil fines and penalties could go, to be distributed to compensate injured investors.[21] In short, since 2010, not only the disgorged ill-gotten gains but ordinary fines also can now flow (through the fund) to victims (instead of the Treasury).

Creation of such a compensation fund is not mandatory for the SEC, and under its own rules, the SEC generally must be able to find that (1) there is an identifiable class of investors that suffered specific, identifiable harms and (2) the money involved is significant enough to justify a distribution (in relation to the number of victims).[22] Still, the SEC has actively used its fund authority, distributing some $14.46 billion to investors between mid-2002 and December 31, 2013.[23] One estimate concludes that these distributions accounted for about 75 percent of the monetary sanctions the SEC collected during this period.[24] More recently, however, the SEC seems to have cut back on this practice, creating fewer funds and distributing less money.[25] Possibly, the administrative burden of distributing small amounts to many victims has made the SEC more reluctant to create fair funds.

The Consumer Financial Protection Bureau (CFPB) has a similar compensation program, which is mandatory.[26] Its procedures work differently, as it pools all penalties received without attempting to match specific penalties with the specific victims injured by the conduct in that case. Through the end of fiscal 2017, the CFPB has deposited some $560 million into its fund.[27] This may be the superior system, because it avoids the "feast or famine" prospect that arises if victim compensation funds are established on a case-by-case basis, because the amounts paid by one defendant in one case may provide little compensation, while the amounts paid in another case will yield very generous compensation. Pooling in effect ensures that most victims will receive some compensation and tends to award a blended average.[28]

Are there lessons to be learned from the SEC and CFPB experience? Even if we were interested only in deterrence, some prescriptions seem obvious: First, these are only two agencies, and the same practices could be generalized and used, for example, by the Federal Trade Commission, the Commodity Futures Trading Commission, the Federal Deposit Insurance Corporation, and most other agencies that protect consumers, investors, or the public. Another possibility is that the Department of Justice should have its own victim compensation fund (rather than determine whether to seek restitution on a case-by-case basis).[29] Legislation would be necessary in these cases, but any misconduct that generates identifiable victims could be addressed through such a compensation fund. Second, if our goal is to induce a judge (in either the civil or criminal justice system) to impose a higher fine (for deterrent purposes), the fact that the money will go to victims and not "down the drain" to the Treasury may supply a justification that encourages higher fines. Certainly, it provides a counterweight to defendants' predictable argument that high fines will produce layoffs, defaults, or bankruptcy.

Beyond victim compensation, fines in the federal system are diverted from the Treasury to fund two other purposes: the compensation of whistle-blowers and the Department of Justice's own expenses.[30] Whistle-blowers will be covered in the next chapter, but this chapter will suggest still another possible use for fines and penalties: namely, to fund the compensation of plaintiff's attorneys retained on a contingent fee basis by an agency for a specific case. Ideally, these cases would be those that were too big, too risky, or too specialized to be brought by the agency's own in-house legal staff. Obviously there are two distinct assertions here: (1) administrative agencies should hire private counsel to handle major cases, and (2) such counsel should be compensated at market rates, on a contingent fee basis out of the recovery, if any, generated by the litigation.

Putting the Bounty Hunter to Work

Private litigation in the United States typically compensates the plaintiff's attorney in a personal injury case through a contingent fee. Such an attorney in effect "eats what he or she kills" and gets nothing if he or she loses. Generally, this compensation is paid based on a percentage of the recovery. Thus, if you trip on an icy sidewalk and break your leg, you may wish to sue the shopkeeper who did not shovel the snow and ice off that sidewalk, and you would probably hire a plaintiff's attorney under a standard fee agreement that paid him one-third of your recovery.

That's a simple example, but the same rules apply in the more complicated work of class actions. Financial institutions are regularly sued by disappointed investors in securities class actions, and the fee awards in these cases are typically computed on a percentage of the recovery basis. The court (which must approve the fee request in a class action) generally uses a "declining percentage of the recovery" formula.[31] Thus, the plaintiff's attorney may get 25 percent of the first $100 million recovery but only a much lesser percentage (say, 2–5 percent) of the recovery over $1 billion. Recoveries are almost always by way of settlement (as both sides prefer to avoid trial), and a number of these settlements in securities class actions have exceeded the $1 billion level. Of course, to obtain such a recovery, the plaintiff's attorney must pay out of the attorney's own pocket millions of dollars in costs (including the salaries of the attorney's own legal staff). This is risky, and many have failed. But there is a well-organized plaintiff's bar bringing securities class actions on a steadily increasing basis, and the leading practitioners on the plaintiff side in this field probably make annual incomes at least as high as those of the leading defense practitioners.[32]

Would plaintiff's attorneys be interested in representing an administration agency in enforcement litigation against large financial institutions? The answer is of course! But their use would only be feasible in cases in which the expected recovery (i.e., the likely fine or penalty) would exceed some minimal level (say, $15 million). Anything below that level represents too cheap a payoff to attract the risk-taking legal entrepreneur who specializes in securities class actions. Such cases may be plentiful, however, because the SEC can seek disgorgement of ill-gotten gains and restitution,[33] which in many cases would typically fund a more than adequate recovery for the plaintiff's attorney. The plaintiff's attorney would also gain prestige and the reputational advantage of having represented the United States, which would carry over to other cases. Finally, such a plaintiff's attorney would face much better litigation odds than in the standard private case. Juries are more likely to trust counsel for the United States (or the SEC) in comparison to counsel for an unknown individual plaintiff (whose client often has credibility or other problems associated with the individual case).

What would the administrative agency gain from using an attorney that it retains from the private plaintiff's bar in a big case? First, there are huge cost savings. The agency would pay virtually nothing out of its own budget, as the retained attorney would look only to the recovery as the source for his or her legal fees. Moreover, the agency can probably negotiate a lower percentage fee than plaintiff's lawyers today are awarded in federal court class actions (in part because plaintiff's lawyers want the reputational benefit of having been retained by the SEC or CFTC). Also, plaintiff's lawyers may accept a lower contingent fee because there is less risk of defeat when they are serving as the agency's counsel.

Consider this point in context: in a major securities or antitrust litigation, the plaintiff's side may need ten lawyers to handle discovery, motions practice, and briefing plus paralegals, other support personnel, and expert witnesses (who counsel must pay over the interim). But all this can be supplied by a plaintiff's law firm that is in the business of trying large cases. This solves not only the agency's cost constraints but also its manpower problem. If the case required ten experienced lawyers to prepare the case for trial, the enforcement division of an administrative agency may be simply unable to spare such personnel—without suspending or dropping its existing cases. That is unthinkable. Moreover, big cases come in an unpredictable fashion. None may occur for several years, and then several may arise at once. By itself, the agency could not digest such a sudden increase in its caseload. But it can retain one, two, or more plaintiff's firms.

Next, there is the factor of skill and "stardom." An agency such as the SEC is highly regarded for its able personnel. But they are paid at civil service salaries, which fall way below the annual compensation of "star" litigation partners (who today may earn $5 million a year or more at some large defense firms). Are stars really needed? Sadly, the answer is yes. The Antitrust Division won a major victory over Microsoft when they were able to recruit David Boies, possibly the best known trial counsel in the country, for that litigation.[34] His very successful deposition of William Gates (Microsoft's CEO) was a key factor that forced Microsoft to settle. At a minimum, the presence of a star litigator is likely to affect the settlement negotiations and raise the likely settlement value of the case.

Also, as good as the attorneys for some enforcement divisions may be, they often lack much trial experience, particularly in massive cases with millions of documents and dozens of issues. They have instead spent more of their career negotiating settlements in the marketplace. This involves haggling about whether this case is stronger or weaker than earlier SEC cases and using those earlier SEC settlements as the frame of reference for valuing this settlement. Bring in a major plaintiff's law firm, however, and they will instead compare this case to their prior settlements (which have often settled much higher).

Even more important is the downside. There is always the possibility that the government might lose its case. If it expended $10 million in expenses plus a quarter of its staff's time on this case, it may have exhausted its budget and will have difficulty explaining its decision to invest so heavily in this case (and, in so doing, not prosecuting lesser but arguably more meritorious cases). Also, the acute fear of embarrassment may cause the government to cave in and settle too easily in the settlement negotiations on the eve of trial. In contrast, the "star" plaintiff's lawyer has likely lost cases before and can explain that only he and his firm bear the losses. A loss (even a much publicized one) is a less humiliating defeat for the government when counsel is retained on a contingent fee basis. In such a case, the government can explain: "It cost us nothing, and the issue needed to be decided." In short, all the logistical, budgetary, and risk issues that may constrain administrative agencies from aggressively pursuing major defendants are potentially solved by this tactic of retaining outside counsel.

What then are the reasons agencies do not frequently retain private law firms to handle the big case? Actually, some administrative agencies do (as is discussed later in this chapter). But most do not. The SEC (probably the administrative agency that handles the most enforcement litigation) disdains specially retained counsel. Their position is that their own staff is good enough. Alas, that is a polite myth, at least when the facts are complex or ambiguous.

Although the SEC's legal scorecard has few ignominious defeats, it has had many weak settlements. That is the real cost of relying exclusively on your in-house team of lawyers. Either because the opposition has a good chance of winning or because the SEC just has an impossible caseload, the SEC often settles cases for very little relief (as Judge Rakoff publicly noted, which caused a firestorm[35]). Corporate defendants do not behave this way. They use their own in-house legal staff for recurring and less important cases, but when they face a "you bet the company" legal battle, they go into the market and hire the best attorney available (and accept that he or she will cost much more).

Actually, this problem is a variant of a classic business decision: the "make or buy" decision. Is it better to have a permanent in-house legal staff (the "make" option) or to retain highly paid specialists (the "buy" option)? The optimal strategy for most large corporations is to do both: use the in-house staff for smaller cases and the typical recurring case, but go outside for the major case. This makes sense because it would be uneconomic to retain highly paid "stars" if "major" cases were few and far between. But if this strategy works well for sophisticated defendants, why is it not followed by sophisticated agencies as well? Here, the real answer is probably that it would demoralize the enforcement staff of the agency. They would in effect be told that their own agency lacked confidence in them, that they were not good enough. Although maintaining the morale of the agency's staff may be a worthy goal, it is not a paramount one.

Another reason that SEC staffers have given for resisting use of outside counsel is that it would in their view necessarily sacrifice prosecutorial discretion.[36] This is shallow nonsense. Although prosecutorial discretion is important and should not be abandoned, the use of outside counsel does not require its sacrifice. To see this, we only have to look across the courtroom aisle and see how corporate defendants behave. The corporate defendant may hire an outside law firm, but it does not surrender its discretion to that firm. At what price it will settle, what other terms it will accept, whether it will take the risk of going to trial—these issues remain very much matters for the corporation's general counsel and its board to decide. Similarly, the agency's general counsel (or the director of its enforcement division) would retain oversight and all authority over whether to sue in the first instance and what settlements could be accepted. No outside counsel would even be retained until an initial decision to sue had been made within the agency.

Settlements would still occur regularly (as plaintiff's counsel know very well that settlement avoids years of costly appellate litigation), but the contest between the opposing sides would be more a battle of equals.

TABLE 2 Comparison of Class Action Recovery to SEC Recovery against Same Defendants

Company	Securities Class Action Recovery	SEC Recovery
Enron	$7.242 billion	$450 million
WorldCom	$6.194 billion	$750 million
Tyco International	$3.2 billion	$50 million
AOL Time Warner	$2.5 billion	$308 million
Bank of America	$2.425 billion	$150 million
Citigroup	$1.320 billion	$75 million
Nortel Networks	$2.217 billion	$35 million
Merrill Lynch	$940 million	none
American International Group	$937.5 million	$800 million
HealthSouth Corp.	$804.5 million	$100 million
Xerox	$750 million	$44 million
Lucent Technologies	$667 million	$25 million
Wachovia	$627 million	none
Countrywide Financial	$624 million	$48.15 million
Lehman Brothers	$600 million	none
Washington Mutual (WaMu)	$208 million	none
National City	$168 million	none
New Century	$125 million	$1.5 million
Wells Fargo (MBS)	$125 million	$6.5 million

Do we have any realistic basis for assuming that retained private counsel would outperform and secure a higher recovery than the agency's own civil service staff? Table 2, prepared by a leading plaintiff's attorney in securities litigation, shows that the margin between private and public recoveries against the same defendant is often 10:1 (or even greater).[37]

Of course, this table is to an extent comparing apples with oranges, as the parallel cases involve different causes of action and different measures of damages. Still, the disparity is so striking as to strongly suggest that retained counsel will do better. Why? It is not simply quality of counsel but even more that the private counsel will not be constrained as much by budgetary limits. It can invest in the action up to the point that it believes that the marginal return no longer exceeds the marginal cost to it.

Existing Experience with the Use of Outside Counsel

Although many federal agencies do not retain outside counsel for even their most important litigation, others do. Three agencies—the Federal Deposit Insurance Corporation (FDIC), the Federal Housing Finance Agency (FHFA), and the National Credit Union Administration (NCUA)—have made significant use of private counsel.

At the state level, most of the states retained private counsel to litigate against the tobacco industry, and under a master settlement agreement entered into between the tobacco industry and all fifty states, they achieved the largest settlement on record ($246 billion) in 1998 (of which some $14 billion was paid to private trial attorneys retained to represent the state on a contingent fee basis).[38] The state attorney generals justified their use of contingency fee arrangements on the grounds that they lacked the personnel, resources, or experience to undertake very costly litigation on their own (whereas the plaintiff's bar had already accumulated considerable experience in suing the tobacco industry). Since then, states and municipalities have used contingent fee agreements to compensate private counsel in suits against lead paint manufacturers, companies selling handguns, and, most recently, opioid distributors. The states' frequent justification for using the contingent fee has been that these cases were too high risk to justify using taxpayers' money. That provides another argument for private counsel: they are superior risk bearers. To be sure, this is what they do in their ordinary professional practice: assemble a portfolio of cases that allows them to prosper even if they win in only a minority of these cases. Rationally, private plaintiffs' counsel would not take a case on a contingent fee basis if they believed it to be a sure loser. In this light, private plaintiff's counsel would be an additional filter assuring us that truly frivolous cases are not brought (and they probably have greater experience in appraising them).

On the federal level, the agency that has made the greatest use of private counsel is the FDIC.[39] When a bank insured by it fails, the FDIC will pay off the bank's depositors and thereby incur losses. If it believes the bank's failure was attributable to director or officer negligence, it has a cause of action against the insolvent bank's directors and officers, which it regularly asserts. In these suits, the FDIC hires outside counsel. The FDIC developed this practice during the savings and loan crisis between 1989 and 1993. In an elaborate self-study, the FDIC listed three reasons for its use of privately retained counsel: First, the savings and loan crisis had overwhelmed its internal resources because of the "limited number of in-house legal staff in relation to the growing number of receiverships."[40] Second, it faced a "wide variety of legal issues . . . that required specialized knowledge of state laws and legal practice."[41]

And third, "the diverse geographic location of the receiverships" posed a challenge.[42] Hiring private counsel enabled it to find experienced lawyers in private practice who knew and had practiced for years in the local court where the case was pending. In contrast, the SEC regularly sends lawyers from Washington to a distant court before which they have never previously practiced—and sometimes they receive a chilly reception.

The FDIC's recent track record is instructive. Following the 2008 crash, the FDIC sued former officers of IndyMac Bank (which had been heavily involved in the distribution of subprime mortgages). After IndyMac failed in 2008, the FDIC retained private counsel and sued IndyMac's officers in California, winning a jury verdict for $169 million in 2012.[43] Contemporaneously, the SEC sued the CEO of IndyMac (who had settled with the FDIC, paying it a $1 million settlement) and basically lost, eventually settling for only a minimal $80,000.[44]

That comparison may seem to be only an anecdote. Perhaps it is, but there are few SEC actions for damages against bank directors and officers, and other comparisons are thus hard to find. Nonetheless, a 2013 study by Cornerstone Research, an economic consulting firm, found that the FDIC had brought suit in some thirty-two cases just in 2013.[45] Cornerstone further found that, among all the financial institutions subject to FDIC jurisdiction that failed in 2009, the FDIC has sued or settled with 41 percent of their officers and directors.[46] This shows a consistent (but not automatic) policy of enforcement (and not the blanket targeting of all directors). In fact, the FDIC has developed an elaborate desk book to set forth its relationship with private counsel in such suits. Use of contingent fee compensated counsel is achieving the FDIC's goals.

The FDIC's successful experience has been noted by both the FHFA and the NCUA, which have each followed in its footsteps. The FHFA has sued most of the major banks that handled subprime mortgage securities before the 2008 crash (and it has already received $5.1 billion in a settlement that JPMorgan entered with all the major regulators).[47] Interestingly, it has been represented in these suits by Quinn, Emanuel, Urquhart & Sullivan LLP, a leading litigation firm. This representation has been on a blended contingent fee, or "success" fee basis, under which the law firm receives a percentage of the recovery above some agreed benchmark level. Such a compromise reduces the prospect that the law firm will receive a windfall for an easy recovery that any firm could have obtained (and thus dampens the likelihood of public criticism).

These developments have not escaped congressional attention. Congressman Darrell Issa (R-CA), chairman of the House Committee on Oversight and Government Reform, challenged in 2013 the NCUA's use of contingency fee arrangements (which were used in securities litigation it brought over mortgage-related securities).[48] The NCUA's inspector general responded that the costs of the litigation involved "analyzing hundreds of securities containing thousands of mortgage loans, issuing administrative subpoenas, taking testimony of hundreds of witnesses, reviewing tens of thousands of pages of documents," and would have been prohibitive.[49] Moreover, it knew that the litigation might have yielded no recovery. In a nutshell, that is the issue in both the criminal and civil enforcement contexts: the costs of such litigation could exhaust the agency's budget, require a material proportion of its manpower, and yet might not gain a recovery that even covered these costs. Hence, these causes will not be brought—unless private counsel can be used on a contingent fee basis.

Are Contingent Fees Lawful in Public Litigation?

Since the 1998 multistate settlement between the states and the tobacco industry that awarded large contingent fees to private counsel retained by the states, industry groups and others have attacked such an enforcement structure, questioning even its constitutionality.[50] To date, however, courts have upheld such contingent fee agreements by public bodies—with one important caveat: the state must maintain control and oversight over the litigation.[51] That seems the appropriate balance: wholesale delegation without oversight is an impermissible abdication by the public agency.

To ensure proper oversight, the optimal procedure should involve the agency first investigating sufficiently to decide that it wanted to sue the defendant, then retaining the outside law firm in those cases that would impose a burden or a level of risk that it could not feasibly accept. The enforcement division's own staff would continue to litigate the traditional caseload and emergency injunctive actions. The retention agreement with private counsel would further require that all material decisions in that litigation would have to be approved by the agency's general counsel or delegate. Although some will object that this might expose defendants to extortionate litigation, the reality is that the plaintiff's bar seldom takes long shots. Those plaintiff firms capable of large investments in an action cannot afford a string of losses and probably want to see at least a fifty-fifty prospect of a lucrative recovery.

Although courts have upheld contingent fee agreements by states and other public bodies (and much of the current opioid litigation is being financed on this basis), that is not the end of the story. In 2007, President George W. Bush issued an executive order (Executive Order 13,433) prohibiting federal agencies from paying contingent fees.[52] No real justification was given for this rule, other than that contingent fees would be costly. In reality, this edict was probably the result of the tobacco industry settlement (which paid billions in attorney's fees to primarily Democratic law firms). How then did the FDIC, the FHFA, and the NCUA escape this ban? They take the position that they are suing as receivers or conservators and thus stand in the shoes of the failed institution that is (in their view) the body paying the contingent fee. In theory, they are simply exercising the failed institution's own right to sue its officers and directors derivatively.

Still, this theory will not work for the SEC or CFTC, which would be relying on federal statutes authorizing them to sue as a public agency. Thus, repeal of Executive Order 13,433 is a prerequisite to this proposal, but any future Democratic administration could easily do that.

Funding Enforcement

Earlier, it was noted that the Department of Justice collects 3 percent of fines and penalties that it collects to fund its enforcement costs. Originally, this levy went only to cover Justice's expenses in suing to collect fines or penalties that were generally imposed by other agencies. More recently, Justice has applied this 3 percent "tax" to fund its own initial enforcement costs (i.e., its costs in suing a defendant rather than the costs of suing to collect a fine).[53] Once this line is crossed and this 3 percent fund is directly covering Department of Justice enforcement costs, it becomes more relevant to ask whether this tax should be increased—say, hypothetically—to 10 percent.

For constitutional reasons, there needs to be a clear limit. If an agency could pocket the fines it collects, this could raise a due process issue. Could the agency be objective and fair if a major case would solve its budget deficit or allow it to hire fifty new staffers (or raise salaries for existing personnel). In *Tumey v. Ohio*,[54] the Supreme Court struck down an Ohio law that rewarded public officials (including the judge in that case) for successfully prosecuting cases related to Prohibition. The Court said that it violated due process when the judge "has a direct, personal, substantial pecuniary interest in reaching a conclusion" against the defendant in a criminal case.[55] To be sure, no single official in the Justice Department would have a "direct, personal, substantial pecuniary interest" in finding against a defendant simply because the Department of Justice taxed the settlement by 10 percent rather than 3 percent. Still, the agency as a whole could at some point be seen as conflicted. In short, while a problem could arise at some level, raising the tax from 3 percent to 10 percent seems relatively safe. The greater problem may be that Congress may resist because it wants to micromanage federal agencies and thus does not want to give them alternative sources of funding.

Conclusion

This chapter has proposed several ideas: (1) greater use of victim compensation funds by both federal agencies and the Department of Justice; (2) greater coordination among enforcement staffs; (3) the retention of outside counsel to handle very large cases or those that are more risky than the agency feels comfortable handling itself; and (4) allowing a greater portion of the monetary sanction recovered in civil enforcement to be retained by the agency to cover its own costs. Some of these proposals will be resisted because they encroach on Congress's appropriation power, and at least the use of outside counsel will be resisted by those agencies that have large enforcement staffs (who will feel slighted and disrespected by such an idea). But the reality is that large complicated cases are simply not brought by many agencies that face budgetary constraints, or, to the extent they are brought, they are often settled cheaply. Retention of private counsel on a contingent fee basis is now well established at the state and municipal levels and has been successfully implemented by several federal agencies (most notably, the FDIC). Most importantly, this is the most feasible way of maximizing prosecutorial resources and manpower (as there is simply no chance that legislatures will vastly increase their appropriations for enforcement).

Although such a reform will be bitterly resisted by agencies with large enforcement staffs (most notably, the SEC), the public pays a high price for the refusal of these agencies to utilize private counsel. Ironically, the United States is a nation that celebrates its entrepreneurial style and successes. It is fully consistent with that American approach to allow a measure of entrepreneurial enforcement in public agency litigation—at least so long as the agency carefully monitors its new agents and preserves prosecutorial discretion. The business community can also be expected to resist this proposal, but in their case, it is because they see its logic and fear it.

PART 3

Specific Reforms

Introduction to Part 3

THIS PART TURNS to specific proposals. How do we reduce the high cost of investigations? Corporate internal investigations can cost $100 million or more. One answer may be to rely less on developing information in investigations and instead rely on buying information in the marketplace. The one new strategy that has worked best in white collar crime is the provision of bounties to whistle-blowers. Paying high rewards for information that incriminates is the core of the SEC's and CFTC's whistle-blower bounty programs. Chapter 7 examines this strategy and proposes that it be generalized and extended to all federal enforcement agencies, including the Department of Justice.

Chapter 8 examines possible changes in corporate criminal law, including the *responsible corporate officer* doctrine, which imposes strict liability. Still, chapter 8 concludes that changes in the substantive law are unlikely to change outcomes dramatically.

Chapter 9 considers what penalties should be imposed on convicted corporations and explores the expanded use of corporate probation. Such a sentence (which can be combined with a fine) should include restrictions on executive compensation and particularly on the use of incentive compensation. Put simply, the excessive use of such compensation is criminogenic. Also, restricting the use of incentive compensation for the period of probation confronts all corporate employees with a potential threat and may unite them in a common desire to avoid illegality (for their own good). Threatening employees may be a far more effective strategy than threatening widely dispersed and often passive shareholders with high fines on the corporation.

SEVEN

The Whistle-Blower as Bounty Hunter

THE INITIAL BARRIER to white collar prosecutions of the corporation or its officers is the cost of acquiring information. Suppose prosecutors want to investigate whether high-ranking executives were aware of serious risks associated with a new product but still marketed the product aggressively, despite this knowledge. Where do prosecutors begin? If prosecutors just send out subpoenas for all records and emails broadly relating to this topic, they may be swamped with millions of documents that they cannot absorb or assess. To be sure, they can use the grand jury, but this is no panacea either. Information overload may make such an investigation slow, costly, and infeasible.

What is the simplest way to gather critical information? The short, blunt answer is to offer to pay for it. Some employee somewhere within the organization will know where the "smoking guns" are hidden. Either out of fear or simply loyalty to the organization, they will seldom volunteer this information—unless they are offered some inducement. Plea bargains with sentencing discounts have long been the principal inducement that prosecutors offered, but these require that prosecutors have something on the informant so that he or she needs to cooperate. More recently, regulators have been offering cash in the form of a percentage of the penalty or other recovery that the government obtains. This tactic motivates those who are not guilty. It is working, but symptomatically it is being used only sparingly.

In overview, offering bounties for information about legal violations is a form of outsourcing. The investigation now begins not with the enforcement agency but with the whistle-blower. To be sure, the enforcement agency can decline to pursue allegations that do not match its priorities, but the starting point for the investigation begins with the outside whistle-blower. Earlier, this book suggested that the SEC should outsource some of its fraud enforcement litigation (but only in large cases) to private counsel, who would be compensated on a percentage of the recovery basis. Traditionalists will respond that this is unthinkable (although it is in fact happening). Yet Congress has recently compelled the SEC to outsource much of its work in fraud detection to private parties (called whistle-blowers) who also are rewarded (when successful) on a percentage of the recovery basis. The two efforts—that is, paying outside counsel and paying whistle-blowers—are more closely related than they initially appear.

How is this effort working? So far, it has been dramatically successful. Since the passage of the Dodd-Frank Act in 2010, the SEC and the CFTC have been required to establish whistle-blower programs that essentially pay bounties to persons who report information to these agencies, at least when the result is to enable the SEC to obtain substantial monetary penalties for violations of the laws they enforce.[1] In effect, Congress created a bounty hunter system to supplement the SEC's own investigatory efforts, and it insisted on strong economic incentives to inform for private citizens (typically present or former corporate employees). This is a form of outsourcing, and it was done largely because Congress was very dissatisfied with the SEC's long-running inability to detect Bernie Madoff's Ponzi scheme. Even when whistle-blowers, such as, most notably, Harry Markopolos, repeatedly gave the SEC detailed memoranda showing the near certainty that Madoff was running what had to be a Ponzi scheme,[2] the SEC just was not willing to take on a detailed investigation and audit Madoff rigorously. Madoff may have been far more flagrant and egregious than Lehman, but both were treated with undue deference, and Congress saw a pattern.

The SEC's Program

As a result of the SEC's seemingly persistent blindness and Congress's belief that the SEC had been far too easy on industry titans, Congress enacted section 21F of the Securities Exchange Act, which directs the SEC to pay an award to a whistle-blower if such person voluntarily provides "original information" that results in the SEC obtaining monetary sanctions exceeding $1 million.[3] The amount that the SEC must pay to the whistle-blower must be not less than 10 percent and not more than 30 percent of the total monetary sanctions collected by the SEC in the case.[4] Given that the SEC often imposes penalties over $100 million, the whistle-blower informer can collect a substantial amount in many cases, and to date, the largest award has been $80 million (shared among three individuals).[5] Not surprisingly, a number of

TABLE 3 SEC Whistle-Blower Payments by Fiscal Year

Fiscal Year	2015	2016	2017	2018
Amount of Payments	$37 million	$57 million	$49 million	$168 million

plaintiff's law firms have established special divisions to represent whistle-blowers (for a percentage of the whistle-blower's recovery).

Brief as the experience to date is, it is obvious that SEC payments to whistle-blowers have quickly accelerated, as table 3 shows.[6]

In the SEC's report to Congress for fiscal year 2017, the SEC disclosed that it had received over 18,000 tips under this program.[7] In its fiscal year 2018 report, the SEC noted that from the inception of this program to the end of fiscal 2018, it had awarded in the aggregate over $326 million to fifty-nine individuals.[8] That comes to an average award of nearly $5.53 million per recipient. In short, this is a major subsidy for information about unlawful behavior. All told, the SEC has ordered defendants to pay over $1.7 billion in monetary damages over the life of its whistle-blower program as a result of these awards—not bad for only $326 million in total whistle-blower awards (in effect, a 19 percent contingent fee award based on a $1.7 billion total recovery).[9]

Although this suggests that incentivizing whistleblowing is an effective strategy, one must note the considerable disparity here between the number of tips (over 18,000) and the number of recipients (59); on this basis, about 1 in every 305 tippees seems to be rewarded. Of course, this ratio may be a product of a variety of factors, including that (1) much information is unreliable, often only unverified gossip, (2) some whistle-blowers are opportunistic free riders who claim to be providing "original information" that the SEC already knew, and (3) many cases that will legitimately generate future whistle-blower awards may still be in the pipeline, thus creating a significant timing gap between the tip and the bounty.

Nonetheless, this ratio raises the possibility that the SEC is unable or unwilling to process or verify all the material and credible information it receives. Consistent with this hypothesis is the fact that, between 2012 and 2016, the SEC received some ninety-nine claims filed by self-described whistle-blowers seeking bounties in cases where there had been a recovery, and it rejected sixty-four of these (or roughly two-thirds).[10] This could mean either that many claims for awards were frivolous or that the SEC resists sharing credit with outsiders. Three different possibilities suggest themselves: (1) the SEC is simply overloaded with tips; (2) as a matter of choice and style, the SEC only responds to tips when the tipper is able to provide a highly factual and easily verified dossier; and (3) the SEC has its own priorities and does not pursue tips that fail to match its priorities. Even when it utilizes information, the SEC seems reluctant to pay awards. At present, it is hard to reach a bottom-line evaluation here,[11] but the SEC may be internally divided about how eager it is to incentivize whistle-blowers.

A related problem also needs attention here. Under the Dodd-Frank Act, the whistle-blower can provide either original factual information or "independent analysis."[12] Harry Markopolos, the analyst who kept identifying Madoff to a resistant SEC, would seem to be the paradigm of the latter type of whistle-blower who performs an independent analysis (but did not have nonpublic information). Important as such an informant may be, it is hard to identify cases in which an award to someone like a Markopolos has been made. This may suggest that the SEC is reluctant to admit that someone made an incisive analysis that they missed. In any event, whistle-blowers like Markopolos need to be encouraged, and current law and practice do not seem to do that adequately.

Other Whistle-Blower Programs

One way to evaluate the SEC's program is to compare it with others. Both the CFTC and the Internal Revenue Service (IRS) maintain active whistle-blower programs. In its most recent report to Congress for fiscal 2018, the CFTC reported that it had made five whistle-blower awards in that fiscal year, amounting in total to more than $75 million (with the largest award being for approximately $30 million).[13] Since the inception of the program, the CFTC has issued nine awards totaling approximately $87 million.[14] Thus, the CFTC program looks like a smaller version of the SEC's program, with relatively few awards but some for very large amounts. Of course, the limited number of awards could be a product of the fact that the CFTC is much less well known than the SEC.

In one respect, the CFTC has recently behaved quite differently from the SEC. Uniquely, it has distributed "alerts" to the investor and securities industry communities, proclaiming its readiness to pay bounties for information and in fields well outside its normal domain, such as money laundering, foreign corrupt practices, insider trading, and cryptocurrency fraud.[15] The CFTC appears markedly more eager than the SEC to attract whistle-blowers. Indeed, the SEC may be particularly uncomfortable with advising the world as to what information it most wants. But this is exactly what agencies should be doing. If the SEC has heard on the grapevine that fraudsters are engaging in a specific form of market manipulation or are offering a particular type of cryptocurrency to retail investors, it should make clear that it wants specific information relating to those practices. In short, instead of passively reviewing the random submissions of various whistle-blowers, it should tell the market what it most wants and is willing to pay for. One can here trust the market to respond (given the bounties established by law), and this will produce more relevant and useful submissions.

Even if the CFTC has the better approach, it is also behaving very cautiously. In fiscal 2018, the CFTC received some 760 whistle-blower tips on Form TLR (the form it prescribes for such reports) but made only five awards.[16] Thus, the question persists with respect to both agencies whether they are responding overcautiously to material tips, possibly because they do not have the manpower or resources to more aggressively prosecute such cases. Here it is still too early to reach a bottom-line judgment.[17]

The IRS provides another basis for comparison. Although it has long paid bounties to informers for information about tax evasion, its procedures were significantly changed by the Tax Relief and Health Care Act, which was passed in 2006.[18] Under section 7623(b) of the Internal Revenue Code, which that act adopted, the tip must be signed and submitted under penalties of perjury and must relate to an action in which the proceeds exceed $2 million and certain other size conditions are satisfied. Thus, even more than in the case of the SEC, the tip must relate to a sizable dispute.

What has been the IRS's experience? In its report to Congress for fiscal 2018, the IRS reported the data shown in table 4.[19]

Thus, comparing the two agencies, they pay similar percentage awards to whistle-blowers, but the SEC has obtained total payments of only $1.7 billion over the life of its program, while the IRS collected over $1.4 billion just in 2018. That differential may be partly explained by the likelihood that there are far more persons or entities who have engaged in tax evasion than persons or entities that have engaged in securities fraud (which is a more specialized endeavor). The IRS, however, clearly processes more tips (paying between 217 and 418 awards a year), while (as noted above) the SEC has only paid awards to an aggregate of 59 individuals since its program began. Of course, the IRS is structured to be primarily a collection agency, but the SEC does seem more reluctant about paying awards.

TABLE 4 Amounts Collected and Awards under IRC § 7623

	FY 2016	FY 2017	FY 2018
Total Number of Awards:	418	242	217
Total Amounts of Awards:	$61,390,910	$33,979,873	$312,207,590
Proceeds Collected:	$368,907,298	$190,583,750	$1,441,255,859
Awards as a Percentage of Proceeds Collected:	16.6%	17.8%	21.7%

The point here is that much valuable information about fraud and corruption may be going to waste because the SEC simply cannot process it all. But maybe others could. For example, Ivy League universities (and other selective schools) cannot admit all qualified applicants. But the fact that they cannot take all qualified students does not mean that those denied admission by them do not go to college. Other schools accept them. Similarly, either because of budgetary limitations or as a matter of style, the SEC may "cherry-pick," bringing a few good cases but disdaining many more credible ones. What then should be done to deal with credible allegations that the SEC or CFTC passes on? In overview, there are two basic possibilities: (1) these allegations could be passed onto other federal agencies (possibly by asking the whistle-blower to file them with a centralized databank); or (2) the allegations could be enforced by private enforcement. Based on this premise, this chapter makes two proposals.

The Qui Tam Action

First, the whistle-blower's allegations could be used to support a qui tam action in federal court. Such actions have a long history, tracing back to medieval England.[20] Private citizens are authorized under a federal statute (the False Claims Act) to sue on behalf of the federal government when the latter has suffered an economic loss. Although not all whistle-blower complaints allege a loss to the federal government, a growing share do, because, for example, the losses in health care cases fall back ultimately on the Medicare system and thus the U.S. government picks up the tab. In recent years, some qui tam actions have resulted in very large recoveries.[21] Successful plaintiffs in these qui tam cases receive a bounty based on the recovery to the federal government.[22]

The real difference between the whistle-blower and the *relator* (which is what the plaintiff in a qui tam action is called) is that the plaintiff's lawyer plays a much larger role in a qui tam action. Now, the plaintiff's lawyer must not only assemble credible allegations but must prove them in court (or at least plead a sufficiently credible case to justify a settlement). If the whistle-blower's allegations are plausible but not highly persuasive, the plaintiff's attorney may be willing to support the whistle-blower (at low cost to the attorney) but not sue on a contingent fee basis. When the plaintiff's attorney is willing on a contingent fee basis, this reflects the attorney's judgment that the case is sufficiently meritorious to justify the attorney investing in it.

Thus, the more we can convert frustrated whistle-blowers into relators, the more we are encouraging and rewarding higher-quality allegations that an objective attorney has screened. This does not imply that we should in any way discourage whistle-blowers or force them to sue, but those who do not receive the agency's endorsement should be encouraged to seek to find an attorney willing to take their case. The contingent fee attorney who takes such a case is expressing confidence in it, and that may be as meaningful as a federal agency opening an investigation.

Actually, the plaintiff's bar could do this on its own without governmental assistance, but many attorneys may prefer the less costly task of just supporting the whistle-blower and hoping for the best. One way to encourage this transition would be for the federal agency running a whistle-blower program to advise would-be whistle-blowers at the time they decline to pursue their allegations of the availability of the qui tam option and provide them with a list of plaintiff's firms or others interested in bringing such actions.

A Proposal for Generalizing the Whistle-Blower

As we have seen, at least three agencies (the IRS, the SEC, and the CFTC) have had a successful experience with paying bounties to whistle-blowers. That is a relatively small number of federal agencies, and clearly this number should be expanded. Ideally, Congress should do that, but Congress will probably find such a proposal too controversial to enact in the near future.

Empirically, important research has found that a significant percentage of corporate frauds are detected and reported by individuals (usually present or former employees).[23] Today, the conclusion seems inescapable that this valuable source of information is not being adequately put to use. Although, as just noted, three federal agencies have had a successful experience with encouraging informants with bounties, the vast majority of federal agencies have done little or nothing (because, of course, Congress has not authorized them). Ironically, the whistle-blower bounty is the rare reform that costs the taxpayer virtually nothing; rather, the experience to date shows that it greatly profits the federal government to pay a bounty based on the proceeds received as a result of the information.

What other agencies could implement this information? Obvious candidates could include the Federal Trade Commission, the Antitrust Division, the Environmental Protection Agency, the Consumer Financial Protection Bureau, and a host of others. If legislation could be enacted,[24] it would authorize each agency to pay out only a percentage of the proceeds and penalties collected and send the balance to the Department of the Treasury.

Some issues are open to reasonable debate. For example, should the Department of Justice pay bounties out of criminal fines and other penalties that are paid in connection with the resolution of criminal charges. Some will feel that this creates an undue incentive for perjury in a context where liberty interests are at stake. One obvious compromise would be to pay whistle-blower bounties only out of criminal fines and penalties that the corporation pays (and not out of similar payments made by individuals). Because the corporation cannot be sent to prison, the civil/criminal distinction is less critical for it; it is only paying a monetary sanction in either case.

Sadly, the foregoing suggestion that Congress should generally authorize whistle-blower bounties is unrealistic in terms of what Congress is likely to do. Because corporations and other defendants will resist broader legislative authorization of whistle-blowers, it is necessary to ask if there is any way to implement a broader use of whistle-blower bounties without legislation. Actually, there is! One means to this end would be to condition eligibility for a deferred prosecution agreement on the corporation placing a significant amount in an account to fund payments to whistle-blowers in the future. For example, suppose the deferred prosecution agreement would have required the defendant corporation to pay $100 million as a penalty. Instead, this amount could be reduced to $90 million, with the $10 million difference being placed in a court-supervised trust fund to reward whistle-blowers who later tipped regulators (or prosecutors) as to misconduct by that defendant.[25] At the end of some defined period, any unused amount could revert to the corporation (or to some master whistle-blower fund that covered all whistle-blowers).

Is this unfair to corporate defendants? No! There is no right to a deferred prosecution agreement (or any other reduced and relaxed disposition, and a future Democratic administration could well abolish the nonprosecution agreement entirely). These dispositions are a gratuitous benefit to the corporation that society is entitled to condition on safeguards against recidivism. Also, because this money would never be received by the agency (but would instead be transferred to a fund overseen by a trustee appointed by the court), this structure skirts the statutory obligation that requires the agency to turn over penalties that it receives to the Treasury.[26]

The key idea here is that the defendant is posting an award for its own future apprehension. Why is this justified? The short answer is that the defendant is admitting its own misconduct by means of the deferred prosecution agreement and thus acknowledging that there is a future risk of recidivism. Fundamentally, this is not different from the defendant agreeing to appoint a monitor to supervise its conduct, except that the monitor receives a fixed payment and the whistle-blower a contingent one. Both monitors and whistle-blower funds are preventive safeguards. In principle, the reward to the whistle-blower still comes out of the penalty imposed on the defendant (just as in the traditional whistle-blower program that Congress has authorized for some federal agencies), but the key difference is that because the defendant consents and never pays the amount covering the bounty to the regulator, this can be done without legislation. Defendants might not agree to this condition, but then they would lose eligibility for a deferred prosecution agreement.

Conceivably, such a whistle-blower fund could also pay bounties to informants who reported misconduct of the same nature elsewhere in the industry (for example, such a fund established by a Volkswagen could pay bounties to whistle-blowers who later reported emission fraud at a GM or Fiat). In this variation, the defendant would be funding a program that monitored not only it but all its competitors as well, and this might be more acceptable to the defendant.

The feasibility of this proposal depends on how much a defendant wants a deferred prosecution agreement (and on how certain it is that it can avoid violating similar laws again in the near future). Because the deferred prosecution agreement reduces the prospect of reputational damages and the risk of collateral liability in follow-on civil litigation, these benefits should still provide adequate motivation to accept a mandatory whistle-blower fund. Ultimately, a whistle-blower fund is a bonding device, as the defendant is effectively proclaiming that it is so confident that it will not be a recidivist that it is willing to pay a reward to those who successfully turn it in.[27]

To sum up, successful prosecutions—civil or criminal—must begin with credible information. This is costly. Today, the government may already be receiving more information than it can process and so responds to relatively few whistle-blower disclosures. The answer to this dilemma is that the government needs to communicate more clearly the types of information it most wants—in effect, advertising through alerts and releases the information it will pay for. Predictably, the market will respond. In particular, employees are one of the best (and cheapest) sources of such information.

To the extent that whistle-blower bounties have been used, they have worked. But, symptomatically, they have been used only sparingly. The sad truth is that even when a reform works, it does not follow that it will be used.

EIGHT

Reforming Corporate Criminal Law

TO THIS POINT, we have focused on procedure (and that is the focus of this book). But another approach to reform would be to refashion corporate criminal law. As a matter of federal criminal law, organizations (including corporations) are today vicariously liable for the acts of their employees and agents.[1] Conceivably, corporate executives could also be made subject to some similar form of vicarious liability, including liability based on negligence, for criminal violations by their corporation or by their subordinate employees. These ideas are not new, but they have recently reentered the public debate with the 2020 presidential campaign. This chapter will be brief, both because we need to cover a range of options and because this author ultimately doubts that these proposals will solve the deeper problems.

Perhaps what is most striking is that liberals and conservatives seem to agree on some proposals for totally different reasons.

Abolish Corporate Criminal Liability?

Traditionalists have long objected to corporate criminal liability because the corporation, being a legal fiction, has no mind and thus must lack mens rea.[2] More recently, some liberals have come to a similar position for a very different reason: corporate criminal liability, they argue, shields executives and makes it easier for prosecutors to settle on a plea agreement with the corporation (for a large financial penalty) that results in practice in sparing individual executives from prosecution. The net result, they assert, is that the corporation can tolerate the penalty as a cost of doing business, while the executives can predict that they will not be held personally accountable. This is not a frivolous argument, and it properly recognizes that both prosecutors and defense counsel can maximize their own interests with a symbolic (but hollow) victory, while leaving the public's interests unprotected.

As this book has earlier argued, the case for corporate liability is not that the corporate entity is itself too culpable to allow it to escape liability but that (1) prosecutors cannot always identify the individual decision makers with the certainty that the criminal law demands and (2) the corporation is typically the best source of the information necessary to prosecute high-ranking executives. In short, it is not an either-or choice between the corporation and its executives, and the best strategy is to pursue both in the hope that each can be induced to turn on the other. Accordingly, this book will not pursue further the case for abolishing corporate criminal liability.

Strict Liability for Executives: The Crime of Being a Boss

Prevailing law does permit the legislature to impose strict liability on senior executives for certain offenses committed by their corporation. Current law may only permit such convictions in the case of what are called *public welfare offenses*, but, as later discussed, this is a category that is ill defined and potentially very expandable.

Two Supreme Court decisions must be considered here. In the first, *United States v. Dotterweich*,[3] the Supreme Court in 1943 upheld a criminal conviction of a corporate president who had "no personal connection" with the underlying facts of the crime but was in "general charge" of the business.[4] His company, Buffalo Pharmacal Company Inc., was a "jobber"—that is, an intermediary who purchased prescription drugs from manufacturers and repackaged them under its own label, shipping them to retail pharmacies. Neither he nor anyone at his company appears to have been aware that the drugs they were shipping were misbranded because the manufacturer had diluted them in violation of the Food, Drug and Cosmetic Act (FDCA). Despite his lack of knowledge, the Supreme Court upheld his conviction on a bluntly utilitarian rational. The FDCA, it wrote, "in the interest of the larger good . . . puts the burden of acting at hazard upon a person otherwise innocent but standing in responsible relation to a public danger."[5] Perhaps, in 1943 in the middle of World War II, it was easy for the Court to see the need to subordinate the interests of the individual to the public good.

Nonetheless, commentary on *Dotterweich* has generally been critical, viewing it as an unfortunate departure from Anglo-American criminal law's traditional focus on mens rea. Many expected that *Dotterweich* would be limited by later decisions. But that did not happen. Instead, in 1975, the Court returned to the FDCA when it faced a case in which the CEO of Acme Markets Inc., a nationwide retail grocery chain, was charged with a criminal misdemeanor because rats had been detected in one of its warehouses.[6] Acme had some 874 retail outlets and 16 warehouses. Although rats may be a fact of life in some urban areas, legally evidence of rat infestation meant that the foodstuffs stored in that warehouse were "adulterated" as a matter of law and had then been introduced into interstate commerce in violation of the FDCA.

One fact also distinguished this case from *Dotterweich*. Unlike in *Dotterweich*, John Park, the CEO of Acme, had received a letter from the FDA stating that rat infestation had been detected at Acme's Baltimore warehouse. He gave instructions to subordinates to correct this problem, but when the FDA again inspected the warehouse several months later, it again found evidence that rats were present. Thus, the defendant Park (unlike the defendant Dotterweich) had actual knowledge but feasibly could only delegate matters to lower-level staff. The FDA did not accept this defense and charged the CEO Park with a misdemeanor under the FDCA. Following his conviction on this misdemeanor charge, he was sentenced to pay a charge of $50 on each count.[7]

Obviously, cases with stakes this small seldom make it to the Supreme Court, but the industry saw a chance to overturn, or at least curtail, the responsible corporate officer doctrine. They guessed wrong. The Court carefully rejected the idea that any officer could be held criminally responsible under the FDCA and limited prosecutions to those who "had authority and responsibility to deal with the situation."[8] Such officers, it added, had a duty, imposed on them by the FDCA, "to seek out and remedy violations when they occur" and "to implement measures that will ensure that violations will not occur."[9] At best, this was a very modest concession on the scope of the FDCA.

The decision in *Park* differed from that in *Dotterweich* only in that the Court recognized an impossibility defense under which the defendant may escape liability by proving that he was "powerless to prevent or correct the violation."[10] To date, however, this defense seems not to have succeeded.

Since *Park*, the responsible corporate officer doctrine has been increasingly relied upon in new contexts, including environmental cases, drug prosecutions, and even the Sherman Antitrust Act.[11] The doctrine is inapplicable if the underlying statute requires proof of mens rea (or even negligence), but many state and federal statutes are written broadly, do not explicitly reference any requisite level of mens rea, but simply forbid "any person" from engaging in the prohibited conduct.

Does this mean, for example, that a statute covering some aspect of banking or financial regulation could be deemed subject to this doctrine? For example, suppose a statute required "any person" at a national bank to make certain disclosures and made no reference to any level of knowledge or intention that was necessary to violate this statute. Here, the answer may depend on whether the statute can be viewed as a public welfare offense. This category of offenses was intended to protect the public from unsafe products (generally food or drugs) and has now been stretched to cover environmental defenses that also expose the public to unknown harms.[12] Generally, public welfare offenses carried short sentences (typically less than a year) and were not viewed as "true" crimes.[13] If the hypothetical statute discussed above was intended only to inform an agency so that it could monitor the bank, this does not seem a classic public welfare offense, but if it was an effort to directly protect the public against some dangerous practice, the issue is closer and can be debated. The length of the authorized sentence might also be given considerable weight (with a longer authorized sentence leading a court to reject the public welfare offense characterization). Of course, Congress or a state legislature could explicitly reject the need for a statute to require any level of mens rea, and *Dotterweich* and *Park* suggest that such a statute would be upheld (unless the authorized sentence were too long). Still, legislatures rarely write statutes in this fashion; instead, they tend simply to ignore the issue.

Because *Park* was decided over forty-five years ago, it can reasonably be asked whether the current (and more conservative) Supreme Court would still follow it. Fair as that question may be, the Court seems to be actively ducking this issue. Most recently in *United States v. DeCoster*,[14] the father and son owners of Quality Egg LLC pled guilty to shipping salmonella-laden eggs in interstate commerce in violation of the FDCA. The sentencing court sentenced each to three months in prison, and the defendants appealed these sentences on the theory that public welfare offenses could not justify prison time (no prison time having been imposed in either *Dotterweich* or *Park*). The Eighth Circuit upheld the sentences, and certiorari was sought. Numerous amicus briefs were filed with the Supreme Court by business groups, asking the Court to curtail *Park*'s broad scope. Nonetheless, the Court denied certiorari.[15]

To summarize, the Supreme Court has compromised, consistently construing ambiguous statutes to require some level of mens rea but leaving alone convictions under clearly public welfare offense statutes.[16] Nonetheless, it remains highly uncertain whether Congress could extend strict liability and public welfare offenses to the context of financial institutions or to ordinary business decisions that did not involve an inherently dangerous product. To be sure, *Park* and public welfare offenses could be extended, hypothetically, to the operators of nuclear power plants or even to the manufacturers of aircraft (such as Boeing), but banks may be a bridge too far. Even if public welfare offenses could be stretched this far, few would be satisfied with a sentence of one or two months for the CEO of a Lehman or an AIG—but that is all that the public welfare offense doctrine has traditionally justified.

Negligence-Based Liability for Executives: Elizabeth Warren's Approach and a Variation

If strict liability is thus an unpromising route, a better option may be to impose negligence liability on senior executives. But for what crimes? Seemingly, the CEO of Greyhound should not be liable if a single Greyhound bus speeds (at least absent evidence that its buses were encouraged by its executives to speed). Nonetheless, in 2019, Senator Elizabeth Warren introduced legislation—the "Corporate Executive Accountability Act"—that could go that far. Under it, executives at every corporation with more than $1 billion in annual revenues could face prison time of up to one year if they negligently permit or fail to prevent

> (1) Any criminal violation of Federal or State law for which their corporation was convicted or entered into a deferred or non-prosecution agreement;
> (2) Any civil violation of Federal or State law for which their corporation was found liable or entered into a settlement with any state or federal agency if the violation affects the health or safety, finances, or personal data of not less than 1% of the American population or not less than 1% of the population of any state; or
> (3) Any criminal or civil violation of Federal or State law for which their corporation is liable if it was the second civil or criminal violation for the corporation.[17]

This is fairly sweeping. Under this language, two speeding tickets to Greyhound might make its senior executives liable, and the senior executives of Pacific Gas and Electric would face prison for a year if the fires caused by its power lines endangered the safety of 1 percent of California's population.

This language obviously is modeled upon the public welfare offense doctrine but it transcends that doctrine by covering civil offenses as well. Perhaps this statute was intended more as a political statement than a legal one, but it does raise the question of how such a statute might be modified and downsized to become more palatable. It is clearly constitutional because it requires proof of negligence (which is viewed by American law as a variety of mens rea), but it may still give less than fair notice. Here, the key questions will be: How does one show negligence by an executive (for example, the chief financial officer) who has little connection with the company's operating side? How broadly or deeply is such an executive expected to monitor? What precisely is the duty to monitor and prevent that is imposed on executives? These types of questions are not unanswerable, but they have not yet been seriously addressed by this statute.

Senator Warren is, however, quite correct that if we wish to enhance deterrence, we should focus on executives more than on the corporate entity. The limited empirical evidence shows this.[18] In this light, a more feasible approach to hers would be to authorize enforcement agencies to impose administrative penalties on corporate officers (including but not limited to the CEO) for negligence that "substantially caused or contributed to" the same conduct that Senator Warren would criminalize; in addition, this administrative penalty (which might be up to $5 million) could also be imposed for the failure to disclose to a federal agency with jurisdiction over the area any "known risk or condition" that could cause loss of life or serious injury to employees, consumers, or other foreseeable victims. Such a penalty could be imposed by administrative law judges and would not be subject to indemnification. Essentially, by making this a civil offense rather than a crime, the agency would not have to prove its case beyond a reasonable doubt but only by a preponderance of the evidence.

Some will respond that such penalties will make corporate executives far too risk averse and shareholders will suffer. Nonsense! Shareholders will predictably respond by offering executives greater and greater incentive compensation to accept risk. Thus, the next chapter will argue that the convicted corporation should be placed on probation under conditions that restrict its use of incentive compensation.

Mandating Closer Attention and the Problem of Conscious Avoidance

Although negligence-based liability can certainly be imposed on corporate executives (at least if done with more precision and detail than the Warren bill currently contains), the more traditional approach would be to hold corporate executives liable for criminal charges requiring proof of knowledge if "conscious avoidance" or "willful blindness" could be shown with respect to the executive's awareness of the corporation's criminal conduct. In most common-law countries (and certainly the United States), conscious avoidance of knowledge is treated as the functional equivalent of actual knowledge.[19]

But what must be shown to prove conscious avoidance? Here, a recent Supreme Court decision has sown considerable confusion. In *Global Tech Appliances, Inc. v. SED S.A.*,[20] the Supreme Court defined the standard for showing "conscious indifference" in a civil patent infringement case and seemingly raised the standard.[21] But whether this decision applies in criminal cases also or whether the prior standard remains unaffected is a question on which subsequent federal courts have divided.[22]

This question could be debated at length, or it can be legislatively resolved by a statute that simplifies the showing that prosecutors must satisfy to show conscious avoidance and thus convict defendants of crimes where only knowledge must be shown.[23] If willfulness must be proven, then more than conscious avoidance must be shown, but that spares corporate executives from conviction in cases involving exceptionally serious charges (such as, for example, homicide) unless intention can also be proven. That may be a fair compromise.

A Duty to Certify?

If we want a mechanism by which to require corporate executives to focus on health and safety problems relating to their consumers and employees (and thus to provide a basis for criminal liability based on either negligence or conscious avoidance), one means to this end is suggested by the Sarbanes-Oxley Act. Passed in 2002 after Enron, WorldCom, and a series of other major corporate failures that seemingly showed corporate managements concealing major problems, section 302 of that act instructed the SEC to adopt rules requiring the chief executive officer and the chief financial officer of public companies to certify that they had reviewed their company's annual and quarterly financial reports and concluded that "based on the officer's knowledge, the report does not contain any untrue statement of a material fact ... [and] the financial statements, and other financial information included in the reports, fairly present in all material respects the financial condition and results of operations of the issuer."[24]

This approach could obviously be extended to other contexts. For example, one could ask a CEO of a pharmaceutical company to "certify that he had personally reviewed the company's activities and received reports from all subordinate officers having relevant experience or responsibility in the area, and based on that, believed the company was in full compliance with its legal responsibilities, including with regard to the safety of its products." Such a certification might be perceived by the officer as placing a noose around his neck, and, in some circumstances, that could be a desirable form of deterrence. Indeed, the Sarbanes-Oxley Act contemporaneously amended federal criminal law to make it a felony (punishable by up to ten years in person) to knowingly provide a false certification.[25]

There are two sides to this strategy. In favor of it, this approach obviously creates a greater deterrent (and is less constitutionally troublesome) than a public welfare offense. Fair notice is certainly also given. On the other side, it has its own obvious problems. First, it is difficult (or impossible) to draft a list of questions to pose to all CEOs. One size never fits all. Even in the case of the pharmaceutical CEO discussed above, the questions need to be more specific: Is there evidence that the company sold opioids to drug mills? Has it produced drugs with a dangerously high potency? Second, the experience with Sarbanes-Oxley has shown that CEOs and CFOs responded to its certification duty by requiring their subordinates in turn to certify to them that the company's financial statements and other related disclosures were accurate in all respects. This made it unlikely that they could be convicted of a knowingly false certification when they were relying on sworn certifications to them. The net result was probably to insulate the CEOs and CFOs, and prosecutions have been few, if any, under this provision. Third, inducing Congress to pass such a sweeping certification provision will not be easy; it would likely cause a political firestorm.

Thus, the proposal here made (in the next chapter) is that such a certification should not be required of all corporations but only of those hereafter convicted of a crime. In their case, it could be made a mandatory condition of probations (which could be imposed in addition to a fine or other sanctions). This special vantage point would allow the sentencing court to frame the required certification in a manner appropriate to the specific corporation and its recent history.

A Summary

One could impose strict liability on corporate executives, but this is troubling from a civil liberties perspective and would face constant challenges in court. Not only would its constitutionality be attacked (at least if more than very short sentences were imposed), but courts would be regularly seeking to trim the statute's application or interpret it strictly. Strict liability is unpopular with courts and even prosecutors.

One might therefore fall back to a negligence standard (as Senator Warren has done in her proposed bill). But one needs to specify what the duty is in a manner that is both sensible and gives fair notice. Under the Warren bill, two violations (criminal or civil) make the CEO liable if he or she was negligent in not preventing them. But, sooner or later, a Greyhound or another transportation company will acquire two or more traffic tickets, and a chemical company will occasionally spill something toxic into the water—on two or more occasions. Was the CEO liable for negligently allowing this to occur? This may give too much discretion to both prosecutors and juries. One statute cannot reasonably define what the duty should be for all corporations, because they are a very diverse group, operating at very different risk levels.

Thus, this chapter has proposed (and the next chapter will spell out) an approach that looks backward and applies to corporations that have been convicted of a felony. It would require (for a probationary period—probably five years) that their CEOs and CFOs file annual certifications that would be tailored by the court to the specific circumstances of their crime.

Finally, this chapter has recommended that the legal doctrine that treats conscious avoidance of knowledge as the equivalent of knowledge needs to be updated in light of recent decisions. Specifically, it should be sufficient that the CEO was subjectively aware that there was a probability that the company was acting in violation of law and took no steps to inquire further. For example, if the CEO of an auto company knows that the company has been unable to comply with applicable federal or state emission controls, it should not be necessary for this officer to know specifically how the company was cheating to escape those controls. Alone, such knowledge of the company's inability to comply could show "willful ignorance" or "conscious avoidance." But this CEO would escape liability if the company's general counsel certified to him that the company was in compliance with its environmental and emission responsibilities. That would not solve everything (but the general counsel might then be prosecuted for a false or reckless certification).

As the next chapter will stress, the better course is not to focus the threat of criminal liability on all corporate executives for a single act of negligence but to instead reduce the incentive to take risks and mandate fuller disclosure of the risks that are taken.

NINE

Dealing with the Convicted Corporation

WHAT SHOULD BE DONE with the convicted corporation (including one that enters a deferred prosecution agreement)? Obviously, it can be fined. But what else? In fact, corporations in the federal system are sentenced in a high majority of the cases to a term of probation (in addition to a fine),[1] but very little thought has gone into what probation conditions are appropriate. Determining what should occur at sentencing involves dividing what is best done ex ante (i.e., before conviction) from what can be better done ex post (i.e., after conviction). Ex ante, legislatures can revise the criminal law, prosecutors can negotiate a plea bargain, and everyone can pressure the firm to identify and provide evidence against its responsible executives. Ex post, much less can be done,[2] but a treatment plan tailored to the specifics of the convicted corporation's case can be better designed at this stage. This chapter will survey and assess this design problem.

Ex post, the court is faced with a specific defendant and not general policy issues. Of course, the court will seek to impose a sentence that deters (both the individual corporate defendant and other corporations similarly situated). But should anything else be done? Today, little more is attempted. Professionally, prosecutors are interested in winning trials, not reshaping corporate governance. Nonetheless, this chapter will suggest that the focus at a sentencing of a large corporation for a serious crime should be on the prevention of recidivism. As others have shown, public corporations are far more likely to be recidivists than corporate executives.[3] As a practical matter, the convicted executive is effectively barred from the industry by his or her conviction, but the reverse is true in the case of the corporation. One cannot bar an Exxon from the energy business without creating an energy crisis or an Apple without

131

panicking the stock market. Realistically, they are "too big to bar," because the economy would suffer.[4] Possibly as a result, some large companies have experienced a string of convictions.[5] This may be because fines can be absorbed by them as a cost of doing business or, alternatively, because corporate culture is hard to change. Either way, this pattern suggests that the court's attention needs to be focused on reducing the risk of corporate recidivism. Put more bluntly, the goal is not to rehabilitate the convicted corporation but to incapacitate it.

How does one do this? This chapter will suggest four strategies. First, the court needs to eliminate or reduce those pressures and incentives that are criminogenic (that is, that encourage the corporation to pursue short-term profit maximization with reckless zeal). Second, the court should compel the corporation (through its high-ranking executives) to regularly certify to its board, the court, and regulators that it is not engaged in specified conduct that resulted in (or at least contributed to) its prior violation. Effectively, this means that we need to adapt the effort made by the Sarbanes-Oxley Act with respect to CEO and CFO certification of the company's financial statements so that it applies as well to other, even riskier, areas of corporate behavior. Third, the corporation's internal circuits may need to be rewired to encourage or require internal reporting to those most able and prepared to intervene (such as the corporation's audit committee). This could involve the use of corporate monitors. Fourth, corporate sentencing needs to address the factor of shame. The goal here is not to denigrate the corporation's products or render the firm less able to compete but to keep the fact of the corporation's conviction front and center in the corporation's memory and to make the experience sufficiently discomforting for its employees that they will resist any reoccurrence. Shame is in effect a group sanction that can be designed to deter. Each of these topics are considered below.

Incentive Compensation and Corporate Recidivism?

The evidence is clear that when corporations use incentive compensation to motivate their executives, they also induce them to take increased risk.[6] Today, most of the compensation received by the CEO and other senior executives at a public corporation comes in the form of equity compensation, paid on an incentive basis, generally in the form of stock options and stock awards.[7] This may be desirable in order to cause executives to listen to the market, change, and adapt, but the available data also show that incentive compensation can incline executives to engage in financial misreporting.[8]

Here, two very brief case studies are useful. First, Valeant Pharmaceuticals International has recently been the subject of much controversy and litigation.[9]

What particularly attracted attention to Valeant was its practice of buying patents on prescription drugs (or the companies owning those patents) and then raising the prices of those drugs by up to 600 percent or more.[10] Eventually, after deceptive behavior by Valeant was publicly disclosed, it attracted congressional hearings and a criminal investigation, and its stock price cratered.[11]

For our purposes, Valeant's immediate relevance lies in its executive compensation agreement with its chief executive officer. That contract made extreme use of incentive compensation. Designed by a hedge fund that wanted to motivate Valeant's CEO to accept risk, it paid the CEO only $1 million in cash but also an assortment of contingent equity awards (stock and options) valued at $16 million.[12] Under this contract, the CEO would receive performance stock units that would vest only if Valeant achieved the following three-year compounded total shareholder returns:

1. Three-year total shareholder returns < 15 percent: 0 shares vest
2. Three-year total shareholder returns of 15 to 29 percent: 407,498 shares vest
3. Three-year total shareholder returns of 30 to 44 percent: 814,996 shares vest
4. Three-year total shareholder returns > 45 percent: 1,222,494 shares vest

In short, if shareholder returns over three years went up 14 percent (or less), the CEO would not receive any incentive compensation, but if shareholder returns went up by more than 45 percent, a reward of 1,222,494 shares would be paid to the CEO. This incentivizes the CEO to gamble (and in turn to raise drug prices exorbitantly). Other senior executives at Valeant received similarly scaled awards. For the hedge funds that owned most of Valeant, this created the ideal incentives to push management to maximize profits—at all costs.

Next, consider a second case: WorldCom Inc. Its failure in 2002 was probably the final precipitating cause of the Sarbanes-Oxley Act. After the SEC sued, Judge Jed Rakoff appointed a corporate monitor, Richard C. Breeden, who had been the former chair of the SEC. Far more energetic than most monitors, Breeden conducted an elaborate study and made some seventy-eight specific recommendations. But at the very outset of his report, in his executive summary, Breeden pointed to the key problem:

> The compensation practices of WorldCom allowed lavish compensation, far beyond any rational calculation of value added by senior executives.... Compensation abuse at WorldCom is most vividly symbolized by more than $400 million in "loans" from shareholders to Ebbers (its CEO) that were put in place initially by two directors who were longtime associates of Ebbers.... Massive volumes of stock options were granted to Ebbers... and other executives, representing hundreds of millions of dollars in value at the time.[13]

Breeden concluded that the existence of these loans and the massive stock grants placed WorldCom's executives under irresistible pressure to maintain (and inflate) WorldCom's stock price, using a variety of accounting tricks and misstatements.

Now, assume that Valeant or WorldCom (or a similar company with a similar executive compensation structure) is convicted of a crime and brought before the sentencing court. If recidivism is to be curbed, it should be obvious that the perverse incentives created by its compensation structure need to be curtailed.

But how? One possibility is to place the corporation on probation for some period (say, five years, which is the usual limit on probation) and impose probationary conditions that are intended to minimize the risk of recidivism. For example, one such crime-reducing probation condition might be a restriction on incentive compensation. Such a condition might limit incentive compensation to no more than 25 percent of the executive's total salary for the period of corporate probation. As a consequence, the executive will be economically less motivated to behave as a risk preferrer.

Critics will respond that such a restraint will make the convicted corporation uncompetitive and its executives will flee to other positions at its competitors. Strenuously as some economists will make this argument, it does not ring true. Corporate executives at a convicted corporation will not find it easy to transfer elsewhere at a higher salary. Their reputations have been damaged, and the desire to flee may be interpreted as a sign that they have a dim future with their current employer. Nor was Valeant's extreme compensation package one that other companies had copied or are likely to adopt in the future; hence, its preclusion will not affect the market for executives generally. Even if some executives do flee to other firms, they may be precisely the executives most likely to engage in risky practices. Good riddance to them!

Some will regard such a probation condition as an unjustified interference with the market, but interference with the market is most easily justified when the market has produced a dysfunctional outcome, and here such interference will only occur when the corporation has committed a serious felony. Recent history has shown that extreme levels of incentive compensation can lead a bank to pressure its employees to cross sell (and even falsify customer accounts, as happened at Wells Fargo) or to cause a pharmaceutical company to market especially high-strength opioid tablets (even though they knew this greatly increases the risk of addiction among patients[14]).

Other problems will be raised with respect to such a probation condition. Is the condition authorized by statute or rule? Here, there are good but legally untested arguments that probation conditions can reduce the risk of recidivism. If a probation condition seems likely to do so, existing sentencing law and the Federal Sentencing Commission's rules imply that it should be upheld.[15] Cases in which a probation condition has been struck down as unreasonable are rarer but do exist.[16] Although, at federal law, a corporation cannot decline probation, conditions must be specific and give fair notice to be enforceable. And they must be within the corporation's power to perform.[17] For example, even if the probation condition can bar new compensation contracts with high incentive compensation for the probationary period, what about preexisting contracts containing that feature?[18] Presumably, a preexisting contract gives enforceable rights to the executive. Arguably, although such a contract would remain in force, the probation condition could bar the employment of anyone so compensated as an executive officer (and any such termination would be without prejudice to the terminated executive's right to be paid under the contract). This chapter cannot address all these issues in detail, but the design of probationary conditions to prevent recidivism remains an unexplored field. Prosecutors and courts simply have not thought sufficiently about how to discourage recidivism through probation conditions.

This example of a probationary condition restricting incentive compensation is just one illustration of a probation condition that seeks to reduce the pressure for short-term profit maximization, which may encourage firms to use legally dubious tactics. Other possible conditions aimed at this same end could do such things as (1) establish a whistle-blower fund (created by a donation by the defendant corporation, as described in chapter 7) to reward whistle-blowers who provide credible information with respect to the defendant; (2) establish a twenty-four-hour-per-day hotline for employees to report misbehavior on an anonymous basis; (3) establish internal programs that alert employees for conduct that is suspicious and should be reported upward; or (4) specify the duties and powers of a corporate monitor. Such conditions certainly have an obvious crime-prevention justification.

Corporate monitors present a more complex topic. They have been criticized both for doing too much and too little (depending on the particular critic's perspective).[19] But these criticisms may in part be attributable to the fact that they are seldom clearly given a meaningful role to play. At one end of the continuum, some monitors have been content with a lucrative sinecure and have done nothing. At the other end, the activism of Richard Breeden stands out. He made some seventy-eight specific recommendations for how WorldCom's corporate governance should be restructured.[20] Such cases are likely to be rare (in part because former SEC chairs are seldom available for this assignment). But the procedure followed in this case should be copied. The court appointed the monitor (from a list submitted by the SEC), thus avoiding the danger of a monitor captured by the defendant. The monitor, who should have some corporate governance experience, should be asked by the sentencing court to analyze the defendant's compensation structure and other governance practices and make recommendations.

Holding Management Responsible—Vicariously

Instead of seeking to convict senior executives for negligence and impose lengthy terms, an alternative approach would be to impose restrictions on incentive compensation in the case of a convicted corporation for the period of corporate probation. Corporate penalties normally fall on shareholders, who often have had little knowledge of the corporation's illegal actions. In contrast, some executives typically have knowledge of the corporation's unlawful actions, even though they are not prosecuted. Restricting incentive compensation makes senior executives bear a collective penalty. Arguably, they deserve to face such a vicarious liability at least as much as the shareholders (who may have less knowledge or ability to act). In this light, one result of restricting incentive compensation is to create an unintended but useful *frankpledge system* in which senior executives face some loss if their corporation is convicted.[21] Such a system creates collective responsibility because all (or most) executives would lose incentive compensation for some period. This should deter dangerous risk-taking and may even cause those who become aware of potential illegality to report it up the ladder within the corporation. If all executives will suffer, the executive tempted to commit an illegal act may hesitate or desist because of loyalty to his or her colleagues. In this way, loyalty to one's peers (a nearly universal trait) can be put to work as a force for law compliance.

Expanding the Duty to Certify

As noted earlier, the Sarbanes-Oxley Act requires the chief executive officer and the chief financial officer to certify the accuracy of the firm's periodic reports to the SEC and also "that information contained in the periodic report fairly presents, in all material respects, the financial condition and results of operations of the issuer."[22] Let's think about how such a duty could be extended and generalized in the case of the convicted corporation. Suppose this company had been convicted of an environmental offense. One could respond by asking specified senior executives, as a condition of the convicted corporation's probation, to certify regularly to the Environmental Protection Agency, the sentencing court, and the SEC (1) that the company was to the best of their knowledge, after reasonable inquiry, in compliance with all environmental laws and regulations; (2) that all reports it submitted to the EPA were accurate and complete; and (3) that these reports fairly presented in all material respects the company's activities that could have a significant impact on the environment. Failure to provide such certified reports would cause the corporation to violate this condition of probation and could result in corporate fines and a lengthened term of probation.

Corporate Rewiring

All public corporations have systems of internal controls, and sometimes Congress revises these. In the wake of Enron and WorldCom, the Sarbanes-Oxley Act required the public corporation's auditor to report to the corporation's audit committee, which alone was given the authority to hire, fire, or discipline it.[23] The goal here was to make the outside auditor more independent and less subservient to management. Although there is no dispositive proof that this worked, the idea seems sound, and it imposed little cost on the corporation.

This reform, which rewired internal reporting, suggests others. Particularly in the case of a convicted corporation, society wants the corporation's general counsel to give independent legal advice and not be simply a lackey for the CEO or CFO. One low-cost means to this end would be to make the general counsel report to the audit committee and not be replaceable by the CEO alone. To be sure, this reform is no panacea, and it is not suggested as justified in every case. But where there is evidence that legal risks were ignored, it makes sense, because it virtually compels the general counsel to take sensitive problems to the audit committee (which otherwise may never hear of them).

When the corporation is seeking a deferred prosecution agreement, prosecutors have additional leverage. They can even raise the issue of whether all personnel are fit to remain in office. As a condition of such an agreement, some executive heads may need to roll. Termination of responsible executives may be harder to justify as a condition of probation, but an entirely reasonable condition of probation could require an internal investigation and appropriate discipline. Nonetheless, such measures are best taken at or before sentencing (when the court's attention is fully engaged).

The rewiring of the corporation's internal circuits that might have the greatest potential benefit would be to place the corporate monitor into direct and continuing contact with the corporation's auditors (both internal and external). Under the Securities Exchange Act, the outside auditor has a statutory duty to follow "procedures designed to provide reasonable assurances of detecting illegal acts" that would have a material effect on the company's financial statements[24] and to "determine whether it is likely that an illegal act has occurred."[25] If it finds that it is likely that such an illegal act occurred, it must inform the appropriate level of management and "assure that the audit committee... is adequately informed."[26] Although this provision dates back to the Sarbanes-Oxley Act in 2002, it has not to date produced any celebrated cases in which auditor-discovered illegality broke into the open. Auditors do not appear eager to enforce this duty. What then might breathe greater life into this duty? One logical answer would be to require a corporate monitor and the outside auditor also to consult and to specify that the auditor inform the corporate monitor (who usually has a clearer commitment to law compliance) of any relevant information it has learned. This could be mandated by a probation condition or simply by a contractual term in a deferred prosecution agreement.

Also, instead of waiting for the auditor to inform it, the monitor should be instructed regularly to inquire of the auditor (in writing and at least on a quarterly basis) whether it had learned any facts or circumstances that made it suspect that it was "likely that an illegal act has occurred."[27] If a written response were required of the auditor, it might produce more valuable information than has yet come to light.

Shame

Should the convicted corporation be deliberately subjected to shame? Clearly there are two sides to this question. Sentencing has long expected the defendant to "accept responsibility" for the crime, and the defendant who is not contrite at sentencing risks disaster. But what the corporation says (through its lawyers at sentencing) has little impact on its employees, who seldom learn that information. Do we therefore want employees to feel some sense of embarrassment about working for a convicted corporation?

Some will argue that this will just increase employee turnover and weaken or demoralize the company. The converse position is that shaming can be a powerful deterrent. If employees can anticipate that their company will be made to bear shame, this may to some degree motivate them to avoid actions that appear risky (and may even induce some to become whistle-blowers).

Realists must recognize that, unless some continuing public recognition by the corporation of its conviction or deferred prosecution agreement is mandated, that incident will quickly become a nonevent, which no one dares mention. Thus, if we want the corporate culture to change, we cannot allow the corporate memory to forget (or repress) the fact of its conviction.

Still, how does one institutionalize shaming without engaging in silly or pointless charades of self-condemnation? In the case of a serious crime (for example, a multimillion-dollar bribery incident in violation of the Foreign Corrupt Practices Act), one could mandate a compulsory reference to the conviction in certain SEC required documents (annual reports, proxy statements, prospectuses, etc.). More meaningfully, one could require a section in every quarterly report filed with the SEC dealing with how the corporation has responded to its conviction, including a periodic update from any corporate monitor. Desirable as such a rule may be, it still sounds overly formal; employees, particularly at lower levels, tend not to read the company's SEC disclosures.

Thus, if we want to influence the corporate culture and make it more law compliant, we need an official who would visit the company's divisions and offices (domestic and foreign) to discuss the conviction and explain the warning signals of similar misbehavior—in effect, to preach the gospel of law compliance. Who could do this? This could be among the principal responsibilities of a corporate monitor (although it has not been one of the monitor's standard duties to date). Alternatively, the general counsel could go on the road to visit local offices to perform this missionary role (and this does happen).

Still, another approach to institutionalizing shame would be to require the CEO to appear in court at the plea of guilty and sentencing stages, both to express the corporation's remorse and to answer the court's questions. This would be distasteful to the CEO and therefore deterrent. Revealingly, this seldom happens today, as the CEO delegates everything to the lawyers.

Conclusion

Modest as these reforms may sound, they will be highly controversial. Auditors do not want to report corporate illegality (and they have seldom done so). Expanded certification requirements may over time land some executives in jail. Finally, restrictions on incentive compensation will be intensely resisted. In the final analysis, the case for restricting such compensation at a convicted corporation is that unindicted executives should not wholly escape the corporation's conviction without bearing any cost. If corporate culture is to change, these are good starting points. Moreover, such reforms are considerably less Draconian than sending CEOs to prison for decades for negligence because an airplane crashed (which assigns too much standardless discretion to the jury).

One last generalization should be noted here: today, our system of criminal justice administration effectively ends at sentencing. It does so in large part because prosecutors define success in terms of trial victories. They want a significant sentence largely because a modest one undercuts their victory;

otherwise, they have little interest in corporate probation. Probation officers basically know even less about corporate governance. Thus, there is a gap here that needs to be filled. The court could hire experts, or it could ask the advice of the SEC, but letting this opportunity pass without even considering preventive restrictions is a mistake. Corporate history, if ignored, repeats itself.

Conclusion

Rebalancing the Carrots and the Sticks

THIS BOOK HAS RAISED a number of themes, and now it is time to connect them. Today, the prosecution of complex corporate crime is characterized by underenforcement: that is, prosecutors rarely get to the top of the corporate hierarchy (or even near the top). A leading cause of this shortfall is that federal prosecutors must (and do) outsource their investigation of corporate misconduct to the defendant corporation. Not surprisingly, the resulting "internal investigation" is necessarily compromised. Low-level employees may be detected and prosecuted, but the investigation rarely finds its way into the corporate headquarters.

This outsourcing occurs because federal prosecutors lack the resources or staff to conduct a thorough investigation themselves. To be sure, this generalization is not always true, but it becomes increasingly accurate as the complexity of the alleged misbehavior grows or as the investigation crosses international boundaries. For example, in a foreign, corrupt-practices investigation, where suspect payments may have been made on multiple continents, there is little chance that federal prosecutors can unravel the scope of the conspiracy without the corporation's assistance. Logistically, the costs and necessary staff are well beyond what a small team of prosecutors can undertake, even if they are assisted by paralegals, staff accountants, translators, and (sometimes) borrowed SEC staffers.

What should be done in response to this problem of underenforcement involves several interrelated questions.

How Can Public Policy Economize on the Costs of Investigation?

In overview, federal prosecutors can gather information in three basic ways.

The Traditional Investigation

Using the grand jury and possibly the record already developed by civil enforcement officials, prosecutors can pursue defendants successfully when they begin their investigation with a fairly good idea of who was responsible. But this technique does not allow them to question hundreds of witnesses or review several million records or a typically much larger number of emails. To be sure, prosecutors do "flip" lower-level defendants and induce them to testify against potential higher-level defendants. But to build a bridge from the individuals actually involved in the crime to the executive suite would require a serial succession of flips that seems never to occur. Senior executives rarely become involved in the details of price fixing, unlawful payments, or other white collar crimes. When CEOs or other senior executives are convicted, it is usually in the case of smaller companies with thin management teams where the persons directly involved in the crime did communicate with senior executives.

The Outsourced Investigation

Needing assistance (including a party that can fund the costs of the investigation), prosecutors have turned to the corporation and offered deferred prosecution agreements (or even nonprosecution agreements) in return for a thorough internal investigation. As stressed throughout this book, the corporation has the comparative advantage at investigation because it can compel its employees and agents to cooperate (or face termination) and it can more easily search its own records and corporate emails. But the terms of this bartered exchange have usually favored the corporate defendant: it picks the counsel and directs the investigation, and the result is generally to collect only the low-hanging fruit. Moreover, the more we attempt to change this arrangement by permitting the federal prosecutors to choose (or become involved in the choice of) counsel, or the more we permit the prosecutor to direct the investigation, the greater the risk becomes that the Fifth Amendment will be violated, meaning that compelled testimony will be inadmissible and any evidence or witnesses that are discovered may be excluded at trial as "fruit of the poisonous tree." Indeed, defense counsel will be duty bound to raise this issue in almost any such case, and significant litigation risk will surround every such case.

Purchased Information

The one new technique by which prosecutors can economize on the high costs of acquiring information is to buy it. This is essentially what paying bounties to whistle-blowers accomplishes. This technique is working well (sufficiently so that the Trump administration is seeking to cut back on it), but at present only a few federal agencies are authorized to acquire information in this fashion. Thus, the most obvious practical reform would be to permit the Department of Justice and other federal agencies similarly to use this technique. But rather than rely on the submissions of random whistle-blowers, the government needs to indicate more clearly the information it most wants. For example, the agency could indicate to the employees of one or more corporations that it wanted information from persons with direct knowledge about payments or monetary transfers to specific companies or persons within a given time period and that it was authorized to pay substantial amounts for such information if it proved useful. When the bounties are high, whistle-blowers will predictably appear and respond.

At present, there is uncertainty as to how much the contemporary pattern can be changed without courts reacting hostilely. The bargain between corporations and prosecutors under which a thorough internal investigation is exchanged for a deferred prosecution agreement would certainly be fairer to the prosecution if they could choose (or at least influence the choice of) the counsel conducting the investigation. But, as earlier noted, if the prosecution moves too far in this direction, the investigation will be attributed to the government (and thus any compelled testimony will be excluded).[1] Many intermediate points on this path are possible (e.g., the prosecution could provide a list of counsel from which the corporation chose), but it is premature today to predict what will work.[2]

Still, assume the worse. Even if investigations in which the prosecution exercises some influence are attributed to it, it still may be better for prosecutors to choose the counsel and direct the investigation. Although this implies that compelled testimony will be barred, much information can nonetheless be assembled, and the internal investigation will not wear blinders if the prosecutors can influence who is interviewed. Some witnesses may waive their Fifth Amendment rights (even after consultation with counsel) because it is difficult for a senior officer of a public company to remain in office after refusing to testify.[3] However, if prosecutors were compelled to surrender the ability to compel testimony in internal investigations, the next question becomes whether such an "attributed" investigation really justifies a deferred prosecution agreement—or only some lesser sentencing leniency. After all, the government has not quite received the value that it hoped for if testimony cannot be compelled. That brings us to a more general topic.

When Should Deferred Prosecution Agreements Be Tolerated?

Many reformers would simply abolish them, and future Democratic administrations may curb them to some degree. But such a preclusive approach would leave the government with far less ability to ensure a thorough internal investigation. Prosecutors would thus remain in the dark, and transparency would suffer. Also, in some circumstances, a deferred prosecution agreement seems entirely appropriate. For example, suppose the corporation self-reports the crime and fires those clearly responsible. Significant credit should be given in such a case (although a full internal investigation still needs to be conducted).

If an absolute ban on deferred prosecution agreements thus goes too far, what is the best compromise here? Because one cannot judge the adequacy and quality of an investigation until after it has been conducted, the decision whether a detailed and costly internal investigation truly justifies a deferred prosecution agreement should not be made in advance. Today, there is too often an implicit understanding that the corporation's internal investigation assures it a deferred prosecution agreement. Indeed, the Trump administration is moving in the direction of accepting that a "robust" compliance should alone justify a deferred prosecution agreement.[4] In contrast, the policy here favored would require the investigation to produce significant results (of which the government was not already aware). If the investigation yielded only small fish, the corporation would still be prosecuted on felony charges, but it would normally be given some sentencing leniency (although not immunity from conviction). This might motivate the corporation to select a counsel for the internal investigation that it knew in advance would please the prosecution— in the hopes that this would contribute to a decision to grant it a deferred prosecution agreement. Also, if the corporation self-reported the crime (before the prosecution was hot on its trail), this would even more clearly justify a deferred prosecution agreement, but merely conducting an elaborate investigation would guarantee nothing.

Assume (quite plausibly) that a future administration might wish to condition the deferred prosecution agreement on more substantial concessions or services by the defendant. One means to this end would be to return to the Department of Justice's former position (of a decade or so ago) when Justice regularly pushed the corporation to waive its attorney-client privilege. That would make everything available to the government, and little could be hidden. This former position was modified under intense pressure from the business community (and rumblings in Congress) in 2008,[5] and today such waivers are rarely, if ever, required. It would be an extremely controversial policy change to require privilege waivers as the price of a deferred prosecution agreement, but it is clear that a corporation can constitutionally waive its attorney-client privilege, and such a waiver would truly make the exchange of an internal investigation for a deferred prosecution agreement a much more equal bargain.[6]

Would corporations still want deferred prosecution agreements at this price? Today, their answers would likely differ. Banks (and some other corporations) might be desperate, at least if a conviction could bar them from the banking industry.[7] If this risk seemed real, they predictably would do whatever was necessary. Other corporations, however, would resist. In their case, the threat would need to be enhanced. Here, we need to return to what is probably this book's most radical proposal: the equity fine.

Is the Equity Fine Justifiable?

As has been argued, cash fines seldom deter, in part because they fall on widely dispersed and very diversified shareholders, who do not respond to these penalties and in any event cannot easily take collective action. Even if extreme monetary penalties would deter, they would still fall on relatively innocent constituencies (i.e., employees, local communities, and creditors), and over time this would likely prove politically unsustainable.

In contrast, an equity fine (say, of 20 percent of the outstanding shares) solves these problems. First, it could not be ignored by management—in part because it could make corporate control contestable.[8] Even the issuance of a 20 percent block would enable insurgents or activists to threaten a change in corporate control (particularly if the stock were sold at an auction). Management cannot be indifferent to this prospect. Second, the equity fine minimizes externalities. Creditors and employees are not affected (except to the extent that stock held by executives is diluted, and that may also be desirable for its deterrent value).

The proceeds of the stock sale would go to either the state or a victim compensation fund, and the corporation might be barred from repurchasing these shares for a defined period. Thus, the intended result is to dilute shareholders (without affecting other constituencies).

Is this so harsh as to violate the Constitution? Although the Eighth Amendment does preclude "excessive fines,"[9] the fact that the penalty is harsh does not make it unconstitutional. Individuals may face sentences of twenty or twenty-five years for the same conduct. Moreover, a sensible analysis should also consider the cost to society if the corporation is not deterred. Finally, the real impact of corporate penalties is largely borne by diversified and often indexed institutional shareholders, which results in a more diffused injury. In the end, the equity fine should be viewed not as the harshest of possible penalties but as a means of reducing the inevitable overspill of criminal penalties on the blameless.

Do These Proposals Trample on the Rights of Defendants?

Clearly, some of these proposals (particularly, any required waiver of the attorney-client privilege to qualify for a deferred prosecution agreement) place increased pressure on the corporation. Is this unacceptable or, at least, ill advised? Here, we need to begin with a background reference point. Individuals in the American criminal justice system today are often faced with a choice between a charge carrying a twenty- or twenty-five-year sentence if they go to trial (and are convicted) or a much lesser disposition if they plead guilty. Some defendants even face the prospect of capital punishment if they spurn a plea bargain and go to trial. The Supreme Court has shown little sympathy for claims that such pressure is unfair or unjust.[10] All that is different when we consider corporate prosecutions is that we are focusing on an inanimate defendant. Those who feel pain when it is convicted are its shareholders, and they bear it to a much lesser degree.

More generally, American criminal law has long played hardball. Most criminal dispositions are by way of a plea bargain, and trials in the federal system are becoming increasingly rare as defendants cannot accept the risk of a long sentence following a guilty verdict after trial. Sentences are long if you are convicted after trial but much shorter if you plead guilty in a plea bargain. The cost of declining a plea bargain can be prison for the rest of your life. If this is the reality for individual defendants, why do corporations merit a much gentler fate?

A few will argue that a stricter application of the criminal law to corporations (and more prosecutions of corporate executives as the result of increased pressure on corporations to identify responsible executives) will harm the economy. This argument can be asserted but not proven. The cases that we have focused on (Volkswagen, the opioid epidemic, the production of dangerous products) have involved long-term, persistent violations of law and significant loss of life (an estimated 400,000 just in the case of opioid overdoses). Arguably, the introduction of some new products or services might be delayed if executives had to fear criminal prosecutions for hiding safety problems (consider here the case of the Boeing 737 MAX). On the other hand, greater caution and prudence might save many lives and seems worth the delay.

Ten Simple Rules for a Complex World:
The Ten Steps That Most Need to Be Taken

Let's be specific. What should be done?

First and foremost, deferred prosecution agreements need to move from the presumptive disposition in the case of a corporate investigation to a more exceptional disposition that had to be truly earned. An investigation that uncovered the involvement of higher-ranking executives or a decision by the corporate defendant to self-report can justify such a disposition, but not simply an investigation that identifies several low-ranking traders manipulating a benchmark or index (although in these cases substantial sentencing leniency in the fine imposed on the corporation could be earned). Ending the promiscuous use of deferred prosecution agreements could be achieved without legislation, simply by amending the Justice Department's own rules (which are set forth in a document now called the *Justice Manual*).

Second, the nonprosecution agreement needs to be abolished (possibly by legislation to make this change truly mandatory but at the least by revision of the *Justice Manual*). Plea bargains need to be subject to at least some judicial oversight.[11]

Third, an element of stigma and shame needs to be reintroduced into the criminal justice system in cases involving the corporation. Today, a deferred prosecution agreement reads like a corporate indenture drafted by skilled corporate lawyers, and no sense of guilt or culpability surrounds it. The better procedure, both for guilty pleas and deferred prosecution agreements, would be to require the corporation's CEO to appear in open court, either to plead guilty on behalf of the corporation (and acknowledge the key facts) or to accept responsibility under the deferred prosecution agreement.

Fourth, when the corporation pleads guilty to a crime, it should not only be fined but also sentenced to a term of probation (probably extending for five years). Presumptively, one probation condition would be the appointment of a corporate monitor, chosen by the court (possibly off a list of nominees submitted by the parties[12]) and with specific duties assigned to the monitor by the court. Certain corporate acts might require the monitor's advance approval.[13] When the corporation instead receives a deferred prosecution agreement, functionally similar probation conditions should be specified in the agreement (with the appointment of a monitor again being presumptively required).

Fifth, a probation condition that needs to be mandated (particularly in the case of banking and financial corporations) is a restriction on incentive compensation. This would serve multiple purposes. First, incentive compensation can be criminogenic. The toxic securitizations that caused a financial collapse in 2008 were packaged by financial executives who were intent on earning extraordinary bonuses. Of course, restrictions on incentive compensation need not be completely prohibitory; the goal should rather be to reduce the level of such incentive compensation at a convicted corporation to well below the industry average.

This restriction also serves additional purposes. Even if a rigorous investigation is conducted, it will not likely uncover or identify all the persons in the organization who had some awareness of the misconduct as it was occurring (e.g., those who knew that dubious payments were being made abroad to obtain business but said nothing). Whether or not these persons are viewed as coconspirators, they were in a position to report the misconduct up the ladder (but did not). They are in effect an outer concentric circle surrounding the inner circle of actual conspirators, and this outer circle would be affected by restrictions on incentive compensation in two ways: first, they would be punished for their inaction, and second, they would be motivated in the future to report up the ladder misconduct of which they become aware (if only to preserve their entitlement to incentive compensation). If they know their own compensation will likely be affected by misconduct committed by others, this has deterrent value, and they are incentivized to alert compliance personnel and superiors to protect their future compensation. At last, they would have a stake in law compliance.

Sixth, although this book has emphasized that the goal of reform is to increase individual accountability (and not simply indict more corporations), it has also stressed that the best way to encourage the corporation to turn on its executives is to increase the threat the corporation faces. This could be done in a variety of ways. For example, if federal prosecutors would indict financial institutions for money laundering, the pressure to cooperate might become irresistible (because a conviction on that grounds could bar them from the banking industry[14]). The likely result would not be a conviction on money laundering but real cooperation from the corporation that entitled it to a deferred prosecution agreement.

Another means to this end would be the equity fine. Its use could conceivably threaten a bank with a loss to its shareholders (through dilution) of perhaps $20 billion in some cases, but the goal would be less to impose such a penalty than to make the bank an "offer it could not refuse": cooperate or else!

Seventh, the optimal negotiating strategy for prosecutors to follow is shown by the prisoner's dilemma. If both the corporate entity and its senior officers were threatened with high penalties, the rational strategy for both is to cooperate against the other. To be sure, the formal logic of the prisoner's dilemma works only when the two sides cannot communicate (which is not the case in the real world). But a reasonable approximation of this circumstance can be achieved if control over the investigation and the negotiations were given to an independent committee of the corporation's board. Once contacted by prosecutors, the board or committee is not in a position to cut a backroom deal with senior executives, and it may prove more risk averse than these executives. The rationale for prosecutors insisting that they must negotiate with a board committee (and not the corporation's senior executives) is that the executives are conflicted. Even if there is no chance that the senior executives were personally involved in the misconduct, their future compensation and job security could still be affected by the outcome of the plea negotiations. This would be a major change from current practices, but it could be established by changes in the *Justice Manual*, instructing prosecutors that they could only negotiate a plea agreement with an independent committee of the board.

Eighth, the most efficient means by which prosecutors can obtain information more economically is to encourage whistle-blowers through bounties. Today, only three agencies—the IRS, the SEC, and the CFTC—do this systematically, and this strategy is working well. Although bounties have a cost, this system funds itself out of the penalties paid by the defendant, thereby sparing the government most out-of-pocket costs. To be sure, payment of bounties reduces the total proceeds that go to the Treasury Department to reduce the federal debt, but in percentage terms this is a trivial cost. Were this bounty system expanded to cover all federal agencies with law enforcement responsibilities, the government might in time be awash in information about corporate misconduct. But to make this system work well, the government cannot passively await future whistle-blowers but rather should solicit the information it most wants through "alerts" and press releases. Inelegant as it may sound, the high costs of acquiring information can best be reduced if the government advertises what it wants.

Ninth, civil enforcement agencies (and particularly the SEC and the CFTC) face two basic problems in litigation that create a mismatch between them and corporate defendants. First, violations come in spurts that produce a crisis. Suddenly, we learn that many companies are making foreign payments that violate the Foreign Corrupt Practices Act; or we learn that many companies have backdated stock options in a manner that cheats their shareholders. This sudden concentration of violations occurs in part because firms copy each other, but it exceeds the agency's capacity to respond and forces the agency to rely on modest and standardized settlements. Second, the personnel at many federal agencies are more expert in settling cases than in trying them. They and defense counsel know the current "going rate" for settling most violations, but these enforcement personnel have had little experience with multiyear litigation in which elaborate discovery is conducted. The answer to both problems is for the agency to retain private counsel that has had such experience and that can fill any sudden gap in the agency's resources.

Such counsel would be compensated on a contingency fee basis that does not strain or break the agency's budget. Indeed, the government can probably negotiate lower contingency fee rates than are currently awarded by federal courts in class actions.

Although the use of privately retained counsel has worked well for those federal agencies that have used it and has been used recurrently at the state level, this proposal will be resisted ferociously by enforcement divisions at those agencies that have not used this procedure. They will see it as a reproach that views them as substandard. Actually, this proposal views private counsel as having a somewhat different expertise, but the more important point is that this is the only feasible means of multiplying prosecutorial resources in the short run. Legislatures are simply not about to double their appropriations for enforcement, but prosecutorial manpower can be substantially increased by the use of private counsel paid on a contingent fee basis. To be sure, critics will contend that this policy sacrifices prosecutorial discretion, but that is nonsense. Control over the litigation would remain at all times in the agency's legal staff (and this proposal would not apply to criminal litigation[15]). Precisely because they are skeptical of this proposal, senior supervisors at these agencies will not allow private counsel to bring frivolous or long-shot cases simply because they can allege high damages.

Tenth, the impact of the "revolving door" on the response to the 2008 crisis is evident and must be addressed. The key figures at the Department of Justice (Attorney General Eric Holder, Criminal Division chief Lanny Breuer) and various Enforcement Division heads at the SEC all came from major law firms specializing in the representation of financial institutions. This is not to argue that they covered up anything or breached ethical duties but only that they were not inclined (at Lehman, AIG, HSBC, and many other cases) to pursue investigations into the executive suite. Here, the best response is not a statute or rule but the mechanisms of political accountability. Presidents who make future such appointments should face political criticism, and that alone could be self-correcting. This less drastic means should at least be tried first before we attempt very difficult legislation.

All these proposals will encounter intense opposition from the business community. Their position has been (and will continue to be) that corporations invest extraordinary amounts in "robust" compliance plans and that should be sufficient to earn them the right to a deferred prosecution agreement when a crime is later detected. The sad irony here is that the payoff to the corporation chiefly comes when the compliance system fails. In fairness, the amounts spent on compliance are substantial, but a corporation can justify such investments simply in terms of the expected sentencing and charging leniency thereby gained. Whether they also prevent criminal conduct is a more debatable issue.[16] Skeptics believe that skilled managers know how to outflank compliance staff when the criminal behavior is truly important to the corporate entity's success.

In truth, little is known about how successful compliance plans are. Preliminary research, however, suggests that corporations know about an extraordinary amount of financial misconduct that is not reported to regulators. Harvard business professor Eugene Soltes has recently found that, at least for a sample of corporations he surveyed, public enforcement statistics significantly underestimated the amount of serious malfeasance within these firms that was known to these firms.[17] On average, he found that there were more than two instances of internally substantiated financial misconduct per week per firm. At a minimum, this shows that firms know a great deal about internal misconduct, but this misconduct is not being self-reported or otherwise addressed as standard compliance plans require. This suggests that these corporations have informal compliance systems that are not subject to or even well integrated with their formal systems (and may be used to outflank it).

That frames a final issue: the business community and recently the Trump administration have argued that the existence of an adequate compliance plan should be the principal determinant of whether a corporation is charged with a crime.[18] After all, they argue, installing a strong compliance plan is the best that the corporation can do, and it should not be punished simply because a good plan failed in one instance. This book responds that there are both good and bad compliance plans, and the proof is in the pudding. If it was a good plan, it will prevent many crimes and spare the corporation enough penalties and damages to justify the corporation's investment in it. Giving the corporation great leniency simply because of a compliance plan unfortunately incentivizes the corporation to erect elaborate Potemkin villages of compliance, and prosecutors are not well equipped, positioned, or motivated to distinguish the serious plans from the shams.[19]

Predictable Opposition

Of course, the business community will resist most of these proposals. So will the bar, as internal investigations have become its newest profit center. But equally intense opposition may come from the enforcement community. They are not used to criticism (particularly from academics, who should in their view serve as cheerleaders). Proposals, such as the use of private counsel to handle big cases, will be seen as a reproach by many at the SEC. Similarly, prosecutors may not want to risk becoming involved in internal investigations or experiment with new sanctions, such as the equity fine. These may make it harder to reach a settlement or a plea bargain. The simple truth is that old dogs do not learn new tricks—except under some compulsion. Bureaucracies persist in the old ways until they are forced to change. That may prove the largest obstacle to real reform.

The Future

Two paths diverge into the future. Conservatives and the business community want more than sentencing leniency; they want the existence of a robust compliance plan alone to entitle a corporation to a presumptive deferred prosecution agreement or a prosecutorial declination. In contrast, liberals are skeptical of deferred prosecution agreements and doubt that much credit should be given to a compliance plan that failed. At a minimum, liberals should want demonstrated results from the internal investigation before it justifies a lenient disposition. Even when the compliance plan and the investigation seem sufficient, liberals might also want to reintroduce a greater degree of shame into our current system for investigating and charging corporations. Today, the process has become humdrum and mechanical, much as if the defendant corporation were simply resolving its tax liability with auditors from the Internal Revenue Service. This also robs the process of deterrent value.

What compromise might work? The basic default rule should be that the corporation must show us who was guilty if it itself wants to escape guilt. It is too much to argue that no one is guilty simply because the compliance plan was adequate. Nonetheless, we could be headed in that direction, as corporate lobbying will aggressively push their position. Corporate law firms also have a strong vested interest in assuring that the internal investigations that they conduct are given great weight by courts. Together, corporations and their counsel constitute a powerful coalition.

In response, the strongest counter-position is that courts need discretion. The best defense against incomplete or self-serving internal investigations is a judicial power to reject them as inadequate. Today, that power does not exist. Thus, Congress should begin by giving courts greater discretion to approve or reject deferred prosecution agreements, and courts should be prepared to insist that prosecutors justify their decisions to grant such dispositions in open court. In such an environment, executive heads would roll more frequently as the result of internal investigations.

To sum up, a leniency-driven model today increasingly dominates our approach to dealing with corporate misconduct. In actual practice, this is a day-versus-night reversal of the old rule of respondeat superior with regard to corporate criminal liability. Congress never authorized this change; instead, many, including the bar and academics, have quietly ushered in this transition, in the belief that it encourages settlements.[20] That it does, but the cost to society is both a loss in accountability (because the corporate entity is not sufficiently threatened to cooperate) and a serious injury to the ideal of legal equality (because higher-ups escape justice). Sadly, a system of all carrots and no sticks will not deter corporate misconduct (although it will keep the bar gainfully employed).

We are not at this all-carrots-no-sticks point yet, but unless the direction is reversed, we are headed there.

Notes

Chapter 1

1. According to a *New York Times*/CBS Poll taken in 2013, 79 percent of the American public believes that more "bankers and employees of financial institutions [should have been prosecuted] for their role in the financial crisis of 2008." See *New York Times*, September 25, 2013, http://www.nytimes.com/interactive/2013/09/26/us /politics/26poll-results.html. Other polls show similar, if slightly lower, public numbers. This does not prove the reality of underenforcement, but it certainly shows the perception.

2. Following Enron's collapse in 2001, two of its former CEOs, Kenneth Lay and Jeffrey Skilling, were convicted on multiple counts of fraud (and acquitted on other counts). Kenneth Lay died before his sentencing, but Skilling was sentenced to over twenty-four years (later reduced by ten years when the Supreme Court overturned his conviction on some but not all counts). Skilling was released from prison in 2019. When WorldCom failed in 2002, Bernie Ebbers, its CEO, was convicted and sentenced to twenty-five years. He would become parole eligible only in 2028, but in December 2020, he was released after the Bureau of Prisons determined that he was terminally ill. He died in early 2020. Numerous other executives were also prosecuted but none at major banks. Also, because Enron and WorldCom were already bankrupt, there could be no concern about the dangers of driving them into insolvency through criminal prosecutions. Nor did these two firms have a powerful champion in Washington (as banks did in the Federal Reserve Board, which, particularly after Lehman's failure, naturally feared a systemic risk crisis if another major bank became insolvent).

3. The most prominent of these defendants was Charles Keating, the CEO of Lincoln Savings and Loan Corp. The estimate of over 1,000 convictions (and over 30,000 criminal referrals) comes from William Black, a law professor and former bank regulator. See Joshua Holland, "Hundreds of Wall Street Execs. Went to Prison during Last Fraud-Fueled Bank Crisis," September, 17, 2013, https://billmoyers.com /2013/09/17. A more specific estimate is that 839 individuals were convicted in connection with the savings and loan crisis. See Jesse Eisinger, "Why Only One Top Banker Went to Jail for the Financial Crisis," *New York Times Magazine*, April 20, 2014, https://www.nytimes.com/2014/05/04.

4. A detailed accounting follows in chapter 2. At the lowest level of mortgage loan applications, there were over one thousand prosecutions of borrowers who were

alleged to have inflated their assets or income. See Daniel Richman, "Corporate Head Hunting," *Harvard Law and Policy Review* 8 (2014): 265, 267n13. The chief executives of some medium-sized banks and brokerage firms were prosecuted after their institutions failed, but none of these was a Wall Street firm.

5. Although senior officials at the Justice Department have always maintained that they would have brought any promising case they uncovered, they have also acknowledged that they discussed and considered the impact on the economy of criminal prosecutions of banks. Lanny Breuer, chief of the Criminal Division at the Department of Justice during this period, has acknowledged that he discussed with regulators the "economic effect" of bringing a case. See Jason Breslow, "Lanny Breuer: Why Cases Have Not Gone Criminal," *PBS Frontline*, June 22, 2013. As discussed later, foreign banking regulators and government officials also lobbied the Justice Department. See chapter 2.

6. For a strong statement of this view, see Richard A. Epstein, "The Deferred Prosecution Racket," *Wall Street Journal*, November 28, 2006 (describing these prosecutions as extortion, in part because no individual was identified who could have been prosecuted).

7. The film *Dark Waters* follows the efforts of Robert Bilott, a tenacious attorney, who undertook a lengthy legal battle against DuPont with respect to the alleged release of a toxic chemical, PFOA, into the water supply of several Ohio and West Virginia counties. See Nathaniel Rich, "The Lawyer Who Became DuPont's Worst Nightmare," *New York Times Magazine*, January 6, 2016, at pp. 39–40. The movie was based on this article. Although a settlement with DuPont was ultimately reached, its terms were sealed, and hence true accountability was not achieved. That, of course, is typical of private enforcement, where victim compensation is the primary goal. Only public enforcement can generally give us transparency and true accountability.

8. As discussed in chapter 2, the earlier savings and loan crisis prosecutions were generally characterized by self-dealing and severe conflict of interests, which further supports this distinction.

9. Between 1992 and 1995, white collar criminal cases accounted for 19 percent of all federal criminal cases, but this rate fell to just under 9.9 percent between 2012 and 2015. See Jesse Eisinger, *The Chickenshit Club: Why the Justice Department Fails to Prosecute Executives* (New York: Simon & Schuster, 2017), xviii. The Financial Crisis Inquiry Report, prepared at the direction of Congress, also found that the FBI reassigned agents away from white collar crime after 9/11. See FIN. CRISIS INQUIRY COMM'N, FINANCIAL CRISIS INQUIRY REPORT (2011), 162–63.

10. Chapter 2 will discuss DPAs in more detail. Of course, the authoritative work is Brandon Garrett, *Too Big to Jail: How Prosecutors Compromise with Corporations* (Cambridge, MA: The Belknap Press of Harvard University Press, 2014); see also Cindy R. Alexander and Mark A. Cohen, "The Evolution of Corporate Criminal Settlements: An Empirical Perspective on Non-Prosecution, Deferred Prosecution, and Plea Agreements," *American Criminal Law Review* 52 (2015): 537.

11. Arthur Andersen LLP was one of the United States' largest and oldest accounting firms. Once it was indicted, its clients backed away and it failed (because it had audited both Enron and WorldCom—an extraordinarily unlucky or symptomatic collection of clients). Yet its conviction was reversed unanimously by the Supreme

Court in 2005 because the Court, it said, had given an incorrect charge to the jury. See Arthur Andersen, LLP v. United States, 544 U.S. 696 (2005). But by that point, Andersen was insolvent and had been liquidated. As a result, thousands of Arthur Andersen employees were laid off and its pensioners lost their pension benefits, while the Andersen partners themselves largely took their clients to other Big Four firms—and thus suffered only minor losses. This outcome could hardly have been more embarrassing for the Justice Department.

12. For a brief comparison of the investments made by Western nations, see John C. Coffee Jr., "Law and the Market: The Impact of Enforcement," *University of Pennsylvania Law Review* 156 (2007): 229.

13. See chapter 2 infra.

14. The full quotation in which Attorney General Eric Holder expressed a fear that some banks had become "too big to fail" and thus could not be prudently prosecuted is set forth in chapter 2.

15. The fullest statement of this position is in United States v. Fokker Services, 818 F.3d 733 (D.C. Cir. 2016), which is discussed infra in chapter 2.

16. The Yates Memorandum (and its modest impact) are discussed infra in chapter 2.

17. These data will be discussed in chapter 6 infra, but for the fullest recent study of the aggregate penalties imposed on corporations, see Committee on Capital Markets Regulation, *Rationalizing Enforcement in the U.S. Financial System* (Cambridge, MA, June 2018).

18. For the leading decision curbing a federal district judge who refused to accept what he saw as a very weak deferred prosecution agreement, see United States v. Fokker Services, B.V., 818 F.3d 733 (D.C. Cir. 2015). Even earlier, the SEC successfully overturned a much publicized decision that found its settlement with a major bank to be shamefully inadequate. The SEC has long used a "neither admit nor deny" settlement procedure under which (unlike a DPA) the defendant does not have to concede or admit the accuracy of the agency's allegations. United States District Judge Jed Rakoff had been dubious of this procedure and the lack of transparency that it causes. When he refused to approve an SEC settlement with Citigroup, finding that he was unable to conclude that the "neither admit nor deny" settlement was "fair, reasonable, adequate and in the public interest," the SEC sought mandamus, and the Second Circuit reversed Judge Rakoff, finding that he had abused his discretion. See SEC v. Citigroup Global Mkts., 752 F.3d 285 (2d Cir. 2014). The decision effectively implied that a court could not inquire into the merits of an SEC settlement and was required (absent extraordinary reasons) to grant the requested injunction. These cases are further discussed in chapter 2.

19. There is a constitutional dimension to this issue of prosecutorial discretion that may preclude some legislative reforms. To the extent that prosecutorial discretion is an aspect of the executive's power, separation of powers issues surface, and Congress may be restricted in its ability to curb executive power. These issues are explored infra in chapter 3.

20. These issues are discussed infra in chapter 6.

21. Under Garrity v. New Jersey, 385 U.S. 493 (6967), the government may not require its employees to waive the Fifth Amendment privilege under the threat of being

fired. Statements so obtained under such a threat are inadmissible in court. This rule also applies when the conduct of a private employer in obtaining statements from its employee are "fairly attributable to the government." This raises the issue of whether statements obtained in an internal investigation by a private employer are also inadmissible if the state has pressured the employer to obtain the statements and implied that it should use a threat of dismissal. In United States v. Connolly, 2019 U.S. Dist. LEXIS 76233 (S.D.N.Y. May 2, 2019), a district court recently found that an internal investigation conducted by Deutsche Bank was sufficiently influenced by the Justice Department as to make the statements inadmissible. The implications of this case are discussed infra in chapter 10.

22. See chapter 5.

23. Senator Elizabeth Warren has proposed the "Corporate Executive Accountability Act," which would apply to executives of corporations with more than $1 billion in annual revenues who negligently permit or fail to prevent:

(1) Any criminal violation of federal or state law for which their corporation was found guilty, plead guilty, or entered into a deferred prosecution agreement;

(2) Any civil violation for which their corporation was found liable or entered into a settlement with state or federal regulation if the violation affects the health, safety, finances, or personal data of 1% of the American population or 1% of the population of any state; or

(3) Any criminal or civil violation for which their corporation is liable if it was the second civil or criminal violation for the corporation.

Punishment would be up to one year in jail for such a negligent violation (and up to five years for a willful violation). This proposed bill is discussed infra in chapter 8.

Chapter 2

1. For an authoritative overview, commissioned by Congress, see FIN. CRISIS INQUIRY COMM'N, FINANCIAL CRISIS INQUIRY REPORT (2011). This report was approved by six out of the ten members of the commission, who were Democrats, and rejected by the four members who were Republicans. This is symptomatic; nothing about the crash and its causes is uncontested.

2. 544 U.S. 696 (2005).

3. Earlier scandals, involving Waste Management, Boston Chicken, Sunbeam, and Qwest, had already damaged Andersen's reputation. Jesse Eisinger opines that, although all the major accounting firms suffered from "problem clients, the list that Andersen compiled stood out for its length and variety." Jesse Eisinger, *The Chickenshit Club: Why the Justice Department Fails to Prosecute Executives* (New York: Simon & Schuster, 2017), 36. One possibility is that Andersen took on high-risk representations because it received very lucrative consulting fees from its audit clients, arguably as a de facto bribe. Consulting income accounted for a majority of Andersen's revenues, and this could have made it more willing to wink at fraud by Enron's and WorldCom's managements. But this is speculative, and no conclusions on this score are here reached.

4. See Eisinger, *Chickenshit Club*, 36–37.

5. 544 U.S. at 608.

6. Id. at 699.

7. This article appeared on August 28, 2001 and the SEC opened an investigation that day. Id.

8. See Arthur Andersen LLP v. United States, 544 U.S. 696 at 699.

9. Id. at 700 and 701.

10. Id. at 701.

11. The jury deliberated for seven days and then declared it was deadlocked. Id. at 702. The Court then delivered what is commonly called a "dynamite charge" but technically known as an *Allen charge*. See Allen v. United States, 164 U.S. 492 (1896) (upholding jury charge that advises jurors to listen to their colleagues and seek consensus). Often, this charge effectively tells the jury that they are unlikely to have a mistrial declared and need to agree in order to go home. Three days after this charge, the jury returned its verdict of guilty. All this suggests that the case struck the jury as factually complex, and thus the issue of intent may have been important to their decision.

12. See Arthur Andersen LLP v. United States, 374 F.3d 281 (5th Cir. 2004) (also finding that the jury need not find any "consciousness of wrongdoing" in order to convict).

13. See 544 U.S. 696 at 702n7 (citing conflict over section 1512[b] between the Eleventh and Third Circuits). This conflict had existed since at least 1998, suggesting that the Court had not previously seen it as an urgent matter.

14. See 544 U.S. at 704–6.

15. Id. at 706.

16. Id. at 706–7. The standard pattern instruction in the Fifth Circuit in an obstruction of justice case told the jury that the term *corruptly* meant "knowingly and dishonestly with the specific intent to subvert or undermine the integrity" of an "official proceeding." The government asked the court to exclude "dishonestly" and add the term *impede* to the phrase "subvert or undermine." The trial court agreed, and this may have been the prosecution's fatal mistake; it went a bridge too far.

17. Mens rea (Latin for "guilty mind") refers to the necessary mental element in a crime. Under Anglo-American criminal law, most crimes require both conduct (called the *actus reus* in law school classrooms) and a mental element (or mens rea). Although it is possible for the legislature to criminalize conduct and provide that no mental element need be shown, courts historically have resisted such an interpretation—unless the legislature makes its intent very clear. Such "strict liability" crimes generally carry lesser penalties, as discussed later in chapter 8. In *Andersen*, the Supreme Court is not stating that all crimes require "consciousness of wrongdoing" but that crimes that expressly require that the individual have acted both "knowingly and corruptly" should be so interpreted.

18. 544 U.S. at 703–4.

19. See Brandon Garrett, *Too Big to Jail: How Prosecutors Compromise with Corporations* (Cambridge, MA: The Belknap Press of Harvard University Press, 2014), 86.

20. Ibid., 147.

21. For such an assessment, see Gabriel Markoff, "Arthur Andersen and the Myth of the Death Penalty: Corporate Criminal Convictions in the Twenty-First Century,"

University of Pennsylvania Journal of Business Law 13 (2013): 797. Markoff finds that, between 2001 and 2010, no publicly traded corporation went out of business because of its conviction.

22. Drexel Burnham pleaded guilty to six counts of stock parking and stock manipulation in December 1988 and survived (barely) until February 1990 when it filed for bankruptcy. Discredited by its conviction and surrounded by other firms bearing grudges toward it, it could not obtain sufficient financing to survive. Its conviction seems at least the proximate cause of its collapse.

23. Two major bank failures, each preceded by a run by depositors, intensified the 2008 crash. The first was Indy Mac, which is a contraction for Independent National Mortgage Corp. It was a very large mortgage originator before it failed and was seized by the FDIC in July 2008. See Damon Paletta and David Enrich, "Crisis Deepens as Big Bank Fails," *Wall Street Journal*, July 12, 2008. Washington Mutual was an even larger failure (and the largest by a bank in U.S. financial history) when the Office of Thrift Supervision seized it in September 2008. See Eric Dash and Andrew Sorkin, "Government Seizes WaMu and Sells Some Assets," *New York Times*, September 26, 2008, A1. Both failures were preceded by rumor-fueled runs by depositors.

24. For example, Jesse Eisinger dismisses this problem as unworthy of serious attention, writing that "the law . . . cannot condone crimes simply because there are collateral victims." Eisinger, *Chickenshit Club*, 55. At the push-comes-to-shove moment, that may be correct, but it does not mean that intelligent engineering to minimize this problem of externalities should not be considered. We will return to this theme in chapter 5.

25. Even ex-prosecutors, such as Mary Jo White, the former U.S. attorney in the Southern District of New York and the future SEC chair, agreed, stating in 2005, "The Justice Department came under a lot of criticism for indicting Arthur Andersen and putting it out of business. That was justified criticism." See Eisinger, *Chickenshit Club*, 56.

26. The first DPA involving a financial firm was in 1992 in a case involving Salomon Brothers, which, if it had been convicted of a felony, might have been disqualified from underwriting U.S. governmental bonds (to the disadvantage of both Salomon and the U.S. Treasury). Brandon Garrett finds a dozen such DPA agreements in the 1990s. Garrett, *Too Big to Jail*, 55. The first formalization of the policy for DPAs was drafted under then Deputy Attorney General Eric Holder in 1999. But the rules for granting DPAs were not formally specified in detail until the Thompson Memorandum was issued in 2003 (prior to the court's decision in *Andersen*). Ibid., 56.

27. For a similar (but earlier) Supreme Court decision, see United States v. Aguilar, 515 U.S. 593, 600 (1995).

28. For a contemporary account of the problems at these two funds, see Kate Kelly, Serena Ng, and David Reilly, "Two Big Funds at Bear Stearns Face Shutdown," *Wall Street Journal*, June 20, 2007, A1.

29. For a review of Bear Stearns's final days, see Matthew Goldstein and David Henry, "Bear Stearns Bet Wrong," *Business Week*, October 22, 2007, at 50. In its traditional manner (which prefers a subsidized merger to a liquidation), the Federal Reserve induced a solvent bank (JPMorgan Chase) to acquire Bear Stearns by making attractive financing available (which averted the need for a governmental

bailout). Had this same technique been used with Lehman (and an unsuccessful attempt was made to induce Barclays to acquire Lehman), much of the damage caused by Lehman's failure might have been averted.

30. For the indictment, see United States v. Cioffi, No. CR - 08-415 (E.D.N.Y. June 18, 2008). For the SEC's complaint, see SEC v. Cioffi and Tannin, C.A. 08-2457 (FB) (E.D.N.Y. June 19, 2008), http://www.sec.gov/litigation/complaint/2008/comp 20625. pdf. See also, SEC v. Cioffi, 2008 U.S. Dist. Westlaw 4693320 (E.D.N.Y. October 23, 2008).

31. Rumors that Bear Stearns was insolvent led to a silent run on Bear Stearns, which in turn caused the Federal Reserve to induce a sale of Bear Stearns to JPMorgan Chase. Such hastily arranged sales or mergers (supported by Federal Reserve loans to the acquirer) were the standard policy of bank regulators, who did not want to see a bankruptcy filing. See Kate Kelly, "The Fall of Bear Stearns: Fears, Rumors Touched Off Fatal Run on Bear Stearns," *Wall Street Journal*, May 18, 2008, A1.

32. For a review of the indictment against Cioffi and Tannin, see Andrew J. Ceresney, Gordon Eng, and Sean R. Nuttall, "Regulatory Investigation and the Credit Crisis: The Search for Villains," *American Criminal Law Review* 46 (Spring 2009): 225.

33. Under section 32(a) ("Penalties") of the Securities Exchange Act, a defendant must be shown to have "willfully and knowingly" made, or caused to be made, a false statement in any report or document filed with the SEC in order to have criminal liability. The federal wire fraud statute also requires the prosecution to show a "specific intent" to defraud.

34. See indictment in United States v. Cioffi and Tannin at 41 (quoted in Ceresney, Eng, and Nuttall, "Regulatory Investigation," 252).

35. Ceresney, Eng, and Nuttall, "Regulatory Investigation," 252 (citing indictment at p. 45).

36. Ibid. (citing indictment at p. 45).

37. See SEC Litigation Release No. 20625 (June 19, 2008) (summarizing SEC's allegations). For a capsule summary of the allegations, see Lori Martin, David Zetlin-Jones, and Kimberly Chedhardy, *Investment Funds, Mutual Funds and Hedge Funds: Enforcement and Trends*, SRO28 ALI-ABA 755 (ALI-ABA Committee on Continuing Professional Education, Philadelphia, Pennsylvania, 2016).

38. Cioffi was acquitted by the jury on this charge as well.

39. See Eisinger, *Chickenshit Club*, 181.

40. See Zachary Kouwe, "Bear Stearns Managers Acquitted of Fraud Charges," *New York Times*, DealBook, November 10, 2009.

41. See Nancy R. Mansfield, Joan T. A. Gabel, Kathleen McCullough, and Stephen G. Fier, "The Shocking Impact of Corporate Scandals on Directors' and Officers' Liability," *University of Miami Business Law Review* 20 (2012): 211, 242.

42. See Eisinger, *Chickenshit Club*, 181.

43. Lehman, being bankrupt, could not be sued, but securities class actions were brought against Lehman Brothers' directors-and-officers insurer and various underwriters. These two actions resulted in total settlements of $516 million, which were approved by Southern District of New York Judge Lewis Kaplan in 2012.

Lehman's auditor, Ernst & Young, also entered into a $90 million class action settlement, and UBS Financial Services settled claims against it relating to Lehman products for $120 million in 2013. These settlements (totaling over $700 million) were well below the aggregate class action settlements in Enron and WorldCom, but so were the equity and debt offerings engaged in by Lehman. See In re Lehman Brothers Sec. and ERISA Litig., 2012 U.S. Dist. LEXIS 74394 (S.D.N.Y. May 24, 2012) (approving settlements). Particularly because the SEC is usually willing to enter into a "neither admit nor deny" settlement under which defendants concede nothing, it seems unlikely that defendants would have fought the SEC's action (if it had sued), given that they settled with the private plaintiffs (who had to prove considerably more to recover). Thus, the SEC's total inaction supports the political constraint or the logistical overload story, more than a lack of fraud explanation.

44. In particular, the failure of Bernard Madoff, which was roughly three months after Lehman's collapse, confronted the SEC with its largest crisis (and subjected it to the most criticism) in its history.

45. See Eisinger, *Chickenshit Club*, 240–41.

46. Ibid., 241.

47. Ibid.

48. Ibid.

49. Ibid.

50. Ibid., 242.

51. Ibid.

52. For a concise explanation of Repo 105 transactions, see Jacob Goldstein, "Repo 105: Lehman's 'Accounting Gimmick' Explained," NPR, Planet Money, March 12, 2010.

53. See Report of Anton R. Valukas, Examiner in In re: Lehman Brothers Holdings, Inc., No. 08-13555 (JMP) (United States Bankruptcy Court, Southern District of New York) (March 11, 2016) at 18 to 19.

54. Id. at 7.

55. Id. at 16.

56. Id. at 16–17.

57. Id. at 18.

58. Id. at 18–19.

59. Lehman had defined "materiality" for its own internal reporting purposes to include any change that moved "net leverage" by more than 0.1 percent; these transactions moved these ratios by whole percentage points. See Id. at 19.

60. Id. at 20.

61. Id. at 9.

62. Id. at 17.

63. See Eisinger, *Chickenshit Club*, 240.

64. Ibid., 237.

65. Strikingly, no criminal prosecutor ever interviewed Lehman's last CFO, Ian Lowitt. Ibid., 243.

66. Ibid., 238. Eisinger points to Bonnie Jonas as the only such person spending significant time on the case in 2009, and he describes her as diligent and steadfast.

67. Ibid., 238.

68. Rule 10b-5 requires proof only of "extreme recklessness"; moreover, the SEC can generally sue under § 17(a) of the Securities Act of 1933, which is generally satisfied by proof of negligence and does not require a showing of scienter. The point then is that the SEC has a distinct litigation advantage over the private plaintiff.

69. Robert Khuzami and George Canellos were at the relevant times director or codirector of the SEC's Enforcement Division. After four years of service, Khuzami left the SEC to join Kirkland & Ellis in January 2013 (and from there he moved on to become general counsel of Deutsche Bank). After four and a half years at the SEC, Canellos returned to Milbank Tweed (where he had spent most of his career) in March 2014. This is the standard pattern of "revolving door" service in a high position at an agency and then a shift to the other side of the aisle. In fairness, Khuzami was widely regarded as an excellent lawyer, both at the SEC and Justice. For a brief review, see Ben Protess, "Khuzami, S.E.C. Enforcement Chief Who Reinvigorated Unit, to Step Down," *New York Times*, DealBook, January 9, 2013.

70. See Eisinger, *Chickenshit Club*, 292 (noting that "multiple criminal referrals" were made by the FCIC and "all withered away without any significant attention paid to them at all").

71. George Osborne, the United Kingdom's chancellor of the exchequer, made exactly this threat of a global meltdown in the case of HSBC. See text and note infra at note 77. The governor of the Bank of France similarly lobbied hard on behalf of BNP Paribas, and Deutsche Bank brought German officials into the negotiations regarding it. See Jessica Silver-Greenberg and Ben Protess, "BNP Paribas Pinned Hope on Legal Memo, in Vain," *New York Times*, DealBook, June 3, 2014; William Horobin, "France Claims Victory in Paribas Case," *Wall Street Journal*, June 1, 2016.

72. Breuer's testimony was before the Senate Judiciary Committee following the highly controversial HSBC settlement. See Hearings before S. Comm. on the Judiciary, 113th Congress (March 6, 2013), http://www.judiciary.Senate.gov. /meetings/oversight-of-the-U.S.-department-of-justice-2013-03-06. He did not say that he would be swayed by such lobbying but only that predictions of a global disaster had to be considered.

73. Eisinger, *Chickenshit Club*, 238.

74. See Mark Hansen, "Law Firms: Lehman Paid Jenner $53.5M for Report on Collapse," *ABA Journal*, May 21, 2010, http://abajournal.com/news/article/Law -firms:-Lehman-paid-Jenner-$3.5M-for-Report-on-Collapse.

75. Eisinger, *Chickenshit Club*, 233.

76. Ibid., 283.

77. See Christopher M. Matthews, "Justice Department Overruled Recommendation to Pursue Charges against HSBC, Report Says," *Wall Street Journal*, July 11, 2016.

78. See Rupert Neate, "HSBC Escaped U.S. Money-Laundering Charges after Osbourne's Intervention," *Guardian* (U.S.), July 11, 2016.

79. See Aruna Viswanatha and Brett Wolf, "HSBC to Pay $1.9 Billion U.S. Fine for Money-Laundering Case" Reuters, December 11, 2012.

80. See Hearings before S. Comm. on the Judiciary, 113th Congress (March 6, 2013), http://www.judiciary.Senate.gov./meetings/oversight-of-the-U.S.-department-of -justice-2013-03-06.

81. Danielle Douglas, "Holder Concerned Megabanks Too Big to Jail," *Washington Post*, March 6, 2013 (noting that some senators described themselves as "shocked" by this statement).

82. Ibid. (describing Senate report and impact).

83. Jed Rakoff, "The Financial Crisis: Why Have No High-Level Executives Been Prosecuted?," *New York Review of Books*, January 9, 2014.

84. Even before this *New York Review* article, Rakoff had become a heroic symbol to liberal journalists because he had pointed out the weakness in SEC civil settlements that did not even explain what the defendant was alleged to have done or which employees were responsible (and for what). See text and notes infra in this chapter at notes 98 to 103. In 2011, even the readers of *Rolling Stone* learned who Judge Rakoff was. See Matt Taibbi, "Finally, a Judge Stands Up to Wall Street," *Rolling Stone*, November 10, 2011 (calling him a "legal hero of our time").

85. Rakoff, "Financial Crisis."

86. Ibid.

87. Ibid.

88. Ibid.

89. Ibid.

90. Ibid.

91. Ibid.

92. See Robert J. Shiller, *Irrational Exuberance*, 2nd ed. (Princeton University Press, 2009), 76–80.

93. See Daniel Richman, "Corporate Headhunting," *Harvard Law and Policy Review* 8 (2014): 265, 276. I should point out here that Judge Rakoff, Professor Richman, and I all teach at Columbia Law School.

94. Ibid.

95. Ibid.

96. Ibid.

97. For an overview of this much debated topic, see Jeffrey Grogger, "Certainty vs. Severity of Punishment," *Economic Inquiry* 29 (1998): 297, 307 (finding studies suggest that to certainty of punishment has greater deterrent impact than severity of punishment).

98. See SEC v. Bank of America Corp., 653 F. Supp. 2d 507 (S.D.N.Y. 2009). The revised settlement was approved by Judge Rakoff (holding his nose) at 2010 U.S. Dist. LEXIS 15460 (S.D.N.Y. 20120).

99. See SEC v. Citigroup Global Mkts. Inc., 827 F. Supp. 2d 328 (S.D.N.Y. 2011).

100. Id. at 329.

101. The SEC sued Brian Stoker, charging him with securities fraud. The complaint against the defendant Stoker was also based on section 17(a) of the Securities Act of 1933 and thus only had to allege negligence (even though the allegations seemed to

speak in the language of scienter). Judge Rakoff upheld the complaint and dismissed the defendant's motion for summary judgment. See SEC v. Stoker, 873 F. Supp. 2d 605 (S.D.N.Y. 2010). The jury acquitted Stoker but, amazingly, wrote a note to the SEC asking it to bring more and stronger cases.

102. Under a legal doctrine, known as *offensive collateral estoppel*, a plaintiff can ask a court to accept the defendant's admission in another case as binding on it in the instant case. See Parklane Hosiery Co. v. Shore, 439 U.S. 322 (1979).

103. 827 F. Supp. 2d at 335.

104. See SEC v. Citigroup Global Mkts., 752 F.3d 285 (2d Cir. 2014).

105. United States v. Fokker Services B.V., 79 F. Supp. 3d 160, 167 (D.D.C. 2015).

106. Id. Fokker Services had turned itself in for possibly violating sanction restrictions that prohibited the shipping of U.S.-origin goods to certain foreign countries (Iran and Burma were chiefly involved). This was not the "crime of the century," and no investigation was pending when the defendant notified the Justice Department and sought a settlement.

107. See United States v. Fokker Services, B.V., 818 F.3d 733 (D.C. Circ. 2015).

108. As the DC Circuit said in Fokker, 818 F.3d at 741: "The Executive's primacy in criminal charging decisions is long settled. That authority stems from the Constitution's delegation of 'take Care' duties, U.S. Court. Art. II, §3, and the pardon power, id. §2, to the Executive Branch. See United States v. Armstrong, 517 U.S. 456, 464 (1996)."

109. United States v. HSBC Bank USA, N.A., 863 F.3d 125 (2nd Cir. 2017).

110. Id. at 135–38 (holding that the district court had "no freestanding supervisory power to monitor the implementation of a DPA").

111. Id. at 142–45. In her concurrence, Circuit Judge Pooler suggested that Congress needed to establish standards and to authorize judicial review for compliance with these standards.

112. See Memorandum from Sally Quillian Yates, Deputy Attorney General to Assistant Attorney Generals and U.S. Attorneys (Washington, DC, September 9, 2015) (hereinafter, the Yates Memorandum). The memorandum was entitled "Individual Accountability for Corporate Wrongdoing." Like the Holder Memorandum and the Thompson Memorandum before it, it purported to explain and interpret Justice Department policy, and it produced follow-on changes in the *Justice Manual*. See Matt Apuzzo and Ben Protess, "Justice Department Sets Sights on Wall Street Executives," *New York Times*, September 9, 2015.

113. See Yates Memorandum, 3.

114. For examples of the criticism that the Yates Memorandum attracted, see Michael P. Kelly and Ruth E. Mandelbaum, "Are the Yates Memorandum and the Federal Judiciary's Concerns about Over-Criminalization Destined to Collide?," *American Criminal Law Review* 54 (2016): 899, 900–902 (protesting conflict that it created between the corporation and its employees); Sharon Oded, "Coughing Up Executives or Rolling the Dice? Individual Accountability for Corporate Corruption," *Yale Law and Policy Review* 35 (2016): 49 (arguing that all-or-nothing policy on disclosure of misconduct would produce less corporate cooperation with prosecutors).

115. See chapter 3.

116. A number of bank and brokerage executives did go to prison, but they did not qualify as "Wall Street" executives. For example, Lee Farkas was the CEO and controlling shareholder of Taylor, Bean and Whitaker, which he grew in a decade from a tiny firm to a "top-ten" player in wholesale mortgage lending. He was convicted in federal court in 2011 on fourteen counts of fraud and sentenced to thirty years in prison. Unlike others caught in the crisis, he was accused of misappropriating over $38 million from Taylor, Bean and Whitaker, which failed as a result and also took Colonial Bank (in which Taylor, Bean and Whitaker had acquired a controlling share) with it into bankruptcy. Unlike a Lehman, this was a case of self-dealing. For a brief overview, see Gretchen Morgenson, "Fair Game: Get Ready, Get Set, Point Fingers," *New York Times*, December 12, 2009. For those who think all sentences after the crash were light, Farkas's scheduled release date is in 2037.

The only executive of a Wall Street firm to be convicted because of conduct during the 2008 crash appears to be Kareem Serageldin, who pled guilty to hiding trading losses on the books of his employer, Credit Suisse. He was sentenced to thirty months, but he was far from a senior bank officer. See Jesse Eisinger, "Why Only One Top Banker Went to Jail for the Financial Crisis," *New York Times Magazine*, April 20, 2011.

117. See Brandon L. Garrett, "The Corporate Criminal as Scapegoat," *Virginia Law Review* 101 (2015): 1789, 1802.

118. The Justice Department prosecuted 237 companies in 2014. This was 29 percent below the number they prosecuted in 2004 (and most of these were small, privately held companies). See Eisinger, *Chickenshit Club*, xix (citing data collected by Brandon Garrett and others).

119. See Garrett, "Corporate Criminal as Scapegoat," 1802.

120. Ibid.

Chapter 3

1. See Christina Rogers and Mike Spector, "Judge Slaps VW with $2.8 Billion Criminal Fine in Emissions Fraud," *Wall Street Journal*, April 21, 2017. Some of the background information about this scandal comes from "Volkswagen Emissions Scandal," Wikipedia, last revised January 3, 2020, https://en.wikipedia.org/wiki/Volkswagen_emissions_scandal.

2. See Jack Ewing and Jad Mouawad, "Directors Say Volkswagen Delayed Informing Them of Trickery," *New York Times*, October 23, 2015; Timothy Gardner, Paul Lienert, and David Morgan, "After Year of Stonewalling, VW Stunned U.S. Regulators with Confession," Reuters, September 24, 2015.

3. James Robert Liang, an engineer at Volkswagen's testing facility in Oxnard, California, was indicted and cooperated, explaining that the installation of the defeat device followed the recognition by Volkswagen that it could not satisfy U.S. (particularly California) air quality standards. Also indicted was Oliver Schmidt, the former head of Volkswagen's U.S. emissions compliance program. If guilty of nothing else, Schmidt was clearly guilty of the crime of aggravated stupidity, as he left Germany for a vacation in Miami after the investigation had begun (and was thus arrested in the United States).

4. For a full discussion of this case, see "The GM Ignition Switch Recall: Why Did It Take So Long?," Hearing before the Subcommittee on Oversight and Investigations

of the Committee on Energy and Commerce, House of Representatives, 113th Congress, Second Session (April 1, 2014). For another overview, see "General Motors Ignition Switch Recalls," Wikipedia, last revised December 19, 2019, https://en.wikipedia.org /wiki/General_Motors_ignition_switch_recalls. See also Jeff Bennett, "G.M. to Recall 8.45 Million More Vehicles in North America," *Wall Street Journal*, June 30, 2014; Lauren Pollock, "What You Need to Know about the GM Recalls," *Wall Street Journal*, April 1, 2014.

5. See James R. Healey and Fred Meier, "GM Ignorance Left 'Switch from Hell' Unfixed," *USA Today*, June 5, 2014.

6. See U.S. Attorney's Office, Southern District of New York "Manhattan U.S. Attorney Announces Criminal Charges against General Motors and Deferred Prosecution Agreement with $900 Million Forfeiture," press release no. 15-244, September 17, 2015, https://www.justice.gov/usao-sdny/pr/manhattan-us-attorney -announces-criminal-charges-against-general-motors-and-deferred.

7. All pleaded guilty to the regulatory crime of *misbranding*, which makes it a crime to mislabel a drug, fraudulently promote it, or market it for an unapproved use. The three executives included Purdue's president, its top lawyer, and its former medical director. See Barry Meier, "In Guilty Plea, OxyContin Maker to Pay $600 Million," *New York Times*, May 10, 2007, https://www.nytimes.com/2007/05/10/business /11drug-web.html/module-inline.

8. See Gabrielle Emanual and Katie Thomas, "Top Executives of Insys, an Opioid Company, Are Found Guilty of Racketeering," *New York Times*, May 2, 2019, https://www.nytimes.com/2019/05/02/health/insys-trial-verdict-kapoor.html ?module=inline. John Kapoor, once a billionaire based on his ownership of Insys Therapeutics, received a five-and-one-half-year sentence in January 2020; Mr. Kapoor was then seventy-six years old. See Katie Thomas, "Insys Founder Faces Prison For His Role in Opioid Case," *New York Times*, January 24, 2020, B-4. In addition, Michael Babich, former chief executive of the company, had earlier pleaded guilty to conspiracy and mail fraud charges and cooperated with the prosecution pursuant to a plea bargain. The indictment essentially alleged a conspiracy, directed by Kapoor, to bribe doctors to prescribe their high-potency opioid, Subsys.

9. The four officer-defendants were originally indicted on December 6, 2016 (after the Yates Memorandum); on October 24, 2017, a superseding indictment added John N. Kapoor, the firm's founder, as a defendant. In January 2019, three weeks before the start of the trial of the other defendants, the former Insys CEO Michael L. Babich pleaded guilty to conspiracy and mail fraud charges and testified against the other defendants. Subsys is a fentanyl-based pain medication.

10. See William K. Rashbaum, "For First Time, Pharmaceutical Distributor Faces Federal Criminal Charges over Opioid Crisis," *New York Times*, April 23, 2019, https:// www.nytimes.com/2019/04/23/nyregion/opioid-crisis-drug-trafficing-rochester.html.

11. Although estimates vary, the National Institute of Drug Abuse places the number of deaths from drug overdose in 2017 alone at 70,200, a more than two-thirds increase from 2007 when 36,010 died. Drug overdoses specifically involving prescription opioids rose from 3,442 in 1999 to 17,029 in 2017. See National Institute of Drug Abuse, "Overdose Death Rates" (2018) (Revised January 2019). See Figure 1 (National Drug Overdose Rates, 1999–2017), https://www.drugabuse.gov/related -topics/trends-statistics/overdose-death-rates.

12. See Peter J. Henning, "The Mounting Costs of Internal Investigations," *New York Times*, March 5, 2012, https://dealbook.nytimes.com/2012/03/05/the-mounting -costs-of-internal-investigations/.

13. In United States v. Barclays Bank PLC, No. CR 1:10-cr-00218 (D.D.C. 2010), the prosecutors advised the court that Barclays had spent $250 million on its internal investigation (but still could not find the individuals responsible for the crime). See Garrett, "Corporate Criminal as Scapegoat," 1817. This illustrates both the high cost and limited value of many such internal investigations.

14. In 2008, Siemens, the German engineering company, agreed to pay a record $1.6 billion to U.S. and European authorities to settle bribery charges. This was the breakthrough FCPA case. See Eric Lichtblau and Carter Dougherty, "Siemens to Pay $1.34 Billion in Fines," *New York Times*, December 15, 2008; see also Brandon Garrett, *Too Big to Jail: How Prosecutors Compromise with Corporations* (Cambridge, MA: The Belknap Press of Harvard University Press, 2014), 8–12.

15. See Mary Shaddock Jones, "The High Costs of Non-compliance!," FCPA Compliance & Ethics, http://fcpacompliancereport.com/2012/11/13 (preserved in the Mary Shaddock Jones Archives).

16. Ibid. At 2019's conversion rates, 650 million euros would translate into over $729 million.

17. Ibid.

18. See U.S. Department of Justice, "Deputy Attorney General Rod J. Rosenstein Delivers Remarks at the American Conference Institute's 35th International Conference on the Foreign Corrupt Practices Act," Justice News, November 29, 2018, https://www.justice.gov/opa/speech/deputy-attorney-general-rod-j-rosenstein -delivers-remarks-american-conference-institute-0.

19. Ibid.

20. See Garrett, *Too Big to Jail*, 13 (noting that in two-thirds of the cases involving deferred prosecution or nonprosecution agreements and public companies, no employees were prosecuted).

21. 2019 U.S. Dist. LEXIS 76233 (S.D.N.Y. May 2, 2019).

22. Id. at *6 to *7.

23. Id. at *21 to *24.

24. There is no estimate of the costs incurred by Deutsche Bank in the *Connolly* investigation, but both Deutsche Bank and Paul Weiss stated on the record that it was the most expensive investigation that they had ever been involved in. Id. at 36.

25. 385 U.S. 493 (1967); see also, United States v. Allen, 864 F.3d 63 (2nd Cir. 1967).

26. Any use, direct or indirect, of a defendant's compelled statements obtained in violation of the Fifth Amendment is also unconstitutional. See United States v. Kastigar, 406 U.S. 441, 453 (1972). Thus, even if the defendant's compelled testimony is not used at trial but instead enables the prosecutors to convince others to confess, plead guilty, and testify against the initial defendant, this evidence from these witnesses is likely "fruit of the poisonous tree," and, if so, this requires reversal of the first defendant's conviction.

27. U.S. v. Connolly, supra note 21, at *30.

28. Id. at *36.

29. See Abbe Lowell and Christopher D. Man, "Federalizing Corporate Internal Investigations and the Erosion of Employees' Fifth Amendment Rights," *Georgetown Law Journal Annual Review of Criminal Procedure* 40 (2011): iii. The Court in *Connolly* noted that it was "deeply troubled by this issue." U.S. v. Connolly, supra note 21, at *3.

30. See Eisinger, *The Chickenshit Club: Why the Justice Department Fails to Prosecute Executives* (New York: Simon & Schuster, 2017), xviii.

31. Ibid.

32. See Garrett, *Too Big to Jail.*

33. See Gibson, Dunn, "2018 Year-End Update on Corporate Non-Prosecution Agreements and Deferred Prosecution Agreements" January 10, 2009, https://www .gibsondunn.com/2018-year-end-npa-dpa-update/.

34. See chapter 2 and text and notes at notes 112 to 114.

35. The impact of the Trump administration is discussed below at notes 44 to 45.

36. See Gibson, Dunn, "2018 Year-End Update."

37. Of the twenty-four deferred prosecution and nonprosecution agreements resolved in 2018, fourteen (or 58 percent) were with financial institutions. Ibid., 1.

38. A bank's license to do business may be jeopardized or even forfeited on a criminal conviction, thus necessitating a lengthy administrative proceeding (in which others might intervene). Hence, a DPA is an important protection for financial institutions.

39. See Gibson, Dunn, "2018 Year-End Update."

40. One exception is settlements of Foreign Corrupt Payments Act cases, which are almost always made public.

41. See Gibson, Dunn, "2018 Year-End Update." For the total of twelve declination letters under the FCPA, see Jennifer Kennedy Park, Alex Janghorbani, and Thomas Galvão Graham, "DOJ Issues Twelfth Declination Letter under FCPA Cooperation Policy" Cleary Enforcement Watch, February 19, 2019, https://www.clearyenforce mentwatch.com/2019/02/doj-issues-twelfth-declination-letter-fcpa-cooperation -policy/.

42. See Brandon L. Garrett, "Declining Corporate Prosecutions," *American Criminal Law Review* (forthcoming).

43. Id. at 10.

44. Id. at 6 to 10.

45. Id. at 16 to 17.

46. Id. at 23 to 24.

47. The new policy was announced in a speech by Assistant Attorney General Makan Delrahim, entitled "Wind of Change: A New Model for Incentivizing Antitrust Compliance Progress," July 11, 2019, Remarks at the New York University School of Law Program on Corporate Compliance and Enforcement, https://www .justice.gov/opa/speech/file/1182006/download. See also Karen Hoffman Lent and Kenneth Schwartz, "The DOJ's New Approach to Robust Corporate Compliance Program," *New York Law Journal*, August 13, 2019, 3.

48. Prosecutors do not specialize in corporate law or compliance plans. In contrast, defendants can call highly paid consultants to testify as to the excellence of the defendant's compliance plan. This is likely to be a very uneven contest.

Chapter 4

1. See Brandon L. Garrett, "The Corporate Criminal as Scapegoat," *Virginia Law Review* 101 (2015): 1789, 1802. Professor Garrett finds that in the cases he studied from 2001 to 2014, federal prosecutors entered into 306 deferred and nonprosecution agreements with companies but prosecuted individuals in only 104 of these corporate cases (or 34 percent). Some 414 individuals were charged in these 104 cases. See also table 1 at p. 1804.

2. For the increase in corporate penalties since 2015, see Brandon L. Garrett, "The Rise of Bank Prosecutions," *Yale Law Journal Forum* 126, no. 33 (May 2016). Garrett finds no trend toward more prosecutions of individuals in deferred prosecution cases. Garrett, "Corporate Criminal as Scapegoat," 1803. Indeed, in 2018, there appear to have been only five cases in which individuals were prosecuted along with the corporation (down from ten in 2017). See Brandon Garrett, "Declining Corporate Prosecutions," *American Criminal Law Review* (forthcoming).

3. See, for example, Wallace P. Mullin and Christopher M. Snyder, "Should Firms Be Allowed to Indemnify Their Employees for Sanctions," *Journal of Law, Economics, and Organization* 2, no. 26 (2010): 30, 32 ("We show that deterrence can typically be achieved at minimum social cost by sanctioning the firm alone.").

4. See Cindy R. Alexander, "Corporate Crime, Markets and Enforcement: A Review," in *New Perspectives on Economic Crime*, ed. Hans Sjogren and Goran Skough (Northampton, MA: Edward Elgar Publishing, 2004), 20, 23.

5. There is an elaborate law-and-economics literature that supports the use of leniency as a tool by which to encourage the adoption of compliance plans and internal investigations. See, for example, Jennifer Arlen and Reinier Kraakman, "Controlling Corporate Misconduct: An Analysis of Corporate Liability Regimes," *New York University Law Review* 72 (1997): 687; A. Mitchell Polinsky and Steven Sharell, "Should Employees Be Subject to Fines and Imprisonment Given the Existence of Corporate Liability?," *International Review of Law and Economics* 13 (1993): 239; Reiner Kraakman, "Corporate Liability Strategies and the Costs of Legal Controls," *Yale Law Journal* 93 (1989): 857. This literature has rarely, however, examined the adequacy of the corporate compliance plans and internal investigations that are thereby encouraged.

6. Gary S. Becker, "Crime and Punishment: An Economic Approach," *Journal of Political Economics* 76 (1968): 169.

7. See, for example, Arlen and Kraakman, "Controlling Corporate Misconduct," 687, 730–35 (arguing that corporate law should incentivize internal policing). For probably the most thorough-going assertion that criminal law overdeters and would be wiser to adopt a more lenient policy toward corporate crime, see Assaf Hamdani and Alan Klement, "Corporate Crime and Deterrence," *Stanford Law Review* 61 (2009): 271.

8. The argument here is that without corporate criminal liability, firms would have little incentive to monitor their employees for criminal behavior (at least unless it was also tortious and would give rise to greater claims against the firm than the expected gain to the firm).

9. For one example, see Jonathan R. Macey, "Agency Theory and the Criminal Liability of Organizations," *Boston University Law Review* 71 (1991): 315, 334. This

view assumes that crime is an agency cost committed by opportunistic employees acting contrary to their corporation's best interests. Of course, some crime fits this pattern, but more may be the product of corporate pressure on the employee.

10. See Jennifer Arlen, "The Potentially Perverse Effects of Corporate Criminal Liability," *Journal of Legal Studies* 23, no. 833 (1994): 835–36 (noting that, under varying circumstances, corporations may or may not cooperate with the government).

11. Prior to the adoption of the Organizational Sentencing Guidelines in 1991, corporate fines were trivial. They then grew steadily. Between 2000 and 2012, average corporate fines ranged from $1 to $16,000,000—still well below the current level. See Brandon Garrett, *Too Big to Jail: How Prosecutors Compromise with Corporations* (Cambridge, MA: The Belknap Press of Harvard University Press, 2014), 294.

12. Ibid., 149.

13. Ibid., 150.

14. Ibid.

15. Ibid., 159 (from fiscal 2009 to 2012, the Sentencing Commission reported that no companies had received such a self-reporting credit and only five corporations of over three thousand sentenced had ever received it).

16. Ibid., 160.

17. See Brandon L. Garrett, "The Rise of Bank Prosecutions," *Yale Law Journal Forum* 126 (2016): 33, 40.

18. See Nick Werle, "Prosecuting Corporate Crime When Firms Are Too Big to Jail," *Yale Law Journal* 128 (2019): 1, 11.

19. Ibid.

20. See Devlin Barrett, Christopher M. Mathews, and Andrew R. Johnson, "BNP Paribas Draws Record Fine for 'Tour de Fraud,'" *Wall Street Journal*, June 30, 2014; see also Werle, "Prosecuting Corporate Crime," 11.

21. See William Holobin, "France Claims Victory in BNP Paribas Case," *Wall Street Journal*, July 1, 2014; see also Werle, "Prosecuting Corporate Crime," 11n34.

22. See Garrett, "Rise of Bank Prosecutions," 40.

23. See Garrett, *Too Big to Jail*, 70.

24. See Emily Glazer, Ryan Tracy, and Jeff Horwitz, "FTC Approves Roughly $5 Billion Facebook Settlement," *Wall Street Journal*, July 12, 2019, https://www.wsj.com /articles/ftc-approves-roughly-5-billion-facebook-settlement-11562960538.

25. Ibid.

26. Ibid.; see also Robert Price, "Why Facebook's Stock Jumped Despite Facing a Record-Breaking $5 Billion FTC Penalty: A Slap on the Wrist," *Business Insider*, July 12, 2019, http://www.businessinsider.com/why-Facebook's-stock-jumped-despite-facing -a-record-breaking-$5-billion-FTC-penalty; see also Troy Wolverton, "The FTC's $5 Billion Fine for Facebook Is So Meaningless, It Will Likely Leave Zuckerberg Wondering What He Can't Get Away With," *Business Insider*, July 12, 2019, http://www .businessinsider.com/the-FTC's-$5-billion-fine-for-facebook-is-so-meaningless-it -will-likely-leave-Zuckerberg-wondering-what-he-can't-get-away-with.

27. The twenty-five largest corporate fines were identified using the registry developed by Professor Brandon Garrett, and then the few corporations that did not trade on a U.S. stock market were eliminated. All the examples shown on the prior exhibit are included. That list (from largest to smallest) follows:

1. JPMorgan Chase Bank NA

2. JPMorgan Chase Bank NA

3. Credit Suisse

4. Credit Suisse

5. Citigroup Inc.

6. Barclays PLC

7. UBS

8. Royal Bank of Scotland (2015)

9. Royal Bank of Scotland (2017)

10. Deutsche Bank AG

11. Teva Pharmaceutical Industry LTD

12. UBS

13. Eli Lilly and Co.

14. BP Exploration & Petroleum LLC

15. GlaxoSmithKline LLC

16. Bank of America

17. Bank of America

18. Andarko Petroleum Corporation

19. Citigroup Inc.

20. Citigroup Inc.

21. Pharmacia and Upjohn (Pfizer subsidiary)

22. Verizon Communications Inc.

23. American Electric Power

24. Wells Fargo and Company

25. Goldman Sachs

Obviously, some firms (all banks) received multiple fines. The author wishes to thank his research assistant Roy Cohen for his efforts in conducting this event study. Cohen is a JSD graduate student at Columbia Law School. He used the WRDS (Wharton Research Data Services) Event Study Tool to conduct this study, and the *market model*, the most frequently used model in event studies, was employed. This event study follows a typical timeline, and a default *estimation window* of 100 days was used, with the event window opening ten days before the event (the public announcement of the fine) and closing twenty-five days after the event. This estimation window is the length of the period (in trading days) used to estimate the expected return and residual return variance. Where the penalty was announced in the press prior to the official announcement by the Department of Justice, Cohen chose the earlier date. For example, the *Wall Street Journal* announced on September 25, 2013, that JPMorgan was offered an $11 billion settlement, and the stock went up 4.66 percent within a day. Later, on October 19, this penalty was increased to $13 billion, and the market did not respond; the formal announcement was on November 19 (again with little market reaction). Hence, the September 25 price reaction is used in this study.

28. The t statistic for the abnormal return was 2.18 and is significant at a level of 0.05 (P = 0.038), and the t statistic for the cumulative abnormal return has a p-value of 0.052 on the day of the announcement and becomes more significant in the following days, with p-values of 0.032, 0.029, 0.032, and 0.042 between days 21 and 25 following the event.

29. There is a rich literature on this point. See Jonathan M. Karpoff and J. R. Lott Jr., "The Reputational Penalty That Firms Bear from Committing Criminal Fraud," *Journal of Law and Economics* 36 (1993): 757–802; and Jonathan M. Karpoff, D. Scott Lee, and Gerald S. Martin, "The Cost to Firms of Cooking the Books," *Journal of Financial and Quantitative Analysis* 43 (2008): 581–612.

30. See Parklane Hosiery Co. v. Shore, 439 U.S. 322 (1979). This doctrine is not automatic, but the basic idea is that a defendant who has litigated and had "his day in court" cannot relitigate the facts that were necessarily incident to his conviction.

31. See Garrett, *Too Big to Jail*, 165–68. Garrett notes that British Petroleum and ExxonMobil recurrently violated environmental laws; Pfizer has a series of violations and deferred prosecution agreements; and in the financial field, AIG, Barclay's, Citigroup, Credit Suisse, HSBC, JPMorgan, UBS, and Wachovia repeatedly pleaded guilty or entered into deferred prosecution agreements. To be sure, there is the counterargument that firms that are one hundred times larger than smaller firms should be expected to violate the law more frequently. That is not this book's interest. This book is not accusing large corporations of greater illegality but rather is only seeking feasible means of deterrence.

32. See Mark (Shuai) Ma and Wayne B. Thomas, "Legal Environment and Corporate Tax Avoidance: Evidence from State Tax Codes," June 19, 2019, https://ssrn.com /abstract=3303842.

33. See Garrett, "Declining Corporate Prosecutions." Professor Garrett finds that the number of cases resolved with deferred or nonprosecution agreements fell to twenty-one in 2018 but that the number of cases involving these prosecutions and accompanied by individual prosecutions fell even further to five in 2018 (down from ten in 2017). Ibid.

34. See Garrett, "Corporate Criminal as Scapegoat," 1805.

35. Ibid. (Some 42 of 414 individual defendants went to trial.)

36. The usual rate, as noted in the text, is that between 95 and 97 percent of individual defendants plead guilty.

37. Garrett, "Corporate Criminal as Scapegoat," 1792, 1808.

38. Ibid., 1809.

39. Jesse Eisinger's book *The Chickenshit Club: Why the Justice Department Fails to Prosecute Executives* (2017) derives its title from James Comey's challenge to young prosecutors that if they had never lost a case, they were "chickenshit."

40. See Garrett, "Corporate Criminal as Scapegoat," 1809n89. This translates to a 5.7 percent loss rate.

41. SAC Capital Advisers, a hedge fund, pleaded guilty to several counts of securities fraud and wire fraud, paid a $1.8 billion fine, and was dissolved. Cohen (whose initials are S. A. C.) escaped criminal liability but agreed not to manage money for others for two years. Among the traders at his firm who were convicted was Mathew Martoma. See United States v. Martoma, 894 F.3rd 64 (2d Cir. 2017) (sustaining conviction). Having escaped criminal prosecution, Cohen has opened a new firm—and nearly purchased majority control of the Mets. For an overview of his case, see Frances E. Chapman, Marisma Jennings, and Lauren Tarasuk, "S.A.C. Capital: Firm Criminal Liability, Civil Fines, and the Insulated CEO," *American University Business Law Review* 4 (2015): 441.

42. See Jesse Eisinger, *Chickenshit Club*, 230.

43. Ibid., 231–32.

44. This problem has, of course, been noted before. See S. M. Kriesberg, "Decision-making Models and the Control of Corporate Crime," *Yale Law Journal* 85 (1976): 1091 (noting that decision-making responsibility was diffused broadly within the large corporation). See also John C. Coffee Jr., "Beyond the Shut-Eyed Sentry: Toward a Theoretical View of Corporate Misconduct and an Effective Legal Response," *Virginia Law Review* 63 (1977): 1099.

45. There is always one counterexample. Here, the leading such example is the conviction of Don Blankenship, the former CEO of Massey Energy, a major coal company, for his role in the Upper Big Branch mining explosion in 2010 in which twenty-nine miners died. Blankenship was a unique CEO in that he micromanaged most of the details surrounding the operation of this mine. However, he was only convicted on a single misdemeanor charge and acquitted on all felony counts. He received a very modest one-year sentence.

46. See Brandon Garrett, Nan Li, and Shivaram Rajgopal, "Do Heads Roll? An Empirical Analysis of CEO Turnover and Pay When the Corporation Is Federally Prosecuted," March 25, 2018, https://ssrn.com/abstract=2966823. Using his sample of companies that reached a deferred prosecution agreement between 2000 and 2014 and a larger control group, Professor Garrett and his colleagues found that, following the settlement of the criminal charges, there was evidence of a higher rate of CEO turnover, but for those CEOs who were not terminated, there was no evidence of any reduction in pay or bonuses. Indeed, bonuses among these continuing CEOs spiked in that year.

47. This author has analyzed who pays the settlement in securities class actions at some length elsewhere. See John C. Coffee Jr., "Reforming the Securities Class Action: An Essay on Deterrence and Its Implementation," *Columbia Law Review* 106 (2006) 1534, 1549–51 (finding that, although corporate officers and executives are regularly sued in securities class actions, they contribute less than 1 percent of the settlement).

Chapter 5

1. For a short summary of the prisoner's dilemma, see "Prisoner's Dilemma," Wikipedia, last revised January 2, 2020, https://en.wikipedia.org/wiki/Prisoner's _dilemma. See also "Prisoner's Dilemma," in *Stanford Encyclopedia of Philosophy* (Stanford, CA: Center for the Study of Languages and Information, Stanford University, Stanford, California, 2019). The standard point is that individual and group rationality can differ, and the law needs to exploit this disparity.

2. The Antitrust Division initially adopted a Corporate Leniency Policy in 1978, but few corporations responded to it. See Scott D. Hammond, "The Evolution of Criminal Antitrust Enforcement Over the Last Two Decades," Washington, DC, February 25, 2010, https://www.justice.gov/atr/speech/evolution-criminal-antitrust-enforcement-over-last-two-decades. Hammond was the deputy assistant attorney general for antitrust enforcement, Department of Justice, at the time of this speech. As the Antitrust Division recognized, a greater incentive was needed, and so the policy was revised in 1993 to give the first defendant to apply and cooperate complete immunity from criminal and civil penalties, but only one corporate defendant per conspiracy was eligible to receive this credit. All its officers, directors, and employees were similarly immunized.

3. In 2019, under President Trump, the Antitrust Division's leniency policy was relaxed to allow other corporations (who were not the first to cooperate) to also receive leniency credit if they had an adequate compliance plan. See Kristen Broughton and Dylan Tokar, "Antitrust Compliance Policy Revamps All-or-Nothing Approach to Corporate Leniency," *Wall Street Journal*, August 5, 2019. This seems exactly the wrong move if one wishes to maximize pressure on the corporation to cooperate. Now it has a second-best option: to hold out and not cooperate but then point to its paradigm of a compliance plan if others defect and cooperate.

4. See Scott D. Hammond, "An Update on the Antitrust Division's Criminal Enforcement Program" (paper presented at the ABA Section of Antitrust Law Cartel Enforcement Roundtable, Washington, DC, November 16, 2005), 10.

5. See Joseph Harrington, "When Can We Expect a Corporate Leniency Program to Result in Fewer Cartels," *Journal Law and Economic* 58 (2015): 417, 418; N. H. Miller, "Strategic Leniency and Cartel Enforcement," *American Economic Review* 99 (2009): 750–68.

6. For this estimate by the *New York Times* columnist for White Collar Watch, see Peter J. Hennings, "The Mounting Costs of Internal Investigations," *New York Times*, March 5, 2012.

7. For some financial institutions, it is at least a legitimate fear that an indictment could result in a run on the bank. Some crimes also preclude the convicted defendant from contracting with the federal government or require a revocation of licenses. (The crime of money laundering will be discussed as such an example later in this chapter.)

8. Under section 21D(b)(2)(A) of the Securities Exchange Act of 1934, a plaintiff suing based on rule 10b-5 may only recover money damages if the plaintiff can plead "with particularity facts giving rise to a strong inference" of fraud. This provision, added by the Private Securities Litigation Reform Act of 1995, is the principal obstacle for plaintiffs in most securities class actions because the plaintiff cannot obtain discovery until this high pleading standard is satisfied. To obtain detailed information satisfying this standard, plaintiff's attorneys use a variety of techniques, including hiring former law enforcement personnel to interview employees and former employees of the corporate defendant.

9. David Boies, the founder of this firm, was in fact retained by the Antitrust Division as its special counsel in a long and successful battle that the Antitrust Division fought against Microsoft. Other firms that regularly represent plaintiffs as well as defendants in class action litigation would include Susman & Godfrey LLP

and Quinn, Emanuel, Urquhart & Sullivan LLP. All would be recognized as among the very best litigation firms in the country. Would they welcome such an assignment? My belief is many such firms would accept an assignment in large part for reputational reasons. If the federal government picks you as its champion, that is a major marketing credential.

10. Regarding the "poisonous tree" doctrine, see United States v. Kastigar, 406 U.S. 441 (1972) (any direct or indirect use of compelled statements obtained in violation of the Fifth Amendment is impermissible). Prosecutors can respond to this obstacle by showing that they uncovered the allegedly tainted evidence by other means, and this defense worked in *United States v. Connolly*; see infra note 11.

11. See United States v. Connolly, 2019 U.S., Dist. LEXIS 76223 (S.D.N.Y. May 2, 2019) (finding that the internal investigation was sufficiently influenced by Department of Justice as to make employees' statements inadmissible where employees had been subject to pressure to testify by the corporation). In *Connolly*, the prosecution prudently decided not to introduce the employees' testimony in evidence, but the defense still claimed unsuccessfully that other evidence was fruit of the poisonous tree. The case law here derives from Garrity v. New Jersey, 383 U.S. 493 (1967) (state may not condition employment on waiver of privilege against self-incrimination). For an overview, see Peter Westen, "Answer Self-Incriminating Questions or Be Fired," *American Journal of Criminal Law* 37 (2010): 97.

12. The court finds, relying on Paul Weiss's head partner conducting the investigation, that "there was nothing 'voluntary' about the investigation." See United States v. Connolly, supra note 11, at *6.

13. Id. at *21.

14. Id. at *26.

15. Id. at *11.

16. The court found that, in compliance with *Kastigar* (supra note 10), the prosecution had satisfied its burden of showing that it did not use Black's testimony at trial and did not derive important information from him but rather gained its information from "wholly independent" sources. Id. at *61 to *66. This was fortuitous. On marginally different facts, a *Kastigar* violation would have been found. See United States v. Allen, 864 F.3d 63 (2d Cir. 2017).

17. Id. at *28 to *31 ("In short, . . . everything I have read suggests that the United States outsourced its investigation to Deutsche Bank and its lawyers").

18. Professor Brandon Garrett has reported that no national bank has ever been convicted of a money laundering charge. See Brandon Garrett, "The Corporation as Scapegoat," *Virginia Law Review* 101 (2015): 1789, 1816–17.

19. See 12 U.S.C. §93(d)(1).

20. Although the comptroller of the currency must initiate such a hearing on a conviction for money laundering, the penalty of forfeiture is not mandatory. Indeed, it is far from likely that the bank's ability to engage in banking would be terminated. The hearing would focus on a variety of issues, including whether the bank's senior executives had willfully violated the money laundering statutes and rules and whether adequate controls had been now installed. The prospect that a major bank would forfeit its franchise seems very small (but perhaps not if Bernie Sanders or a similarly minded candidate became president).

21. Sometimes, activist groups do demand that the comptroller of the currency revoke a bank's charter. See Editor, "Public Citizen Calls on Comptroller of Currency to Revoke Rabobank's Charter," *Corporate Crime Reporter*, March 1, 2018. But they get no response.

22. See John C. Coffee Jr., "'No Soul to Damn; No Body to Kick': An Unscandalized Inquiry into the Problem of Corporate Punishment," *Michigan Law Review* 79 (1981): 386. Interestingly, when this author first published this proposal in 1981, he received correspondence from study groups and politicians in countries with socialist governments who liked the idea, except that they wanted the state to continue to hold the shares. Governance ownership (even of a minority stake) is not the aim of the equity fine as here proposed.

23. Under section 3(a)(10) of the Securities Act of 1933, securities issued with court approval are exempt from registration. This exemption would require a fairness hearing (which shareholders would be invited to attend), and the court would be approving the issuance of the shares in exchange for cancelation of a cash fine in equal amount.

24. See Katherine Blunt and Russell Gold, "PG&E Regulators Failed to Stop Crisis," *Wall Street Journal*, December 9, 2019, 1.

25. See Ivan Penn, Lauren Hepler, and Peter Eavis, "Wildfire Deal to Cost PG&E $13.5 Billion," *New York Times*, December 7, 2019, B1.

Chapter 6

1. The reluctance to suing individuals is probably driven in part by the recognition that individual executives generally lack the resources to pay a significant judgment or settlement (unless they are indemnified, which only shifts the payment back to the entity). This matters less in criminal prosecutions where the executive can be sent to prison and thereby satisfy the public's hunger for retribution, but in a civil case, if executives contribute only a modest amount to the settlement, this may offend the public or generate adverse media attention. Alternatively, the real factor may be that the settlement with the corporate defendant is based on an implicit agreement not to sue the corporate executives.

Even if the individual defendant lacks resources, he or she can still be effectively disbarred. For example, the SEC is authorized by section 21(d)(2) of the Securities Exchange Act to ask a court to bar a person from serving as an officer or director of a public corporation, either for a period of years or for life.

In fairness to the SEC, it does frequently name individual executives as defendants in addition to the corporate entity. In fiscal year 2019, the SEC named individual defendants in 69 percent of its "standalone" cases. See U.S. Securities and Exchange Commission, Division of Enforcement 2019 Annual Report at pp. 17 (2019) (November 6, 2019), https://www.sec.gov/reports.

2. See Better Markets, *Wall Street's Six Biggest Bailed-Out Banks: Their RAP Sheets & Their Ongoing Crime Spree* (Washington, DC, April 9, 2019), 5.

3. See Committee on Capital Markets Regulation, *Rationalizing Enforcement in the U.S. Financial System* (Cambridge, MA, June 8, 2018). The committee's director is Professor Hal Scott of the Harvard Law School.

4. Ibid., ix (fig. 1).

5. Ibid., x.

6. Ibid. No data are available for later years.

7. Because this study also finds that the number of enforcement actions peaked in 2012, this suggests a two-year lag for litigation and negotiation before aggregate sanctions peaked in 2014.

8. This figure is simply the sum of the sanctions imposed in 2012 through 2016 from the foregoing chart. Uniquely over these years, the Civil Division of the Department of Justice was the principal enforcement agency, recovering the largest amounts; in other years, it has been the SEC, which, across the entire period, brought the largest number of actions.

9. From 2000 to 2016, the SEC in each year brought the largest number of actions, which did not vary much from year to year. But in the 2012 to 2016 period, the Civil Division of Justice generally recovered the greatest amounts (in some very large settlements with U.S. and foreign banks). The SEC has slightly over 4,500 employees and in 2018 brought some 490 standalone cases. See SEC Division of Enforcement 2019 Annual Report at pp. 11–12 (2019).

10. A recent and controversial example is the SEC's belated decision to sue Volkswagen with respect to its emissions scandal. The SEC's suit, brought in 2019, came well after a global settlement had been reached with public and private enforcers. The court hearing the action characterized the SEC as a "carrion hawk" picking over the remains of a case and pushed the SEC to settle quickly. See David Michaels, "Judge Prods SEC to Settle Fraud Case with Volkswagen," *Wall Street Journal*, August 17, 2019, B3.

11. In 2018, Deputy Attorney General Rod Rosenstein announced new procedures to count the penalties paid to other agencies in order to discourage "piling on," but disagreement continues. See Mike Koehler, "Discouraging 'Piling On' Sounds Great, but It All Depends on What 'Piling On' Means," FCPA Professor Blog, May 11, 2018, http://www.fcpaprofessor.com.

12. While the president can fire his own employees at will, he can only fire or discipline employees of the "independent" federal agencies (such as the SEC or FTC) for "cause." Article II of the U.S. Constitution does require, however, that the president have some removal power over even these employees. See Free Enterprise Foundation v. Public Company Accounting Oversight Board, 561 U.S. 477 (2010).

13. See U.S. Const. art. I, § 9, cl. 7. For an overview, see Gerald E. Frug, "The Judicial Power of the Purse," *University of Pennsylvania Law Review* 126 (1978): 715.

14. See 31 U.S.C. § 3302(b).

15. See Committee on Capital Markets Regulation, *Rationalizing Enforcement*, 106.

16. Ibid.

17. Ibid.

18. Ibid., 106–7.

19. Ibid., 116–19. In fiscal 2014 and 2015 (the last years for which data are available), $526 million and $393.6 million, respectively, were deposited by Justice into the 3 percent fund. Ibid., 118.

20. See section 21B(e) of the Securities Exchange Act. This original authority applied only to amounts recovered as disgorgement of ill-gotten gains.

21. See section 929B of the Dodd-Frank Act (2010) (authorizing the commission to add any civil penalty to its disgorgement fund).

22. See SEC, Rules of Practice and Rules on Fair Fund and Disgorgement Plans, Rule 1100, September 2019, 17 C.F.R. §201.1100 to 1106. For an overview, see Urska Velikonja, "Public Compensation for Private Harm: Evidence from the SEC's Fair Funds Distributions," *Stanford Law Review* 67 (2015): 331.

23. See Velikonja, "Public Compensation," 350.

24. Ibid., 334. Thus, the SEC has numerous fair funds, each established for a particular case. The largest distribution from a fund appears to have been $816.5 million. Ibid.

25. See Committee on Capital Markets Regulation, *Rationalizing Enforcement*, 110 (showing decline from 2007 through 2012). However, in fiscal 2017, the SEC dispersed almost $1.06 billion from its fair funds (which was a substantial increase but not near its highest distribution of over $2.78 billion in fiscal 2004).

26. Section 1017 of the Dodd-Frank Act mandates that the CFPB deposit all civil monetary penalties into the "Consumer Financial Penalty Fund." See 12 U.S.C. § 5497(d).

27. See Committee on Capital Markets Regulation, *Rationalizing Enforcement*, 112.

28. That is, if all defendants contribute restitution to the same fund, this means that in cases where there are high losses (but the defendant has limited assets), the victims can look to the single fund for some recovery. In effect, a single fund implies some damage averaging. Of course, the downside of this is that other victims will receive less than full recovery in cases where their defendant had sufficient funds and paid full restitution.

29. Under federal law, the sentencing court in a criminal case has authority to order restitution. See 18 U.S.C. § 3663 ("Order of Restitution"). Procedures for awarding and enforcing restitution are specified in 18 U.S.C. § 3664. But courts may not want to take on the procedural complexity of supervising awards of restitution to hundreds of victims (and few do). Moreover, by creating a Department of Justice restitution fund, the criminal fine or penalty itself could be used for restitution (not just the amount expressly awarded by the court as restitution). Finally, a Justice restitution fund could also use penalties and monetary sanctions awarded in the civil process. For an overview of some of these issues, see Lionel M. Levenue, "The Corporation as a Criminal Defendant and Restitution as a Criminal Remedy," *Journal of Corporation Law* 18 (1993): 441; "Victim Restitution in the Criminal Process: A Procedural Analysis," *Harvard Law Review* 97 (1984): 931.

30. Under section 21F of the Securities Exchange Act, the SEC is directed to award between 10 and 30 percent of all monetary penalties it receives over $1 million to the whistle-blower who first provided information to the SEC leading to the enforcement action. As noted earlier, the Justice Department has been authorized to award 3 percent of its civil recoveries to a fund to cover enforcement costs. See notes 19 to 20.

31. There are many empirical studies finding that the "declining percentage of the recovery" formula dominates. For an excellent review, see Theodore Eisenberg and Geoffrey P. Miller, "Attorney Fees and Expenses in Class Action Settlements: 1993–2007," *Journal of Empirical Legal Studies* 7 (2010): 248. See also John C. Coffee Jr., "Understanding the Plaintiff's Attorney: The Implications of Economic

Theory for Private Enforcement of Law Through Class and Derivative Actions," *Columbia Law Review* 86 (1986): 669, 686.

32. From decades of working in this field of class actions, the author feels entitled to make this assessment on his own authority. For a description by the author of fee practices and the profitability of plaintiff firms, see John C. Coffee Jr., *Entrepreneurial Litigation: Its Rise, Fall, and Future* (Cambridge, MA: Harvard University Press, 2015).

33. Although disgorgement is a long-standing remedy, the Supreme Court has recently granted certiorari to determine if the SEC is authorized to award it. See Liu v. SEC, 2019 U.S. LEXIS 6599 (November 1, 2019) (granting certiorari). Should the Court strip the SEC of authority to award disgorgement, the SEC will have greatly reduced authority, but no prediction on the outcome (or on any legislative response) is here made.

34. In 1997, the Antitrust Division of the Department of Justice asked David Boies, a very well-known trial lawyer who had successfully defended IBM, to serve as its trial lawyer in its major suit against Microsoft. By most accounts, Boies was at least "an important factor in the government's trial victory." See Howard M. Erichson, "Coattail Class Actions: Reflections on Microsoft, Tobacco, and the Mixing of Public and Private Lawyering in Mass Litigation," *UC Davis Law Review* 34 (2000): 1, 16–18.

35. See Jed Rakoff, "The Financial Crisis: Why Have No High-Level Executives Been Prosecuted?," *New York Review of Books*, January 9, 2014.

36. In December 2012, this author wrote a column in the *National Law Journal* titled "SEC Enforcement: What Has Gone Wrong?" criticizing SEC enforcement for its failure to pursue executives at banks and suggesting that the SEC use private counsel, retained on a contingent fee basis, to fill this gap. See John C. Coffee Jr., "SEC Enforcement: What Has Gone Wrong?" *National Law Journal*, December 3, 2012, at 23–24. This elicited an immediate and angry reply from the SEC's two directors of enforcement, Robert Khuzami and George Canellos, who said that my proposal "ignores critical differences between the SEC's goals as a regulator and those of a litigant seeking monetary damages." See Robert S. Khuzami and George S. Canellos, "Unfair Claims, Untenable Solutions: Professor Coffee Does Not Do the SEC's Enforcement Record Justice," *National Law Journal*, January 14, 2013, at 34. To be sure, the perspectives of a fee-motivated private counsel and a public attorney within a civil service bureaucracy do differ, but this does not mean that the SEC (or any other regulator) has to defer to the private counsel that it hires. Just as corporate general counsels monitor and sometimes reverse their retained private counsel, so could the SEC. What private counsel adds to the mix is both the ability to absorb risk and high litigation (and particularly trial) competence. For third-party reviews of this debate, see Editorial, "Professor Coffee Hits a Nerve at the SEC," *Corporate Crime Reporter*, January 15, 2013; Margaret H. Lemos, "Privatizing Public Litigation," *Georgetown Law Journal* 105, no. 515 (2016).

37. This table was prepared by Max W. Berger, the senior partner of Bernstein, Litowitz, Berger & Grossman, the largest plaintiff's law firm in New York City.

38. See Coffee, *Entrepreneurial Litigation*, 183–84.

39. Ibid., 185–85.

40. Ibid., 184.

41. Ibid.

42. Ibid.

43. Ibid., 185.

44. Ibid.

45. See Cornerstone Research, *Characteristics of FDIC Lawsuits against Officers and Directors of Failed Financial Institutions* (Boston, September 2013), "Report Summary" and 1, https://www.cornerstone.com/Publications/Reports/Characteristics -of-FDIC-Lawsuits-Feb-2014.

46. Ibid.

47. Coffee, *Entrepreneurial Litigation*, 185–86.

48. Ibid., 186–87. Congressman Issa retired from Congress and did not run for reelection in 2018.

49. Ibid., 187.

50. See Martin H. Redish, "Private Contingent Fee Lawyers and Public Power: Constitutional and Political Implications," *Supreme Court Economic Review* 18 (2010): 77.

51. See Santa Clara v. Superior Court, 74 Cal. Rptr. Ed 842 (Ct. App. 2008); State v. Hagerty, 580 N.W. 2d 139 (N.D. 1998); State v. Lead Indus. Ass'n, 957 A.d 2d 428 (R.I. 2008); Kinder v. Nixon, 2000 WL 684860 (Mo. Ct. App. May 30, 2000).

52. See Executive Order No. 13,433, 3 C.F.R. 13,433 (2007).

53. See Committee on Capital Markets Regulation, *Rationalizing Enforcement*, 117.

54. 273 U.S. 510 (1927)

55. Id. at 523.

Chapter 7

1. In the case of the SEC, see section 21F of the Securities Exchange Act (15 U.S.C. § 78 u-6); in the case of the CFTC, see 7 U.S.C. § 26.

2. See Luke Hornblower, "Outsourcing Fraud Detection: The Analyst as Dodd-Frank Whistleblower," *Journal of Business and Technology Law* 6 (2011): 287.

3. The term *original information* is defined in the SEC's rules to require that the information be derived from the individual's own "independent knowledge" or "independent analysis" and not from publicly available sources. See 17 C.F.R. § 240. 21F-4(b). Thus, one cannot either buy the information or learn it in a chain of gossip.

4. See 15 U.S.C. § 78 u-6(b).

5. This award made in 2018 was to three whistle-blowers. (Two shared a $50 million award and the third received $33 million.) See U.S. Securities and Exchange Commission, "SEC Announces Its Largest-Ever Whistleblower Awards," press release no. 2018-44, March 19, 2018. The SEC also made an additional $54 million award in September 2018 (divided also between two individuals).

6. These data come from both *2017 Annual Report to Congress on the Dodd-Frank Whistleblower Program* (Washington, DC, November 15, 2017), 1, 23; and U.S. Securities and Exchange Commission, *2018 Annual Report to Congress: Whistleblower Program* (Washington, DC, November 15, 2018), 9.

7. See 2017 Ann. Report, 1.

8. See U.S. Securities and Exchange Commission, *2018 Annual Report to Congress*, 9.

9. Ibid., 1. It should be remembered that the fact that the SEC has ordered $1.7 billion does not mean that it has been paid this amount; many default.

10. See U.S. Securities and Exchange Commission, Office of the Whistleblower, "Final Orders of the Commission," last modified August 25, 2017, www.sec.gov /about/offices/owb-final-orders.shtml.

11. In fairness, the SEC's inspector general found in 2003 (at the outset of this program) that "the SEC is prompt in responding to information provided by whistle-blowers." See U.S. Securities and Exchange Commission, Office of Inspector General, "Evaluation of the SEC's Whistleblower Program," report no. 511, January 18, 2013, v. Of course, being prompt is not the same as being receptive.

12. See section 922(a) of the Dodd-Frank Act. Under SEC Rule 21F-4(b)(2), "independent knowledge" does not require "direct, first-hand knowledge of potential violations"; thus, a Markopolos should be able to qualify for an award if he performs a complex analysis of financial information. See Hornblower, "Outsourcing Fraud Detection," supra note 2, at 297. But examples of awards for such efforts are not apparent to this author.

13. U.S. Commodity Futures Trading Commission, *Annual Report on the Whistleblower Program and Customer Education Initiatives* (Washington, DC, October 2018), 2.

14. Ibid., 3. Thus, the CFTC program appears to be accelerating with most of its awards and the majority of its payments being made in fiscal 2018.

15. See Rachel Graf, "CFTC Calls for Whistleblower Tips as Enforcement Evolves," LAW360, September 19, 2019, https://www.law360.com/articles/1200344/cftc-calls -for-whistleblower-tips-as-enforcement-evolves.

16. U.S. Commodity Futures Trading Commission, *Annual Report*, 3. This was a 63 percent increase over fiscal 2017, which was in turn a record year to that point.

17. The proper comparison should look to the percentage of awards paid on tips submitted in a given year. Otherwise, there is a serious lag. Awards also cannot be paid until all appeals are concluded. Because the number of tips has risen exponentially, any comparison that matches current awards in a period with the number of current tips received is comparing apples to oranges.

18. See U.S. Internal Revenue System, *Whistleblower Program, Fiscal Year 2018 Annual Report to Congress* (Washington, DC, n.d.), 4.

19. Ibid., 9.

20. For an overview and careful evaluation of the qui tam action, see D. R. Engstrom, "Harnessing the Private Attorney General: Evidence from Qui Tam Litigation," *Columbia Law Review* 112 (2012): 1244.

21. GlaxoSmithKline paid over $3 billion in 2012 to resolve criminal and qui tam actions against it. This appears to be the largest qui tam recovery on record. See Katie Thomas and Michael S. Schmidt, "Glaxo Agrees to Pay $3 billion in Fraud Settlement," *New York Times*, July 2, 2012.

22. Under the False Claims Act (31 U.S.C. § 3729-3733), the government has the option to take over the relator's suit. If it does and it recovers, the relator receives 15 to 25 percent of the recovery (either by settlement or trial). If the government

does not intervene and the relator litigates and obtains a recovery, between 25 to 30 percent of the recovery goes to the relator.

23. See A. Dyck, A. Morse, and L. Zingales, "Who Blows the Whistle on Corporate Fraud?," *Journal of Finance* 65 (2010): 2213–53 (finding that 18 percent of the corporate fraud allegations underlying a sample of securities class actions was brought forward by an employee). This percentage was much higher in some industries.

24. This is because, as noted earlier, statutory law and the Constitution's Appropriations Clause require that amounts received by government agencies go to the Treasury, unless Congress has directed otherwise. See chapter 6, supra, at notes 13 to 15. But one means to sidestep this provision is discussed below.

25. The fund would be under the control of a court-appointed trustee, who would decide the amount of each bounty, using much the same criteria as set forth in section 21F of the Securities Exchange Act, which governs the SEC's whistle-blower fund. If there was no prospect of reversion to the defendant, the defendant could probably deduct such payments for tax purposes in the year of payment (which might also make it more attractive to defendants).

26. See 31 U.S.C. § 3202(b).

27. In traditional corporate governance theory, *bonding* is one of the devices by which managers and shareholders reduce agency costs. See Michael Jensen and William Meckling, "Theory of the Firm: Managerial Behavior, Agency Costs and Ownership Structure," *Journal of Financial Economics* 3 (1976): 305.

Chapter 8

1. Historically, the precedent that established this doctrine (in 1909) was New York Central & Hudson Railroad Co. v. United States, 212 U.S. 481, 494–95 (1909). In essence, the Supreme Court simply adopted for criminal law (with little analysis) the same rule of respondeat superior that applied in civil cases.

2. For examples of this view, see Donald R. Cressey, "The Poverty in Corporate Crime Research," in *Advances in Criminological Theory*, Vol. 1, ed. W. S. Laufer and F. Adler (New Brunswick: Transaction Publishers, 1989); V. S. Khanna, "Is the Notion of Corporate Fault a Faulty Notion?: The Case of Corporate Mens Rea," *Boston University Law Review* 79, no. 355 (1999).

3. 320 U.S. 277 (1943).

4. Id. at 278. For the finding that Dotterweich had "no personal connection" with the conduct in question, see United States v. Buffalo Pharmacal Co., 131 F.2d 500, 501 (2d Cir. 1942).

5. 320 U.S. at 281.

6. United States v. Park, 421 U.S. 658 (1975).

7. Id. at 666.

8. Id. at 674.

9. Id. at 672.

10. Id. at 673 (citing United States v. Wiesenfeld Warehouse Co., 376 U.S. 86, 91 [1964]).

11. See United States v. Wise, 370 U.S. 405 (1961). But see also United States v. United States Gypsum Co., 438 U.S. 422 (1978) (contra).

12. For a brief review of the expansion of the doctrine, see Kimberly Kessler Ferzan, "Probing the Depths of the Responsible Corporate Officer's Duty," *Criminal Law and Philosophy* 12 (2018): 455, 459–69.

13. For the classic article that defined the field, see Francis Bowes Sayre, "Public Welfare Offenses," *Columbia Law Review* 33 (1933): 974.

14. 828 F.3d 626 (2016).

15. DeCoster v. United States, 2017 U.S. LEXIS 3334 (May 22, 2017) (certiorari denied). In this author's view, it is not surprising that the Supreme Court denied certiorari in *DeCoster*, because the defendants conceded their liability by pleading guilty and challenged only their three-month sentences. That issue of sentencing severity is probably not the issue that the Court may have wanted to consider.

16. See Staples v. United States, 511 U.S. 600 (1994) (noting that court had "avoided construing criminal statutes to impose a rigorous form of strict liability"). See also United States v. International Minerals & Chemical Corp., 402 U.S. 558, 563–64 (1971).

17. See S.1010, 116th Congress (introduced April 3, 2019). This bill would amend title 18 of the US Code to add a new section 451 ("Negligence of Executive Officers"), which is closely paraphrased in the text.

18. One recent study finds that administrative penalties imposed on corporate executives worked far better than penalties imposed on the corporation to deter tax evasion. See Mark (Shuai) Ma and Wayne B. Thomas, "Legal Environment and Corporate Tax Avoidance: Evidence from State Tax Codes," June 19, 2019, https://ssrn.com/abstract=3303842.

19. For many years, courts have treated "willful ignorance" or "willful blindness" as the equivalent of actual knowledge. But the formula and phrasing vary significantly among courts. See Alexander F. Sarch, "Willful Ignorance, Culpability and the Criminal," *St. John's Law Review* 88 (2015): 1023.

20. See 563 U.S. 754 (2011). In *Global-Tech*, the Supreme Court synthesized the "conscious avoidance" holdings of all eleven federal circuits to develop a test that it imported from the criminal law to resolve a similar issue in patent law. It found that all federal circuits agreed on two basic requirements for the doctrine's application: (1) the defendant must subjectively believe that there is a high probability that a fact exists, and (2) the defendant must take deliberate action to avoid learning of that fact. This gave rise to an issue whether *Global-Tech* controlled subsequent criminal cases involving the doctrine or otherwise changed the criminal law on mens rea.

21. In particular, the requirement of "deliberate action" in *Global-Tech* raised the bar for prosecutors and discouraged reliance on the doctrine.

22. Compare United States v. Goffer, 721 F.3d 113 (2d Cir. 2013) and United States v. Clay, 832 F.3d 1259 (11th Cir. 2016) (both holding no change in criminal law) with United States v. Jinwright, 683 F.3d 471 (4th Cir. 2012) (finding that *Global-Tech* does apply to "willful blindness" instruction to the jury in federal court).

23. "Conscious avoidance" (or "willful blindness") is treated in most U.S. jurisdictions as the equivalent of actual knowledge, but it is not the equivalent of a specific intent to defraud or "willfulness," which are higher levels of mens rea. Thus, if "willfulness" or "intentionality" must be shown regarding the specific crime, proof of "willful blindness" or "conscious avoidance" will not be sufficient.

24. See section 302(a)(2) and (3) of the Sarbanes-Oxley Act.

25. Section 906 of the Sarbanes-Oxley Act added this prohibition, which is today set forth in 18 U.S.C. § 1350. The maximum penalty goes up from ten years to twenty years for a "willfully" false certification.

Chapter 9

1. For example, in fiscal 2018, ninety-nine corporations were convicted in federal court (94.9 percent by a plea of guilty), and of these ninety-nine, seventy-five (or 75.8 percent) were sentenced to probation. In other recent years, the percentage of convicted corporations sentenced to probation has ranged from 60 to 77.9 percent (in 2013). See U.S. Sentencing Commission, *Sourcebook of Federal Sentencing Statistics*, table 53 (2009–2018), https://www.ussc.gov/research/sourcebook/archive. A sentence to probation is, of course, in addition to a fine and other sanctions.

2. One reason is that prosecutors will be less prepared to grant sentencing concessions at this stage. The defendant corporation has forced the prosecution to go to trial and thus has lost its leverage. If the corporation could receive the same concessions after trial, it would have much less incentive to plea bargain, and thus prosecutors tend to be less willing to offer concessions posttrial.

3. See Brandon L. Garrett, *Too Big to Jail: How Prosecutors Compromise with Corporations* (Cambridge, MA: The Belknap Press of Harvard University Press, 2014), 165–67. As Professor Garrett notes, corporations often plead guilty through their subsidiaries, and this interferes with counting the felonies in which they have been involved. (He emphasizes the case of Pfizer, which has pleaded guilty itself and through its subsidiaries.)

4. Some have argued that the convicted corporation should lose its charter and be denied the right to operate as a corporation. See Mary Krenier Ramirez and Steven A. Ramirez, *The Case for the Corporate Death Penalty: Restoring Law and Order on Wall Street* (New York: New York University Press, 2017). Suffice it to say that this author does not like the death penalty in any form and considers such a penalty vastly disproportionate and likely to be borne by the nonculpable.

5. See Garrett, *Too Big to Jail*, 166 (noting that public companies with multiple environmental convictions include BP, ExxonMobil, McWane Inc.; in addition, Big Pharma companies with multiple convictions include Pfizer, ICN Pharmaceuticals, and GlaxoSmithKline; banks with multiple deferred prosecution or nonprosecution agreements include AIG, Barclays, HSBC, JPMorgan, UBS and Wachovia).

6. See Jeff L. Coles, Naven D. Daniel, and Lalitha Naveen, "Managerial Incentives and Risk-Taking," *Journal of Financial Economics* 79 (2006): 413–68; see also David F. Larcker, Gaika Ormazabal, Brian Taylor, and Donald J. Taylor, *Follow the Money: Compensation, Risk and the Financial Crisis*, Stanford Closer Look Series (Stanford, CA, September 8, 2014).

7. Recently, Equilar, the compensation consultant, reported that the share of total CEO compensation derived from equity was 60 percent (with cash accounting for only 36 percent) for companies in the S&P 500. See Equilar, "2015 CEO Pay Strategies," August 4, 2015, 9, www.equilar.com/press-releases,34-2015-CEO-pay-strategies. Equilar further reports that, from 2010 to 2014, the use of performance-based stock compensation rose 38.1 percent at firms in the S&P 500 Index, and other bonus compensation rose 12.4 percent.

8. Christopher S. Armstrong, David F. Larcker, Gaika Ormazabal, and Daniel J. Taylor, "The Relation between Equity Incentives and Misreporting: The Role of Risk-Taking Incentives," *Journal of Financial Economics* 109 (2013): 327–50.

9. See, for example, Andrew Pollack and Sabrina Tavernise, "Valeant's Drug Price Strategy Enriches It, but Infuriates Patients and Lawmakers," *New York Times,* October 4, 2015; Joe Nocera, "Is Valeant Pharmaceuticals the Next Enron?," *New York Times,* October 27, 2015; Jonathan Rockoff, "Valeant Pharmaceuticals under Investigation by Federal Prosecutors," *Wall Street Journal,* October 15, 2015.

10. See John C. Coffee Jr., "Preserving the Corporate Superego in a Time of Stress: An Essay on Ethics and Economics," *Oxford Review of Economic Policy* 33 (2017): 221–30 (discussing Valeant and its compensation structure).

11. See Julia La Roche, "It's a Hedge Fund Horror Show as Valeant Gets Crushed," *Business Insider,* October 21, 2015; Gretchen Morgenson, "Valeant's High-Price Drug Strategy," *New York Times,* October 2, 2015.

12. See David F. Larcker and Brian Tayan, *CEO Pay at Valeant: Does Extreme Compensation Create Extreme Risk?,* Stanford Closer Look Series, April 28, 2016, 1.

13. See Richard C. Breeden, *Restoring Trust: Report to the Hon. Jed S. Rakoff, United States District Court for the Southern District of New York, On Corporate Governance for the Future of MCI, Inc.* (Washington, DC, August 2003), 2, https://www.sec.gov /Archives/edgar/data/723527/000119312503044064/dex992.htm.

14. At least one well-known manufacturer of opioid drugs employed hundreds of sales representatives, paying them incentive compensation to sell its products to prescribing doctors, and it rewarded sales of high-dosage tablets disproportionately because they gave the company permanent customers (i.e., addicted ones). See Joseph Walker and Jared S. Hopkins, "Purdue Led Its Opioid Rivals in Pills More Prone to Abuse," *Wall Street Journal,* September 20, 2019, 1.

15. The *Federal Sentencing Guidelines Manual* expressly authorizes probation for organizations (including corporations). See U.S. Sentencing Commission, *Federal Sentencing Guidelines Manual* (Washington, DC, 2018), §§ 8D1.1. Under § 8D1.1(a) (6) of that manual, probation conditions can be justified by the need "to ensure that changes are made within the organization to reduce the likelihood of future criminal conduct." Reducing incentive compensation serves this purpose. Also, the Sentencing Reform Act, which authorizes these guidelines, has several stated purposes, the third of which is to protect the public from further wrongdoing by the offender. See 18 U.S.C. § 3553(a)(2)(C) ("to protect the public from further crimes of the defendant"). Generally, probation conditions, even those requiring a corporation to engage in community service, have been upheld. See United States v. Mitsubishi International Corp., 677 F.2d 785 (9th Cir. 1982); United States v. Nu-Triumph, Inc., 500 F.2d 594 (9th Cir. 1974); see also United States v. Tonawanda Coke Corporation, 5 F. Supp. 3d 343 (W.D.N.Y. 2014). This goal of incapacitating the corporate offender so that it will not lapse into recidivism is directly served by probation conditions that reduce the incentives of executives to take risky or unlawful actions. For a more general overview, see John C. Coffee Jr., "Standards for Organizational Probations: A Proposal to the United States Sentencing Commission," *Whittier Law Review* 10 (1988): 77; James Geraghty, "Structural Crime and Institutional Rehabilitation: A New Approach to Corporate Sentencing," *Yale Law Journal* 89 (1979): 353.

16. Such cases in which probation conditions have been struck down as unreasonable or unauthorized do exist. See, for example, United States Missouri Valley Construction Co., 741 F.2d 1542 (8th Cir. 1984) (*en banc*) (striking down probation condition requiring corporation to make a charitable contribution to a charitable organization that had not been injured by its conduct); see also United States v. John Scher Presents, Inc., 746 F.2d 959 (3d Cir. 1984) (same). These cases involve court-ordered payments that were not intended to reduce the risk of recidivism or otherwise incapacitate or deter. This author agrees that mandatory charitable contributions are not authorized by federal law.

17. See United States v. Ashland, Inc., 356 F.3d 871 (8th Cir. 2004).

18. If this compensation contract is not per se illegal (which seems unlikely), it is presumably enforceable by the executive, but the executive does not have a right to continue in office (although his contract must be honored in terms of payment).

19. There has been much criticism of corporate monitors, both for their vague undefined powers and for a tendency toward nepotism in their appointments. For an overview, see Vikramaditya Khanna and Timothy L. Dickinson, "The Corporate Monitor: The New Corporate Czar?," *Michigan Law Review* 105 (2007): 1713; see also Brandon L. Garrett, "Structural Reform Prosecution," *Virginia Law Review* 93 (2007): 853. Although many law-and-economics scholars point out that monitors know much less than corporate managers about the corporation's business (and thus are unlikely to make more efficient decisions), monitors are appointed to help the corporation make more law-compliant decisions (not more efficient ones). Unlike these scholars, this author believes corporate monitors need more, not less, authority.

20. See Breeden, *Restoring Trust*.

21. A *frankpledge system* was deliberately created in Medieval England (probably from the time of Canute the Great in the eleventh century) under which individuals were made joint sureties responsible for causing any man in their tithing suspected of a crime to appear in court. If they failed and the defendant did not appear, those in this tithing were liable for the fine in his place. Collective responsibility gives each in the group an interest in minimizing law violations. See "Frankpledge," Wikipedia, last revised December 20, 2019, https://en.wikipedia.org.wiki/.Frankpledge. Here, executives in effect pledge their future incentive compensation (or some portion of it) that the corporation will not engage in serious crime.

22. This language comes from 18 U.S.C. § 1350 ("Failure of corporate officers to certify financial reports"), which provides for up to a ten-year sentence and a $1 million penalty. Also, false statements in any such certification that is filed with a federal agency or court would be subject to the criminal penalty provided for in 18 U.S.C. § 1001 (which provides for up to a five-year sentence).

23. This provision is now set forth in section 10A(m)(2) of the Securities Exchange Act, which provides that the audit committee of a public company "shall be directly responsible for the appointment, compensation, and oversight of the work" of the auditor relating to the audit report and that "each such registered public accounting firm shall report directly to the audit committee."

24. See section 10A(a)(1) of the Securities Exchange Act.

25. See section 10A(b)(1)(A) of the Securities Exchange Act.

26. See section 10A(b)(1)(B) of the Securities Exchange Act.

27. This is the language of section 10A(b)(1)(A) of the Securities Exchange Act.

Conclusion

1. Although this was the result in United States v. Connolly, 2019 U.S. Dist. LEXIS 76223 (S.D.N.Y. May 2, 2019), which is discussed earlier in chapter 5, one district court decision cannot settle the law in this field, and small factual distinctions may lead to different outcomes. Prosecutors may continue to influence investigation (perhaps more subtly), but if they do, *Kastigar* hearings will become a regular aspect of white collar criminal litigation.

2. This technique was used by Judge Jed Rakoff to appoint a monitor in the SEC's action against WorldCom, and it resulted in the appointment of Richard Breeden, a former chairman of the SEC, as WorldCom's monitor. He proved to be a much more active monitor than most.

3. For example, Martha Stewart waived her rights and talked to the Southern District prosecutors in connection with their investigation into an insider trading case. She was prosecuted and convicted as a result under the false statements statute (18 U.S.C. § 1001). The point here is that high-ranking executives may be unable to continue in office if they do not testify, because of social conventions.

4. In a speech on July 11, 2019, Assistant Attorney General Makan Delrahim indicated that the Antitrust Division will consider a company's compliance plan not only at the stage of awarding sentencing credits but earlier in terms of charging decisions made by prosecutors. See Makan Delrahim, Assistant Attorney General, Antitrust Division, "Remarks at the New York University School of Law Program on Corporate Compliance and Enforcement," July 11, 2019, https://www.justice.gov/opa /speech/file/1182006/download.

5. This change in position was expressed in what has become known as the Filip Memo. See Mark Filip, "Memorandum from Deputy Attorney General Mark R. Filip to Heads of Department Components and United States Attorneys on Principles of Federal Prosecution of Business Organizations" (Washington, DC, August 28, 2008). Legislation had been introduced in both the House and the Senate to bar the Department of Justice from requiring such waivers. See the Attorney-Client Privilege Protection Act of 2007, H.R. 30130. For an overview of these developments, see Daniel Rickman, "Decisions about Coercion: The Corporate Attorney Client Privilege Waiver Problem," *DePaul Law Review* 57 (2008): 295.

6. It is not here suggested that a waiver of the privilege should be required of the corporation in every case (or even in most cases), but it is a factor that should have great importance and should be required when the prosecution nears senior levels of the corporation. As a practical matter, the corporation's waiver may also reveal many incriminating statements by or to its employees.

7. Under 12 U.S.C. § 93(d), if a national bank is convicted of money laundering, the comptroller of the currency must issue to the bank "a notice of the Comptroller's intention to terminate all rights, privileges, and franchises of the bank" and schedule a pretermination hearing. Still, the comptroller is given considerable discretion by 12 U.S.C. § 93(d)(2), and termination seems likely to be an uncommon outcome.

8. Managements and the board of directors rarely own 10 percent or more of a large public company's stock. Institutions (as a group) typically own over 70 percent of

such a company's stock, but individual institutions usually stay below 5 percent (for a number of reasons, including liquidity and SEC reporting requirements). Thus, a 20 percent block is likely to make the purchaser of such a block the company's largest shareholder. An activist shareholder, such as a Carl Icahn, might welcome the opportunity to acquire such a position and might pay a premium above the market price for such a block.

9. The Eighth Amendment to the U.S. Constitution prohibits the federal government from imposing "excessive fines" or cruel and unusual punishments. A fine is usually considered excessive only when it is grossly disproportionate to the gravity of the offense. See United States v. Bajakajian, 524 U.S. 321 (1998) (confiscation of $357,144 from the defendant for failure to report possession of more than $10,000 in cash while leaving the United States was excessive). In general, the Court has emphasized that judgments about punishment (and the limits thereon) belong to the legislature. See Solem v. Heim, 463 U.S. 277, 290 (1983). This prohibition against excessive fines also applies to the states.

10. The Supreme Court has repeatedly held that plea bargaining is constitutional, despite the claim that it is coercive or undermines constitutional rights. See, for example, Brady v. United States, 397 U.S. 742 (1970). As a practical matter, the only litigable issue will be whether the plea was made knowingly and voluntarily.

11. A nonprosecution agreement means that there is no case or guilty plea so that nothing comes to the attention of any court (and no court has jurisdiction). Even if a court had jurisdiction, existing decisions have given courts almost no role to play. Legislation is needed here, and many have made proposals. For a similar view, that nonprosecution agreements should be barred, see Brandon L. Garrett, *Too Big to Jail: How Prosecutors Compromise with Corporations* (Cambridge, MA: The Belknap Press of Harvard University Press, 2014), 274.

12. See supra note 2 (describing such a procedure that was used in WorldCom).

13. For example, if a pharmaceutical company was convicted of "misbranding" because it had recommended powerful opioid prescription drugs for more general and unapproved uses, its advertising and other communications with doctors and pharmacies should be supervised by the monitor, who could block (subject to judicial review) some communications.

14. See supra note 7 (discussing the powers of comptroller of the currency under 12 U.S.C. § 93(d)).

15. No suggestion is made that private counsel should be used in criminal cases. At least three reasons justify a distinction between civil and criminal cases: First, most private law firms have had little or no experience at criminal litigation (but have had a wealth of experience at securities and antitrust private litigation). Second, plea bargains (particular with individual defendants) are a very sensitive matter, which cannot be as safely delegated to private attorneys. Third, contingent fees are not possible in criminal cases, and thus private counsel could not be retained on such a basis.

16. Some sentencing credit to corporations for compliance plans and self-reporting seems intuitively justifiable, but economic models also suggest that, at some point, this credit can become excessive and lead to increased crime. See Masaki Iwasaki, "A Model of Corporate Self-Policing and Self-Reporting," August 28, 2019, https://ssrn.com/abstract=3449512. It is highly unlikely that models or empirical research

will tell us in the near future where the inflection point is at which corporate leniency becomes excessive and encourages crime. Judgements, however, still have to be made.

17. See Eugene Soltes, "The Frequency of Corporate Misconduct: Public Enforcement versus Private Reality," December 5, 2018, https://ssrn.com/abstract=3347159 (forthcoming in the *Journal of Financial Crime*).

18. It should be understood here that, since 1991, the federal sentencing guidelines give a significant credit to convicted corporations that have adopted an effective compliance plan. See U.S. Sentencing Commission, *Sentencing Guidelines Manual*, section 8B2.1. Potentially, the credit can be up to 95 percent. In addition, the Department of Justice has adopted a policy that considers such a compliance plan at the charging stage to determine if the corporation should even be criminally charged. See Department of Justice, "Principles of Federal Prosecution of Business Organizations," *Justice Manual*, § 9-28,000 to § 9-281,300. The new development under the Trump administration is a willingness to give even greater weight in deciding whether to charge a corporation to the existence of such a compliance plan. See supra note 4 (discussing the recent position taken by the head of Antitrust Division that compliance plans should be considered at the charging level as well as in terms of sentencing leniency).

19. Put simply, prosecutors are expert trial lawyers, not experts on corporate governance. Nor do they regard sentencing as their major battlefield. In short, they are neither experts in compliance nor well positioned to litigate these issues. The author does not, however, suggest that all or most compliance plans are Potemkin villages.

20. Although some academics (such as Brandon Garrett) have been highly critical of the trend toward deferred prosecution agreements, other academics who take a law-and-economics perspective have tended to applaud the use of leniency to induce defendant corporations to settle in high numbers. See, for example, Jennifer Arlen and Reinier Kraakman, "Controlling Corporate Misconduct: An Analysis of Corporate Liability Regimes," *New York University Law Review* 72 (1997): 687. Some corporations do monitor carefully, but it remains an open empirical question as to how diligently most corporations monitor their employees. In this light, enhancing judicial scrutiny is the classic technique for inducing managers to monitor more closely.

Index

effect" discussion in, 156n5; federal district court judges issue with, 34–37; policy shift of, 10; "revolving door" practices at, 4, 29, 150, 163n69; "3 percent fund" of, 98, 108, 178n19; Yates Memorandum and, 37–38, 39, 57

Department of Treasury, U.S., 119, 183n24

deterrence, 6, 94–95; abnormal return in, 65, 67f, 173n28; Becker's "expected penalty" and, 59; BNP Paribas example in, 62–63, 87; corporate fines and, 61–62 171n11; corporate officers fines as, 69; difficulties in, 11–12; DPAs shortfall in, 9; expected penalty and expected gain in, 62–65, 76; high penalties and, 58–59; individual executive versus corporate entity in, 57–58, 68–69, 74; law-and-economics scholars in, 57–58; shame as, 138–139, 147; Standard Chartered example in, 63; stock market reaction and corporate fines event study in, 65–66, 66t

Deutsche Bank, Paul Weiss report on, 47–48, 85, 168n24

Dodd-Frank Act, 96–97, 99, 114, 116, 179n26, 182n12

DPAs. *See* deferred prosecution agreement

Drexel Burnham, 19, 24, 160n22

Ebbers, Bernie, 133, 155n2

Eighth Amendment, 145, 189n9

Eisinger, Jesse, 3–4, 9, 22, 27, 32, 158n3, 160n24

Enron, 3, 4, 15–16, 27, 155n2

Environmental Protection Agency (EPA), 41

Equilar, 185n7

equity fine, 56, 87–91, 145–146, 148, 177n22, 188–189nn8–9

executive compensation, 74, 132–133, 174n46

Facebook, 64–65, 87

Farkas, Lee, 166n116

FDCA. *See* Food, Drug and Cosmetic Act

Federal Deposit Insurance Corporation (FDIC), 105–106

Federal Housing Finance Agency (FHFA), 105–106

Federal Reserve, 4, 21, 31, 160–161n29, 161n31

Federal Trade Commission (FTC), 64

FHFA. *See* Federal Housing Finance Agency

Fifth Amendment, 48, 58, 81, 84–87, 142–143, 157–158n21, 176n10

Financial Crisis Inquiry Commission, 28

Fokker Services, 36, 165n106, 165n108

Food, Drug and Cosmetic Act (FDCA), 123–125

Foreign Corrupt Practices Act, 51, 73, 149

France, Anatole, 14

frankpledge system, 136, 187n21

"fruit of the poisonous tree," 48, 85, 142, 168n26, 176n11

FTC. *See* Federal Trade Commission

Fuld, Richard, 24

Garrett, Brandon, 38, 47, 49, 156n10, 160n26, 170nn1–2; on acquittal rate impact, 70–71; on CEOs, 174n46; on corporate fines, 61–62; on DPAs use, 9, 38, 173n31, 173n33, 190n20; on fines and market capitalization ratio, 63; on recidivism rate, 69; on Standard Chartered, 63; on subsidiaries, 185n3

General Motors (GM), 2, 5, 40, 71; DPA of, 43; faulty ignition switch investigation at, 42–43

GlaxoSmithKline, 182n21

Gleeson, John, DPA supervision of, 36

Global Tech Appliances, Inc. v. SED S.A., 127, 184n20

GM. *See* General Motors

Hammond, Scott D., 175n2

Henning, Peter, 45

Holder, Eric, 10, 32, 37, 157n14, 160n26

HSBC, 10, 36; bank regulators consultation and warning in, 31; DPA use in, 31–32; Mexican drug cartels and Iranian terrorists money laundering of, 31; political pressure in, 32; "too big to jail" phrase use after, 32

independent counsel and plaintiffs bar use in, 83–84; independent investigation in, 82–84; internal investigation cost and conduct in, 82–83; internal investigation public or private in, 84–87; leniency competition in, 80–81; leniency incentives in, 81–82; plaintiff and defendant dual representation and ground rules in, 84; shareholder sanction in, 89–90; standard example of, 78–79, 79f; "strong inference of fraud" and, 83–84, 175n8; *United States v. Connolly* case and, 85–86, 176n16, 176nn10–11

prosecutions, 10, 21–22, 40, 49, 52; acquittal rate impact in, 70–71; budgetary and manpower limitations of, 44–45; CEOs and high-ranking executives and, 8, 34, 75; constitutional dimension in, 157n19; decision-making identification in, 72–73, 174n45; DPAs logistical efficiency in, 8, 73–74; Eisinger on Justice Department and, 4; Enron and WorldCom results of, 3, 4, 155n2; financial regulators fear in, 4; Garrett on individual, 38–39; global investigations and, 73; individual resistance phenomenon in, 69–70; Lehman and, 3, 23; money laundering schemes escaping, 5–6; mortgage loan borrowers and, 155–156n4; organizational crime difficulties in, 6; SAC Capital Advisors case and, 72, 174n41; savings banks collapse and, 3, 155n3, 156n8; sex appeal of cases and, 71–72; terrorism reallocation in, 8, 156n9; 2008 crash and, 3–5, 15, 155n1; younger prosecutors choice in, 72

Purdue Pharma Inc.: expected penalty and expected gain in, 64; opioid crisis of, 5, 43; plea bargain and misbranding of, 43, 167n7

Rakoff, Jed, 37, 133, 157n18, 164n84, 188n2; Bank of America and Citigroup SEC settlements rejection of, 35–36; on companies focus shift to individuals, 33–34; *New York Review of Books*

essay of, 32–33; on 2008 crisis and Department of Justice, 32–33
recidivism, 60, 69, 74, 120, 131–132, 134–135, 186–187nn15–16
Richman, Daniel, on prosecutorial resources strain, 34
Rosenstein, Rod J., 46–47, 178n11

SAC Capital Advisors, 72, 174n41
Sarbanes-Oxley Act, 128–129, 132–133, 136–138, 185n25
Schmidt, Oliver, 166n3
Securities and Exchange Commission, U.S. (SEC), 3, 10, 16, 23, 161n33, 177n1, 178nn9–10; Bank of America and Citigroup settlements and, 35–36; bounty program of, 112, 114, 149; class action recovery comparison to, 104, 104t; disgorgement and, 101, 180n33; federal district court judges issue with, 34–35; fraud detection outsourcing of, 114, 141; Lehman's and, 28–29, 163n68; "neither admit nor deny" settlement procedure of, 36, 157n18, 161–162nn43–44; "original information" and awards of, 114–115, 115t, 117–118, 181n3, 181n5; outside counsel use and, 102–103, 180n36; Stoker suit of, 164–165n101; tips and recipients disparity in, 115–116; victim compensation fund of, 98–100, 179n25, 179nn28–29
Serageldin, Kareem, 166n116
Siemens AG, internal investigation and cost of, 45–46, 168n14
Skilling, Jeffrey, 155n2
Stewart, Martha, 188n3
Stoker, Brian, 164–165n101

Tannin, Matthew M., 21, 23
Temple, Nancy, 16
Thompson, Larry, 41
Thompson Memorandum, 41, 160n26, 165n112
Too Big to Jail (Garrett), 9, 156n10
Trump administration, 2; corporate compliance plans and, 53, 150–151, 169n48, 170n5, 189–190n16, 190nn18–19; federal criminal

About the Author

For decades, Professor John C. Coffee Jr. has been recognized as a leading expert in both the fields of corporate law and white collar crime. In recognition of his achievements, he has been elected a Fellow of the American Academy of Arts and Sciences, the American College of Governance Counsel, the American Bar Foundation, and the European Corporate Governance Institute. He has also been three times named to the *National Law Journal*'s list of the 100 Most Influential Lawyers in America.  Repeated surveys have found him to be the most cited author in law reviews on the topics of corporate and business law. At Columbia University, he holds the Adolf A. Berle Chair and is Director of its Center on Corporate Governance. He has also been a visiting professor at Harvard, Stanford, and Virginia Law Schools.

For his work on white collar crime, Professor Coffee was awarded the Donald Cressey Award for Lifetime Achievement by the Association of Certified Fraud Examiners in 2011. He has served as a consultant to the U.S. Sentencing Commission for its Organizational Guidelines and its proposed environmental sentencing guidelines. He also served as a reporter to the American Bar Association for its Model Standards on Sentencing Procedures and Alternatives.

For his work on corporate governance, Coffee received in 2018 the Allen and Overy Law Prize awarded by the European Corporate Governance Institute. Coffee has served as a Reporter to the American Law Institute for its Principles of Corporate Governance (1993), which codifies the fiduciary duties of corporate officers and directors. He has served on the Legal Advisory Committee to the New York Stock Exchange and on the Legal Advisory Board to the National Association of Securities Dealers (which formerly oversaw the Nasdaq).

Professor Coffee has testified before congressional committees on over twenty occasions and has worked on the drafting of the Sarbanes-Oxley Act, the Dodd-Frank Act, and recent insider trading legislation.

Coffee's scholarly books include *Entrepreneurial Litigation: Its Rise, Fall, and Future* (2016); *The Regulatory Aftermath of the Global Financial Crisis*, with Ellis Ferran, Niamh Moloney, and Jennifer G. Hill (2012); *Gatekeepers: The Professions and Corporate Governance* (2006); and *Knights, Raiders, and Targets: The Impact of the Hostile Takeover*, with Louis Lowenstein and Susan Rose-Ackerman (1988).

In addition, Coffee is coauthor or coeditor of several casebooks, including *Securities Regulation: Cases and Materials*, 13th edition (2015), with Hillary Sale and Todd Henderson; *Cases and Materials on Corporations*, 8th edition (2013), with Jesse Choper and Ron Gilson; and *Business Organizations and Finance*, 11th edition (2010), with William Klein and Frank Partnoy.

Dear reader,

Thank you for picking up this book and welcome to the worldwide BK community! You're joining a special group of people who have come together to create positive change in their lives, organizations, and communities.

What's BK all about?

Our mission is to connect people and ideas to create a world that works for all.

Why? Our communities, organizations, and lives get bogged down by old paradigms of self-interest, exclusion, hierarchy, and privilege. But we believe that can change. That's why we seek the leading experts on these challenges—and share their actionable ideas with you.

A welcome gift

To help you get started, we'd like to offer you a **free copy** of one of our bestselling ebooks:

www.bkconnection.com/welcome

When you claim your **free ebook**, you'll also be subscribed to our blog.

Our freshest insights

Access the best new tools and ideas for leaders at all levels on our blog at ideas.bkconnection.com.

Sincerely,

Your friends at Berrett-Koehler